The Black Athlete
in West Virginia

The Black Athlete in West Virginia

High School and College Sports from 1900 Through the End of Segregation

Bob Barnett, Dana Brooks
and Ronald Althouse

McFarland & Company, Inc., Publishers
Jefferson, North Carolina

This book has undergone peer review.

ISBN (print) 978-1-4766-7897-9
ISBN (ebook) 978-1-4766-3875-1

Library of Congress and British Library
Cataloguing data are available

Library of Congress Control Number 2020010518

On the cover: Earl Lloyd, 1950 (courtesy of West Virginia
State University Archives and Special Collections)

———

Printed in the United States of America

*McFarland & Company, Inc., Publishers
Box 611, Jefferson, North Carolina 28640
www.mcfarlandpub.com*

To the African American students,
athletes, coaches, teachers, and administrators
of the segregated schools and colleges
of West Virginia

Table of Contents

Acknowledgments

We would like to express appreciation to the following individuals and institutions who contributed in different ways to this book. A grant from the West Virginia Humanities Council in 1982 funded the initial research.

Several individuals have provided special assistance in transforming our manuscript into this book, including Lysbeth Barnett, who helped with editing, library and archival research, sympathy and provided excellent computer technical assistance, and Dr. Michele Schiavone, who edited the complete manuscript and provided library fact-checking. Both made a huge improvement in the manuscript. Gary Mitchem, the acquisitions editor at McFarland, was there for us every step of the way. Stephanie Martin and Joanne Pollitt skillfully took care of so many small details that turned into a mountain of work for them. Our thanks go to Helen Jackson-Gillison who was among the founders and was the first president of the West Virginia All Black Schools Sports & Academic Hall of Fame. The Hall of Fame inductions regenerated an interest in the history of the all black schools and colleges making the research for this project more productive.

We are deeply appreciative of the help we received from archivists and librarians who assisted us in locating materials in their collections and for the access to materials provided by the West Virginia Archives and History Library, West Virginia State University archives, Bluefield State College archives, Marshall University archives, West Virginia Wesleyan College archives, West Virginia University Athletic Department, Bethany College archives, WVU Tech archives, University of Charleston archives, Glenville State College archives, West Liberty University Athletic Department, Alderson Broaddus College archives, Concord University, Fairmont State University archives, Salem University archives, Shepherd University archives, West Virginia Regional and History Center at the West Virginia University Library, and the Weirton Area Museum and Cultural Center.

We are especially grateful to the following individuals who so generously gave of their time to be interviewed about their experiences: Sonny Allen, Mike Arcure, Shirley Atkins, Larry Barker, Ed Barrett, Benjamin

Baughman, Frank Beach, Horace Belmear, Ancella Bickley, Ken Blue, Ronald Booker, Knute Burroughs, Andrew Calloway, Mark Cardwell, Jr., Phillip Carter, Herb Colker, Gene Corum, Bob Douglas, Beverly Duckwyler, William Dunlap, Warne Ferguson, Garrett Ford, Kevin Gilson, James Green, Jr., Moses Guin, Arintha Poe Hairston, Major Harris, Claude Harvey, Dorothy Hicks, Stephanie Holman, Ruth Jarrett, Dolores Johnson, Floyd Jones, Opal Jones, Bob Kelley, Wilkes Kinney, Donna Lawson, Earl Lloyd, John Mackey, Gerald Martin, Carolyn Matthews, Ed Pastilong, Shirley Robinson, Elizabeth Scobell, Ed Shockey, Ergie Smith, Lacy Smith, John Sorrenti, Edward Starling, Tim Swarr, James L. Taylor, William "Shellie" Trice, William Turner, Bucky Waters, James Wilkerson, Ronald Wilkerson, Elhanier Willis, and Bob Wilson. This is your story. We hope that we have done it justice.

Again, thank you for all your hard work and help.

Preface

This book provides a history of the African American experience in West Virginia on athletic fields and courts. It covers social, cultural, and historical accounts of segregation and integration from the perspective of the 40 black high schools and three black colleges in the state. Beginning in 1900 with the first sports event played by a black West Virginia college, the book describes key contests and the role sports played in segregated schools and in the black community. The impact of these sports extended far beyond the fields of play for the players and teams were a source of community pride, a validation of ability and achievements, and strengthened bonds within the black community. The book traces the changes after the 1954 Brown decision through 1969 when the last black high school closed. *The Black Athlete in West Virginia* explores many of the race relation issues African Americans faced in West Virginia as it seeks to convey what sports meant to individuals and to community development during segregation and to identify what was gained and what was lost through integration.

This is the only book that covers black sports in both high schools and colleges in a state with segregated schools. By including both educational levels rather than isolated examples, it provides a more comprehensive record of the experiences of African Americans seeking equal treatment in a separate educational system and subsequently seeking equality and inclusion in a white world. Looking at their experiences in West Virginia is particularly instructive because of the differences in race relations in different sections of the state. Parts of the state reflected many of the attitudes and policies of its neighbors to the north, making it one of the most progressive of the border and former slave-owning states, yet other parts also reflected the attitudes of the former slave states on its southern and eastern borders and the state remained tightly segregated in most areas well into the 1960s.

This book chronicles an important aspect of African American history that has received insufficient attention because it existed outside of the mainstream of white America. In fact, most of the black high school records and trophies were destroyed during integration. This book corrects this oversight.

It captures the achievements of African American players, coaches, and administrators who demonstrated skill, teamwork, intelligence, and organizational ability while in other aspects of life they were considered second class citizens. West Virginia's achievement in holding the first state basketball tournament for black high schools in 1925 and the subsequent growth and impact of the tournament have been largely overlooked. The book compiles the story of the tournament, the successes of West Virginia high schools in national black high school basketball tournaments, and the state's black national champions in college football and basketball. These were points of pride and their impact as well as the role of sport in providing an opportunity to excel and in creating bonds within African American communities across the state should not be forgotten.

West Virginia demonstrated the bitter sweetness of integration. Most schools in the state integrated within a few years of the *Brown* decision. But integration went only one way in the high schools. The African American students were all sent to white schools and coaches from black schools were demoted. Colleges were somewhat different—white students integrated the two black colleges in the fall semester of 1954, and one year after the *Brown* decision all of the white colleges were integrated. College sports teams were not so quickly integrated, however.

The chapters in this book are topical, not chronological, because the civil rights movement and integration in West Virginia was not monolithic, unified, consistent, nor linear. The state itself was very sectionalized with distinct social, cultural, demographic and economic differences between its regions. The sectional differences were compounded by the state's terrain, which increased the isolation of its small rural communities. The high schools located in the northern part of the state, close to Ohio and Pennsylvania, integrated quickly. The schools in the southwestern, southern and eastern parts of the state next to Maryland, Virginia and Kentucky did not integrate until the 1960s. Marshall University, West Virginia University, the small colleges and the black colleges all had different patterns of integration.

We discuss high schools and colleges separately because their integration patterns were so very different. We trace the development of the individual black high schools in rough chronological order and describe the role of the schools and their athletic teams in developing community leaders and as a source of community pride. In addition, we highlight the black basketball tournament, the first in the United States, which played an important role in bringing the states widely dispersed African American communities together. The tournament's history also reflected the growth of black high schools in the first half of the 20th century and their declining numbers after 1954.

The various colleges experienced markedly different facilitating factors and barriers to integration and to athletic contests between integrated and segregated teams. Consequently, we group similar colleges into chapters. The most important events, accomplishments, or questions that each group faced are a focal point or theme for the chapter. The result is that each chapter is a stand-alone essay.

The chapters are in rough chronological order but shift between chapters on colleges and chapters on high schools during a similar time frame. This leads to some overlap and repetition of contextual information. However, this approach does help the reader maintain a sense of periodicity as each group is discussed separately.

Because so little has been written about black high school and college sports during segregation much of the research is primary. We utilized material from the archives of 10 universities and colleges in the state. We had to recreate the results of 33 years of the WVAU state black high school basketball tournament from newspaper accounts in the *Pittsburgh Courier* and local West Virginia newspapers which are held in the West Virginia Archives and History Library in Charleston. But the richest source of information was from the 60 interviews we conducted with coaches, players, and fans.

This project has been a life's work. In 1982 Bob Barnett received a research grant from the West Virginia Humanities Council to research and write about the black West Virginia Athletic Union (WVAU) state basketball tournament. Since there were no records, nor secondary sources about black high school sports he spent the summer reconstructing the 33 tournaments from newspapers accounts and tape-recorded interviews he conducted with nine of the former coaches in the black high schools. In the summer of 1983, Barnett published an article in *Goldenseal: A Quarterly Forum on West Virginia's Traditional Life.* The title of the article is "The Finals: West Virginia's Black Basketball Tournament, 1925–1957." At the time West Virginia was the only state with a published history of its black high school basketball tournament. He continued to research the topic and made presentations to state and international academic associations and wrote encyclopedia entries in the *West Virginia Encyclopedia* and the *Encyclopedia of Appalachia.* He expanded the topic to include West Virginia's black college sports. In 2013 West Virginia University Press published *Hillside Fields: A History of Sports in West Virginia* which included a chapter on the black high school tournament and a chapter on West Virginia State University sports. Additional research has produced three chapters in this book on the black high school tournament and four chapters on black college sports and the integration of West Virginia's colleges.

As social scientists, Dana Brooks and Ron Althouse wrote the following: "The study of sport takes us to the heart of critical issues of society and cultures." The authors have consistently analyzed the historical, cultural, social, and political factors impacting the African American athletes' experiences at various levels. In 1991, Brooks taught his first class in African American sports. In 1992 with support from the WV Humanities Council, they recorded interviews with people involved in integrating sports at WVU. The textbook *Racism in College Athletics: The African-American Athlete's Experience* was first used in the fall of 1993. Co-authored by Brooks and Ron Althouse, the textbook focuses on the historical analysis of racism in college sports and the impact of race, racism, and gender on the recruitment, retention, and mobility of African Americans in college athletics. They have continued to spread this message through their various professional careers and in the form of written books, book chapters, classes, radio interviews, TV appearances, and presentations at academic meetings. This book is the culmination of 35 years of research.

Because the process was begun 35 years ago, we were able to gather eyewitness accounts of the very early WVAU tournaments beginning with the first in 1925, as well as accounts of participation in numerous high school and college athletic contests. The book is based on careful and extensive research, but we have avoided academic jargon so that it will be accessible to non-scholars interested in the topic.

The research for this book includes a survey of secondary sources and significant primary archival and newspaper research. Bob Barnett's *Hillside Fields: A History of Sports in West Virginia* gave a comprehensive account of sports in the state. Ocania Chalk's pioneer volume *Black College Sports* and David K. Wiggins and Ryan A. Swanson's *Separate Games: African American Sports Behind the Walls of Segregation* provided information on national trends in black high school and college sports. Likewise, Robert Pruter's *The Rise of American High School Sports and the Search for Control*, Charles H. Martin's *Benching Jim Crow: The Rise and Fall of the Color Line in Southern College Sports, 1890–1980*, and Randy Roberts' *But They Can't Beat Us: Oscar Robertson and the Crispus Attucks Tigers* provided good information on black high school sports nationally. *The West Virginia Encyclopedia*, edited by Ken Sullivan, John Alexander Williams' *West Virginia: A History*, and Tim L. Wyatt's *The Final Score* were storehouses of information on the history of West Virginia. Ron Thomas' *They Cleared the Lane* had two excellent chapters on West Virginia State in the 1940s and early 1950s. However, we know of no source that covers the impact of sports in the black high schools and colleges in a single state. Furthermore, this book provides an additional dimension because the participants tell their own stories of a people who succeeded in their struggle to prove themselves equal while being treated as second class citizens.

Introduction

by BOB BARNETT

"We want to induct you into the West Virginia All Black Schools Sports & Academic Hall of Fame," said the woman on the phone. It was Helen Jackson-Gillison, founder and president of the West Virginia All Black Schools Sports & Academic Hall of Fame, established in 2008.

"Why me?" I asked, wondering if she knew that I am white.

"Dana Brooks and Ron Althouse nominated you for writing a history of the black high schools' state basketball tournament. We'd also like to invite you to do a presentation during the first day of the Hall of Fame weekend," she explained. I breathed a sigh of relief. Dana and Ron knew me personally, so my race was not a secret, and I *had* written a history of the state basketball tournament.

The Hall of Fame induction was an impressive black-tie event. The hotel ballroom was packed with former students from the black schools and their families, who clearly wanted to preserve the memories and bonds of community engendered by their shared experiences. Gary District's outstanding football and basketball teams were being honored that year, so I decided to begin my presentation with some background about the early tournaments and to play some excerpts from the tape recording of the interview that I had done in 1982 with Gary District's coach, the late James Wilkerson. As the tape of Wilkerson was playing, I looked up to see the audience's reaction. Grown men were crying, handkerchiefs in hand, tears streaming down their faces, moved to tears just to hear their coach's voice. I returned to the Hall of Fame in 2011 and 2012 to do presentations and to play recordings of interviews with other coaches for family, friends, and former players who cherished hearing their coach's voice. The recordings have now been digitized by the West Virginia Archives and History Division and are cataloged at the Smithsonian. They are available to the public at the West Virginia Archives and History Library in the Bob Barnett Collection which is a collection of the recorded interviews that were given to the library in 2013.

After several Hall of Fame weekends, Dana, Ron and I recognized the need for a comprehensive history of sports at the black high schools and colleges during segregation and the transition to integration. It was a daunting task because none of records from the black high schools had been saved when they were closed during integration. Outside of what we had done there were only a few, small scattered studies on black sports in West Virginia. The accomplishments of the players and coaches and the role of sports as a unifying force and source of pride for the African American community were in danger of being forgotten. This book corrects this important omission in the historical record as it examines sports at West Virginia's 40 black high schools and three black colleges. This is a book about sports and education. But it is also a chronicle of a very visible aspect of the experiences and achievements of African Americans in their struggle for social justice within West Virginia.

Although there were publicly-funded segregated schools in the state, the separate facilities were not equal. Not every county had a black high school. Budgets for the black schools were inadequate, resulting in limited resources in the classrooms and in the athletic facilities where any existed. Many black high schools lacked gyms. For example, the four white high schools in Hancock County had their own football stadiums and gyms, but the only black school in the county, Weirton Dunbar, had no gym and played its football games on a vacant lot next to the city's power station. This was typical of experiences throughout the state. Wheeling Lincoln, in one of the largest cities in the state, practiced and played its basketball games in the Colored Recreation Center. Lewisburg Bolling was permitted to use the gym at Lewisburg High School when it was not being used by the white team, but the Bolling players were not allowed to dress in the locker room. The Bolling football field was on a vacant lot strewn with rocks and broken glass.

Despite those challenges, the black high schools became the center of African American life in the black communities. The teachers and coaches were community leaders and role models. The students were well educated in an environment under the control of African Americans. Sports and school activities provided wholesome entertainment. The sports teams were visible expressions of achievement and excellence. Each black community united around its school, cheering its victories and cherishing its successes.

One of those success stories began on Saturday, March 21, 1925, when 175 fans watched breathlessly as Kimball High School, from the southern coal fields of McDowell County, squared off against a big city team from the north, Wheeling Lincoln High School. They were the best of the 11 teams that had met for the first West Virginia Athletic Union state-wide high school basketball championship—the nation's first state basketball tournament for segregated black high schools.

The final was highly contested to the end a fitting beginning for the tournament, which would continue for 33 years and grow so large that four regional tournaments were introduced to winnow the 40 black high school teams down to an eight-team state tournament.

James Wilkerson saw it all. He had been a student at the West Virginia Collegiate Institute (now West Virginia State University), where the tournament was played and was assigned to be a host for the team from his alma mater, Gary Negro School (later called Gary District). After getting the team settled in the basement of the gym where all the players slept on cots, he was able to watch the teams play day and night in the double elimination tournament. Later as a teacher and coach at Gary District, his teams won the state black basketball tournament two times. "It was what our kids and fans lived for," said Wilkerson.

The three black colleges in West Virginia also developed successful athletic programs during segregation. In 1900, Storer College, a Baptist school, met Howard University in a football game, becoming the first West Virginia black college to play in an intercollegiate game. Storer continued to field teams until it closed in 1955. West Virginia State and Bluefield State, which both opened in the 1890s, developed teams that played at the top level of black college sports and both eventually joined the prestigious Colored Intercollegiate Athletic Association (CIAA), now called the Central Intercollegiate Athletic Association.

Bluefield State's football program won national black college championships in 1927 and 1928 under coach "Big Jeff" Jefferson. West Virginia State won the co-national black football championship in 1936 with coach Adolph Hamblin and West Virginia State claimed the national black basketball championships in 1948 and 1949 under coach Mark Cardwell. In addition, West Virginia State won numerous CIAA championships in the 1940s and 1950s. The success of the black college teams created tremendous pride in the West Virginia black communities.

Through interviews conducted over the past 35 years, other coaches, players and fans add their voices in eye-witness accounts of athletics in black high school and colleges. Their experiences show how sports became a source of pride, an opportunity to excel, and created bonds within African American communities across the state.

All this began to change after the 1954 *Brown v. Board of Education* decision; black high schools gradually closed as integration progressed. By 1961, Gary District was competing in the integrated West Virginia Secondary Schools Activities Commission state basketball tournament where Wilkerson and Ergie Smith led the basketball team to become State Runner-up in 1962 and State Champions in 1965. The year after the championship season, Gary District High School closed and Wilkerson, whose teams had also won state football championships and national honors in basketball, was demoted to assistant coach at the integrated Gary High School. The Gary District experience was repeated across the state as all the black high schools were closed by 1969; their students were sent to white schools; and most black principals, faculty and coaches were demoted.

The colleges integrated quickly with white students entering Bluefield State and West Virginia State immediately and all white colleges integrating within the next year. Sports teams did not integrate as quickly, however, and the book traces the progression of integration as well as the successes of notable black athletes.

The book is designed to trace the impact of sports in black high schools and colleges on West Virginia's African American communities and to provide a picture of the school integration process in the state. It is written so that the book can be read in its entirety or individual chapters can be read and understood by those who are only interested in specific aspects of the story. Regardless of the approach, the reader will find an inspirational account of acting with dignity, working hard, and achieving success despite adverse circumstances.

PART I

School and College Segregation in West Virginia, 1863–1954

A persisting thread running through the garment of the American writing experience is discrimination against blacks; racism is rooted deeply in our history. Black Africans were first brought to colonial America in 1619. By the middle of the 17th century, a slave system among colonial plantation owners had begun and enslaved black Africans who had become a major source of labor. A racist social structure, with blacks at the bottom, was thus created. The Declaration of Independence and the U.S. Constitution condoned racial subordination and discrimination against African Americans. Slavery was sanctioned, and blacks were denied all of the rights of citizenship. It took a civil war and the passage of the 13th amendment to the U.S. Constitution in 1865 to officially end the slavery system. Many states passed Jim Crow laws mandating racial segregation in almost all areas of public life. Jim Crow laws legalized white domination and thus left racism essentially intact. A "separate but equal" system replaced slavery and became an even more efficient instrument of domination and subordination than slavery had been.

The 1896 U.S. Supreme Court decision in the *Plessy v. Ferguson* case institutionalized the "separate but equal" doctrine and ensured nearly a century of white supremacy in America. After the *Plessy v. Ferguson* decision, sport was largely color coded, and African Americans participation on predominantly white high school, college, and professional teams virtually disappeared. Broadly scaled, a chronicle of African American participation in sport can be divided into three periods: (1) Segregation: 1863–1954, (2) Integration: 1954–1968, and (3) Post-Integration: 1968–present.

1

African Americans
in West Virginia,
1860–1969

The state of West Virginia was admitted to the Union in 1863, after separating from Virginia. The new state's citizens had opposed Virginia's decision to secede from the Union and agreed to form their own state that would be admitted to the Union. Yet when the boundaries of the new state were finalized, a significant number of West Virginians favored slavery and in fact were staunch supporters of the Confederacy. The section of the state where a person lived usually defined their attitude toward slavery and continued to influence the treatment of African Americans well into the 20th century.

In 1860, on the eve of the Civil War, the area of Virginia that is now West Virginia had a population of 21,144 African Americans, of whom 2,773 were free blacks and 18,371 were slaves. In comparison, the rest of Virginia had more than a half-million slaves. The distribution of slaves among the various counties in West Virginia demonstrated the schism over slavery within the new state. The Eastern Panhandle counties of Berkeley with 1,650 and Jefferson County with 3,960, along with the counties bordering Virginia such as Greenbrier with 1,525, Hardy with 1,673, and Hampshire with more than 1,000 all had significant numbers of slaves. In addition, Kanawha County, which used slaves extensively in the salt industry, had 2,138 slaves and was strongly in favor of retaining slavery.

The Northern Panhandle counties of Hancock had two slaves, Brooke had 18 slaves, Ohio County, the most populous in the state by far, had only 100 slaves; and Marshall County had only 29 slaves. In addition, the very small rural mountain counties of Webster (3), Calhoun (9), and Pleasants (15) all had fewer than 16 slaves. Ironically, McDowell County, in southern West Virginia, had no African Americans in 1860. But, because of the recruiting of black miners, by 1920 McDowell had become one of the black population centers in West Virginia. The uneven distribution of African Americans in

1860 was another precursor to the strong sectional differences regarding the treatment of African Americans in the state during the next century.[1]

In April 1861, when the state of Virginia's secessionist convention voted 88 to 55 to leave the Union, 32 delegates from what was to become West Virginia voted against secession; 11 delegates voted for it, and four abstained. The contingent from western Virginia hurried home to begin a second secessionist movement, this time from the state of Virginia to form a new state and remain in the Union. The western counties of Virginia had long believed that they were ignored by and underrepresented in the Virginia House of Burgesses. The lack of support for internal improvements such as canals to transport products across the mountains into Virginia, and a belief that slavery hindered the economic development of the mountainous sections of the state were areas of contradiction with many in the eastern part of the state. In October 1861, only 37 percent of the voters located in western counties participated in the voting process to secede from Virginia. Because of the low voter turnout and many voting irregularities, the vote was not a clear directive for separation from Virginia. However, after a series of political maneuverings, West Virginia was introduced to the United States Senate as a slave state to appease a large minority of citizens who favored slavery. Only a last-minute amendment to the state constitution, which aimed to gradually abolish slavery, encouraged the Senate to vote West Virginia in as the 35th state in the Union.[2] After it became a state, the West Virginia Legislature passed a law in February 1865 abolishing slavery and, in December 1865, the United States Constitution was amended to abolish slavery nationwide.

* * *

Early in the state's history, West Virginia extended both voting and education rights to African American citizens. Schools in West Virginia had been segregated from the beginning, but in 1866, the West Virginia Legislature provided for a system of schools for black children.[3] In 1891 the West Virginia Legislature established the West Virginia Colored Institute (later West Virginia State University) and in 1895 the Bluefield Colored Institute (later Bluefield State College) to train teachers for the state's black schools. The 1908 Legislature authorized increased funding to support high schools in the state. This legislation began a mass movement to build high schools for white students. The State Attorney General quickly ruled that schools had to be provided for Negro children on the same basis, where the need was warranted.[4] Public schools throughout the State of West Virginia were added as the black population grew.

African Americans had the right to vote in West Virginia when the state was founded and retained that right through the Jim Crow era when most former Confederate states denied voting to black citizens. By the 1888 election,

African Americans had become such a powerful voting force that Democrats accused Republicans of bringing in African Americans from Virginia to vote illegally. By 1910, African Americans comprised 17 percent of the voters in the state in the era before women's suffrage. Between 1890 and 1921 African American voters influenced the legislature to build two black colleges, provide an orphans' home, build an industrial school for boys and one for girls, a hospital for the insane, and a deaf and blind school for African Americans.[5]

A climate of social injustice, Jim Crow laws, and racial hostility was forged in America during the decades of the 1880s, 1890s, and around the turn of the 20th century. The social and political climate of West Virginia provided some measure of hope.

Several economic, socio-cultural, and political factors continued to encourage blacks from the South to migrate to the coalfields of West Virginia. For example, "Lynching's were fewer, educational opportunities were greater, and voting was not restricted to Whites," according to historian Joe William Trotter, Jr.[6] Coalfields also provided a refuge from racial tension found in the South. However, "compared to the urban north, blacks in the coalfields confronted a legal system of racial segregation," wrote Trotter Jr.[7]

Similarly, compared with other ex–Confederate and border states, West Virginia was much more accommodating for African Americans through the 19th century. However, despite providing schools, voting, and a relatively safe environment, the state remained rigidly segregated in almost all aspects of life. By 1910, the black population in West Virginia had reached 64,000, or about 5 percent of the state's 1,221,119 total population. In 1930 the population of the state was 1,729,119, but the black population had almost doubled to 115,000.

* * *

African American migrants from the Southern states drastically changed the landscape of West Virginia and many Northern cities. For example, migration created the great urban black population centers in the Northeastern and Midwestern cities such as New York, Philadelphia, Pittsburgh, Chicago, Detroit, and Cleveland.

During the first Great Migration, between 1910 and 1930, 1.6 million African Americans moved from the rural south to the urban north. The increase in Jim Crow laws and lynching in southern states coupled with better economic opportunities in the north was much of the motivation for the movement. On the way north, some of the migrants decided to settle in West Virginia, often attracted by the promise of good paying jobs.

The Great Migration changed the African American demographic pattern from rural southern farmers to northern industrial workers.

In the mid–1920s, the Harlem Renaissance, a flowering of African

American musical, literary, artistic, and intellectual life, was beginning to change the outlook of African Americans from one of social disillusionment to race pride. In 1926 black intellectual Alain Locke characterized the movement when he wrote, "Negro life is seizing its first chance for group expression and self-determination."[8]

The work of African American intellectuals, scholars, and educators, such as Kelly Miller, Frederick Douglass, Henry Highland Garnet, and poet Paul Laurence Dunbar was important to African Americans, and some black high schools in West Virginia were named after these important figures. West Virginia contributed Booker T. Washington, the most famous black educator, and Carter G. Woodson, who is recognized as the father of black history, to black education. Both received their early education in West Virginia.

* * *

America's economic and industrial growth during the turn of the century (1900–1930) had a major impact on attracting African Americans to migrate to the North. The demand for more workers in factories during the World War I period encouraged factory owners to widen their recruiting of workers. Northern industrialists sent agents south to recruit black workers. Stories in the black weekly newspapers such as the *Pittsburgh Courier*, the *New York Amsterdam News*, and the *Chicago Defender*, which circulated widely in the South, made the North seem cosmopolitan and attractive. Those newspapers coupled with word of mouth encouragement from relatives and friends who had earlier gone north helped to swell the numbers of new migrants.

The completion of the Baltimore and Ohio, Norfolk and Western, and the Chesapeake and Ohio railroads through the developing coalfields of West Virginia in the 19th century spurred the first increase of the African American population in West Virginia. Many African Americans worked on building the railroads in West Virginia and stayed in the state to mine coal. As the coal mining industry grew, the demand for labor followed. Mine owners, realizing that the best method to increase output was to hire more workers, aggressively recruited blacks from the South to work in West Virginia mines.

Many of the new migrant coal miners and their families took up residence in company towns, with populations ranging from 200 to 500 people. Early coalmine owners encouraged managers to hire married over single men since married men were less mobile. Blacks and whites worked in the same coalmines and, on occasion, shared social activities like playing baseball or attending religious services. When houses in company towns were constructed, bosses' homes were separate from the camp houses and, often, the houses of the "Negroes" were divided from the other miners' houses.

Unlike most blacks who migrated to large cities in the North during the Great Migration, African Americans who moved to West Virginia tended to locate in smaller towns and coal camps rather than cities. The most prominent attraction for West Virginia was high paying jobs in the coal industry, while larger towns and cities offered lower wages and had limited access to jobs. In the early 1900s, southern farm workers were paid between \$.75 and \$1.00 per day and factory workers were paid \$2.50 for a nine-hour day. Miners in West Virginia were paid a much better wage, from \$3.20 to \$5.00 per eight-hour day.[9]

Early in the 20th century, some factories were developing in the small cities in the northern and central parts of the state. For example, Weirton Steel in the Northern Panhandle, which was destined to become the biggest employer in the state with more than 12,000 employees, was built in 1909. In 1913, Weirton Steel recruited their first black workers from southern West Virginia, Georgia, Virginia, Pennsylvania, Alabama, and South Carolina. Blacks worked in the mill beside workers recruited from Yugoslavia, Poland, Wales, Italy, and Greece in an "industrial melting pot." However, the black population of Weirton never exceeded 5 percent of the city's population.[10]

The number of schools expanded tremendously during the period from 1900 to 1930 for both black and white children because of the action of the legislature and Attorney General, who encouraged the building of schools for both races. By 1925, West Virginia had 24 black high schools. Among the earliest black high schools were Parkersburg Sumner (first graduating class 1887), Huntington Douglass (founded in 1891), Wheeling Lincoln (1900), Charleston Garnet (1900), Clarksburg Kelly Miller (1903), Gary District (1922), and Williamson Liberty (1923). In most counties, there was only one black high school, as was the case in Harrison County with Clarksburg Kelly Miller. In that situation and other similar cases, all of the black students from the county attended the one black high school. In counties without a black high school, the black students were transported to other counties or sometimes to other states.

* * *

Along with the growth of high schools came interscholastic sports. By the 1920s, basketball had become a very popular high school sport, leading many states to establish governing groups for high school sports to establish rules for competition and conduct state championship events.[11] The first West Virginia State High School Basketball Tournament (including only white teams) was held in 1914. The West Virginia State High School Athletic Association (now the West Virginia Secondary Schools Activities Commission) was established on June 17, 1916, in Clarksburg, West Virginia, and took over the tournament for white high schools. From 125 high schools in 1913, the Association grew to 233 in 1925.[12] In 1925, West Virginia's association petitioned for and received membership to the National Federation of State High School Athletic Associations.

In 1925, the West Virginia Athletic Union (WVAU), the state governing body for black high school sports, was founded. It oversaw the first black state high school basketball tournament in the United States. In 1933, a track and field meet was added and football and baseball championships were added later. But basketball remained the premier athletic event in the black high schools.

By the 1920s, West Virginia's three black colleges had established athletic programs. Bluefield State and West Virginia State were in the process of becoming four-year colleges as were West Virginia's white normal schools. Storer College, located in Harpers Ferry in West Virginia's Eastern Panhandle, remained essentially a two-year college through most of its existence.

* * *

From the early 1900s through World War II, black communities developed in the coal camps as well as in the growing towns and cities of Wheeling, Weirton, Clarksburg, Fairmont, Bluefield, Beckley, and Charleston.[13] The increased number of blacks in southern West Virginia, along with growing black consciousness and expanded earnings, fostered the beginnings of a small black middle-class in West Virginia.[14] Between 1910 and 1930, the majority of black male professionals in West Virginia were employed as clergymen and schoolteachers. During the same time, black female professionals were primarily employed as schoolteachers.[15]

Black teachers in West Virginia initially came largely from other states, particularly Ohio, Virginia, and Pennsylvania.[16] In the 1890s the West Virginia Colored Institute and Bluefield Colored Institute were established to train black teachers along with Storer College, which had been founded in 1867. By 1932, the number of black high schools increased to 32.[17] Most black teachers were college graduates and were well respected in the communities where they lived.

Historically, the church has been a major social institution within the black community. The church is often credited for promoting the establishment of schools, banks, insurance companies, raising the level of black consciousness, serving as a community meeting facility, and supporting community economic development.

Church leaders were often also coal miners working the mines beside other black coal miners. The tie between the black preacher and the coal company could become a double-edged sword. "If the black preacher wished to remain employed in the mines, he was obligated to preach the company message. At times, black preachers who had a much too cozy affiliation with the company earned miners' disrespect, if not the contempt of his congregation," wrote sociologist David A. Corbin.[18]

The black high schools were the most influential intuitions in the black communities because most communities had more than one black church,

Ohio

Pennsylvania

Weirton·

·Bethany
West Liberty
Wheeling·

Morgantown·

Maryland

Fairmont·

Martinsburg.
Harpers Ferry
Charles Town·

Parkersburg·
Clarksburg·

Moorefield·

Glenville·

·Elkins

Huntington
Institute·   ·Charleston

·Montgomery

·Logan   ·Beckley   ·Lewisburg
·Williamson   ·Hinton
·Mullins

Virginia

Kentucky
Gary· ·Kimball
·Bluefield

The cities, towns, and small villages that were important in the development of black high school and college sports in the first half of the 20th century (map by James Atkinson).

but only one black high school, which often drew from a wide geographic area. The black community felt pride in and ownership of their schools. Schools also provided a place for community meetings and events, entertainment, and cultural events for the black community. School athletic teams, particularly the basketball teams, provided ties between black communities throughout the state.

The state of West Virginia thrived during the first half of the 20th century. Its mines, mills, chemical plants, and small businesses prospered, and its economy grew at a faster pace than the national average. The state's population also grew faster than the national rate, reaching two million by mid-century. As the 1950s progressed, however, the state's economy began to stagnate; but, blinded by pride, West Virginians failed to notice the beginnings of decline in the state's industries, roads, and schools.

By 1960, West Virginia lagged in most measures of social, political, economic, and population growth, and the gap widened as the decade progressed. The results of the 1960 Census shocked West Virginians; between 1950 and 1960 the United States population had increased by 18.5 percent. In contrast, West Virginia had lost 7.2 percent of its population. With the loss of 145,131 people, the state's population had dropped from over two million to 1,860,420 people.

Between 1930 and 1970, more than 4.4 million African Americans continued to migrate north and west. After World War II, black West Virginians joined the migration. The Depression of the 1930s reduced the number of black miners, but the total number of miners declined even more sharply from a high of 141,000 in 1947 to just 45,000 in 1969 because of rapid mechanization in the mining industry. African Americans were eliminated from the work force more quickly than whites. The number of black miners dropped from 12 percent of the work force in 1950 to just 5.2 percent in 1970.[19]

Many unemployed black miners began to leave the state for factory jobs in the East and Midwest. In 1940 the black population in West Virginia had peaked at 117,700, 6 percent of the total state population. By 1980 the black population declined to 65,000, only 3 percent of the state's population. In the 1950s, whites began migrating from West Virginia, although clearly not in the same numbers as blacks.[20]

* * *

Other changes were occurring. In May 1954 the Supreme Court ruled on *Brown v. Board of Education*, mandating integration of public schools. West Virginia's governor William C. Marland and superintendent of schools W.W. Trent quickly pushed for integration. Of the 446,000 students in West Virginia's public schools, only 26,000, or 5.7 percent, were black. Monongahela High School in Morgantown and Riverside High School in Elkins integrated immediately. By the end of the 1956–57 school year, 20 of 55 counties in West Virginia were fully desegregated. Twenty-one had partially integrated and 11 had no black students. Only the three Eastern Panhandle counties were still completely segregated.[21]

With few exceptions, integration went smoothly throughout the state except for some of the counties along the Virginia border, such as Greenbrier and Boone counties. Other counties such as Barbour, Mercer, Berkeley, and Mineral wanted to delay integration until the Supreme Court devised a plan for integration. Meanwhile, all of the colleges in the state, except Glenville, had integrated by 1955–1956, and both West Virginia State and Bluefield State had admitted white students as early as the Fall 1954 semester.[22]

In March of 1969, the all-black Bluefield Park Central High School, located in Mercer County in the extreme southern part of the state, played in the WVSSAC tournament, advancing to the regional tournament where they were defeated by an integrated Gary High School team. At the end of the 1968–69 school year, Bluefield Park Central was finally closed, ending the period of segregation in West Virginia public schools.

* * *

Integration in West Virginia was painful, and in some cases disheartening, for the African American community. Integration went only one way; black students were integrated into white schools. All of the black high schools disappeared with integration as well as the traditions, records, and trophies that were associated with them. The black principals, teachers, and coaches, who were leaders in the black communities, were demoted to lesser positions in the newly integrated schools. West Virginia State College and Bluefield State College became predominantly-white colleges by the mid–1970s.[23]

* * *

The black population in the state in the 2010 census was 63,000, or only 3.4 percent of the state's population. That is a low percentage of African Americans compared with the other border states and the ex–Confederate states. Many black West Virginians continue to live in the coal-producing regions in southern West Virginia. Unemployment remains high in the coal industry because increased mechanization and mountain top removal require fewer workers, environmental concerns have reduced the demand for coal and natural gas has become less expensive than coal. Today, athletes compete on school and college teams for men and women in a pattern that follows national trends. African American athletes participate in a higher proportion in football, basketball and track and field. African American participation is lower in wrestling, soccer, and volleyball.

The black schools are gone but remain a bittersweet memory for the students, teachers, and administrators who attended and taught at those schools. The black schools were a major symbol of a segregated age in the United States; they were also a major source of control and pride for African American communities.

2

Intercollegiate Sports in the Black Colleges, 1900–1954

In 1900, tiny Storer College, located in Harpers Ferry, was the first black college in West Virginia to play in an intercollegiate athletic contest. Their opponent in that historic event was Howard University, one of the most prestigious of America's black colleges. The game was played in Washington, D.C., on Howard's home field. Howard, which had played intercollegiate football since 1894, was a budding football power playing at the highest level of black college football. The more experienced and skillful Howard team easily crushed the fledgling Storer team, 43–0, as they would in every other game against Storer in future seasons. The next season Storer traveled to Institute, West Virginia, to play West Virginia State in the first black college football game played in the state.[1] Those early football games were part of the beginnings of intercollegiate sports programs in black colleges in the United States.

The development of black colleges in West Virginia closely followed the trends set by black colleges in the United States through 1950 in both athletic and academic programs. Around the Civil War, black institutions of higher education were founded by missionary organizations to teach former slaves to read and write. Cheyney Institute for Colored Youth (1837) (now Cheyney University of Pennsylvania), Lincoln University (1854) in Pennsylvania, and Wilberforce University (1865) in Ohio were the first black colleges in the United States. Storer College, founded by the Freewill Baptists in 1868, was among this early group of black colleges. These schools developed basic education for elementary and high school students, but also soon established normal or teacher training programs to help satisfy the desperate need for black teachers.

In 1890, the Second Morrill Act was passed, which provided land grants to build colleges for African Americans in states with segregated schools. The West Virginia Colored Institute (1891) was founded under the Second Morrill

Act. The Bluefield Colored Institute (1895) was established in Bluefield, West Virginia, initially as a "high graded" school.

From 1890 through 1915, Booker T. Washington, the head of Tuskegee Institute (now Tuskegee University) in Alabama, was the leading spokesperson for black higher education. Washington was born a slave in Virginia. After emancipation his family moved to Malden, West Virginia. Washington lived in Malden for seven years while he worked in the coal mines and salt furnaces and saved money to go to college. After graduating from Hampton Institute (now Hampton University) and attending Wayland Seminary (now Virginia Union University), he was appointed the principal of the new Tuskegee Normal and Industrial Institute. Through astute political maneuverings he became friends with presidents and rich, liberal businesspeople who supported his fundraising. Washington preached not challenging segregationist and Jim Crow laws but elevating black people through education and developing industrial and agricultural skills for the jobs available to them, thereby demonstrating that they were responsible and reliable citizens. Most black colleges during that period followed his lead and taught a combination of elementary and high school students, vocational skills, agriculture and teacher training. Remaining loyal to West Virginia, Washington lobbied the West Virginia legislature to have West Virginia State located in the Kanawha Valley near Charleston, and he returned many times to speak on the campus.[2]

After 1920, black colleges began to add more college level courses. W.E.B. DuBois, the first African American Ph.D. from Harvard, agreed with Washington that education was a key for black advancement. However, DuBois believed that black schools should focus more on the liberal arts and an academic curriculum because they would develop a leadership elite who could elevate the race. As a prolific author and co-founder of the NAACP, DuBois, along with the NAACP, took a more radical stand than Washington's by advocating for equal rights for African Americans. The opinions of both Washington and DuBois were influential in shaping the beliefs held by other black educators, state legislatures, and white philanthropists.[3] By the 1920s, black higher education had begun to shift away from vocational education to a more traditional college curriculum and to grant four-year college degrees. In 1926, the North Carolina College for Negroes was established as one of the first public liberal arts colleges for black students. By 1940 all three black colleges in West Virginia were granting four-year college degrees.[4]

Athletic programs were added between 1890 and 1910 as most of America's black colleges began to follow the pattern set by white colleges. Football and baseball were the two most popular sports. The first recorded intercollegiate football game between two black colleges took place between Biddle University (now Johnson C. Smith University) and Livingston College in the winter of 1892. The game was played in a snowstorm in Salisbury, North Carolina. Biddle won the game 5–0.[5]

Football rapidly spread to the South, where Tuskegee Institute lost an 1894 game 10–0 to Atlanta University in the Georgia capital. Later that same year, Howard University and Lincoln (Pennsylvania) University played on Thanksgiving Day in the first game of what was to become the biggest black college football rivalry game of the first half of the 20th century. Lincoln won that first game 6–5. Through the early 1900s, both Howard and Lincoln became football powers among the black colleges.[6]

Black college football began to draw large crowds to major games in the post–World War I period. In 1919, the Lincoln-Howard game was played in Shibe Park, a major league baseball field in Philadelphia that was the home field of both the Athletics and the Phillies. The game drew 19,000 fans. Three years later the rivalry game was held in Griffith Stadium, the Washington Senators' baseball field. Sport historian Ocania Chalk writes in *Black College Sport*, "The stage was set for the biggest extravaganza for Negro Americans."[7] Special trains brought black fans from the major east coast cities. The 25,000 fans were not disappointed as Lincoln won a thrilling 13–12 victory.[8] Those games proved lucrative for the colleges and also provided them publicity in the black press. The series continued to draw big crowds during the 1920s.

Through the first half of the 20th century, other black colleges began to strive for the championship of black colleges, named annually by the black weekly *Pittsburgh Courier*. Tuskegee, Morgan, Virginia State, Hampton, West Virginia State, and Bluefield State in the CIAA, Tuskegee and Morehouse in the south, and Wiley in Texas all received mention for the black college national championship during that period.[9]

Although baseball did not prove as popular at the black colleges as did football, Chalk reports that an early intercollegiate game played by a black college took place in 1894. That game between Howard University and the white Kendall Green College (now Gallaudet University) was played in Washington, D.C., and ended in a dispute, with both teams claiming victory. Baseball spread quickly among the black colleges. In 1896 a league was formed including Atlanta Baptist College (now Morehouse College), Atlanta University, Morris Brown College, and Clark University. By 1911 most of the major black colleges had baseball teams.[10]

* * *

Storer College, founded by the Freewill Baptist Church, which had been active in the abolitionist movement, was established to educate the newly freed slaves in the Shenandoah Valley. The college was named for a white Maine businessman named John T. Storer, who endowed the college with a gift of $10,000. Harpers Ferry was selected as the site for the college because of the historic symbolism of abolitionist John Brown's Raid, which climaxed at the Harpers Ferry armory, and for its proximity to the Shenandoah Valley. A more practical reason for establishing Storer in Harpers Ferry was that it was on the main line of the B&O Railroad and had easy access by rail to much of Virginia, Washington, D.C., and Baltimore. But the deciding factor was a grant from the federal government of four large brick houses which had been the residences of the former officers of the federal armory destroyed during the Civil War.[11]

When the boundaries of the new state of West Virginia were established during the Civil War, the federal government wanted the B&O railroad, which ran through Jefferson, Berkeley, and Morgan counties of Virginia, to be part of the new state. Those counties, now known as the Eastern Panhandle of West Virginia, were pro–Confederate and had a large number of slaveholders. Storer College's location in Jefferson County, on the very eastern margin of West Virginia, surrounded on three sides by Virginia and closer to Maryland and Washington, D.C., than most of West Virginia, provided Storer with better transportation and closer cultural ties to those areas than to West Virginia. The remote location from the rest of West Virginia, on the eastern side of the crest of the Appalachian Mountains, was of little importance to the Freewill Baptists, but it essentially isolated the college from the rest of the state.

Storer College opened in 1867 with 19 students. The residents of Harpers Ferry did not welcome the new college; towns people threw rocks at the teachers and the campus was vandalized. Students and faculty often attended classes armed because they feared personal attacks from numerous Confederate sympathizers who lived in the area. The majority of the teachers, as well as the college presidents, were whites from the North. Some were intimidated by the hostile atmosphere and returned home. Even as late as 1944 a cross was burned on the lawn of the college's first black president.[12]

Although called a college, Storer was initially a sub-collegiate institution that taught only the basic subjects of religion, reading, and mathematics, similar to many other schools established to teach former slaves in the post–Civil War period.[13] Storer soon added a rudimentary normal or teacher training program to train black teachers. "The training of African Americans to go back to their communities to teach other African Americans remained one of the main missions of Storer throughout its history," according to James Green, Jr., a local historian whose parents were both Storer graduates.[14]

The West Virginia Board of Education subsidized Storer College from 1881 through 1954, for both the training of teachers and to pay tuition for black high school students in the preparatory program. There was no black high school in Jefferson County until 1938, when Page-Jackson High School was opened in nearby Charles Town. Those subsidies from the West Virginia legislature were important sources of income for the often-struggling private school. Storer became a four-year college when Charles Town's Page-Jackson became fully operational in the 1940s. Following the *Brown* decision in 1954, all subsidies from the state ended because formerly white schools and colleges were now available to black students.[15]

Athletic programs began at Storer in 1900 with the establishment of football and baseball teams. During the first few decades of the 20th century, Storer played against a mix of colleges, clubs, and high schools instead of playing a complete intercollegiate schedule, because the majority of its students were in the high school or preparatory program. During this same period, football competition was developing among the black high schools in Washington and Baltimore, including the Baltimore Colored High School, Morgan College Preparatory School, and Washington's M Street High School.[16]

In 1913, the Storer Athletic Association published eligibility rules stating that a player had to be a full-time student and in school for two months before the season opened unless by mutual agreement with the opposing team. Athletes were also prohibited from using tobacco or liquor.[17] The opponents Storer played were usually either in Washington, D.C., or in the local areas of Virginia, Maryland, or even Pennsylvania, because teams in those states were closer and more accessible by train from Harpers Ferry than other parts of West Virginia.

In 1900, Storer scheduled and lost the historic first game with mighty Howard University. Later in the season Storer defeated the Charles Town Athletic Club 23–0 and then played an intramural game on Thanksgiving Day between campus teams.[18] In 1901, Storer opened the football season on November 9 against Morgan College of Baltimore at a neutral site in Frederick, Maryland. Storer's Howard Bird opened the scoring with a 50-yard end run. The score was tied at halftime. But Morgan, substituting liberally, came back to score in the final minutes of the game to win 10–5 (touchdowns counted five points until 1912). The *Storer Record*, the campus newspaper, commented, "Morgan outweighed Storer, but they were poorly conditioned and the game seemed like a contest between a tiger and an elephant."[19]

Later that 1901 season, Storer played a Thanksgiving Day game at West Virginia State. A student reporter traveled with the team to Institute and provided in-depth coverage of the event in the *Storer Record*. Colorfully describing the midnight train ride over the snow-covered Allegheny Mountains to Parkersburg, West Virginia, he went on to report that on Thanksgiving morning almost the entire school, the corps of cadets, and both teams took a riverboat from Institute to Charleston, where everyone went to the Missionary Baptist Church for church and dinner. After dinner, both teams went to Riverside Park for the game. The game was less exciting as West Virginia State's Yellow Jackets scored two touchdowns in the first half and kicked the extra points for a 12–0 lead. The Yellow Jackets scored again in the second half, but Storer managed to tackle the West Virginia State quarterback in the end zone for a safety to make the final score West Virginia State 18, Storer 2.[20] That game was one of the very few contests between the two colleges because of the difficulty of traveling between Institute and Harpers Ferry.

By 1909, Storer scheduled games against high school teams because the majority of the male students were enrolled in the high school program. But with the sprinkling of college men, Storer was competitive with the large high schools in Baltimore and Washington. Storer defeated Baltimore High School 5–0 but lost to M Street High School of Washington, D.C., 12–0. In 1912, Storer again lost to M Street 21–18, the Howard University Academy or high school team, 3–0, and two athletic clubs. The only win was over a high school pick-up team in Washington for a 1 win 4 loss season record.[21]

From 1900 to 1920, Storer fielded a baseball team but played most of their games against local black athletic clubs. In 1910 Storer played a nine-game schedule, including two games that were lost to Howard University. Storer finished the season with a 5–4 record. The 1912 season highlight for Storer was a doubleheader split on Easter Monday with Lincoln (Pennsylvania) University.[22]

Those games were typical of the early Storer College athletic schedules, which usually had a number of high school and local athletic clubs. Storer had difficulty competing with the larger colleges because of the small number of college students; it was more competitive with the high schools and clubs. In addition, playing high schools and club teams was easier and less expensive than traveling long distances to play college teams.

* * *

The black population of West Virginia grew by almost 80 percent from 1910 to 115,000 in 1930, stimulating the growth of the black state colleges to train teachers. During the 1920s, white two-year normal schools began to teach advanced classes and, by the late 1920s, schools such as Marshall, Fairmont, Shepherd, and Concord began awarding four-year degrees. The black colleges, like the white colleges, expanded their teacher training programs and became four-year colleges. In 1929, the West Virginia Colored Institute became West Virginia State College and Bluefield Colored Institute changed its name to Bluefield State Teachers College in 1932.

However, through the 1920s, Storer College only increased its offerings of college classes to the level of a junior college while remaining under the control of the American Baptist Church (which had merged with the Freewill Baptists). The Storer athletic program expanded in the 1920s with the addition of men's and women's basketball teams and more games added to the football schedule. Basketball was played as early as 1912 when Lorenzo Bird,

An early Storer College women's basketball team. Storer's women's teams were called the Zephyrs (a gentle wind); men's teams were the Tornadoes (courtesy West Virginia and Regional History Center, WVU Libraries).

who had been a football player around the turn of the century, returned for a visit to the campus, and, seeing the need for expanded physical activity, had baskets and back boards installed in the tiny gym on campus where the girls had physical education.

In 1919, the first boys' basketball team lost all five games.[23] In 1921, pledges of $3,400 were secured to refurbish a barn on campus for a gym. Work on the basketball court began in the fall and was completed in December 1921.[24] "It really was a barn and there was not much seating. Most of the fans stood," said James Green, Jr.[25]

Storer attempted to upgrade their athletic image and football schedule in the 1920s in the hope of attracting more college students to enroll. In 1922, the football team took the field in new uniforms. "New old gold and white jerseys gave them the classy look they have before needed," reported the *Storer College Record*.[26] In 1926, the Storer boys' teams took on the name the Golden Tornadoes, while the girls' teams became known as the Zephyrs.

The 1926 football schedule was upgraded to include the games against colleges and one athletic club. Storer was overmatched from the opening game of the season against Lincoln University because most of the Storer team were still high school students who were outweighed by 10 to 20 pounds

The 1922 Storer College Golden Tornado football team (courtesy West Virginia and Regional History Center, WVU Libraries).

per man. The *Storer Record* writer quipped, "The teams were like pigmies and giants, but the Tornadoes played with such speed and skill that Lincoln led by only 27–0 at the half."[27] The final score was Lincoln 63–0. A 20–0 loss to Morgan College was followed with a 20–7 homecoming defeat at the hands of Bluefield State, who was also in their first full season of college competition. Only a 34–0 win by Storer over the Stella A.C. of Hagerstown, Maryland, kept the season from being a total disaster.[28]

Following this difficult 1926 season, Storer reduced the football schedule by playing more high school and club teams and fewer college teams. Storer could not attract enough college men to successfully play against the black college teams that were growing stronger during the 1920s.

During the 1930s, money was a constant problem for Storer College. The American Baptist Church, facing financial difficulties during the Depression, withdrew most of its funding from Storer and many of the other 10 black colleges it was supporting. Also, in 1930, enrollment dropped to 118, only 39 of whom were considered college students; the remaining 79 were high school students.[29]

Because of the problems with finances and uneven enrollment, Storer found it increasingly more difficult during the Depression to compete in football against college teams. The 1931 season was a good example of Storer's football schedule during the decade. The season consisted of five wins over athletic clubs in nearby Charles Town, West Virginia; Winchester, Virginia

(2); Hagerstown, Maryland; and Carlisle, Pennsylvania. With an undefeated record, the Golden Tornadoes traveled to Bordentown, New Jersey Industrial School for the annual Thanksgiving game, a tradition that had begun in 1928. The day turned extremely cold and was made more uncomfortable by the strong wind blowing off the Delaware River, which was only 500 yards from the playing field. The cold hands of the Storer players caused eight fumbles, leading to a 0–0 tied game, the only blemish on a 5–0–1 record that season. The basketball team played a limited schedule of athletic clubs, but also added Delaware State College (now Delaware State University) and the Morgan College junior varsity.[30]

In the late 1930s Storer began to add courses with the intent of becoming a four-year college. By 1939 the enrollment had increased to 144, of whom 83 were college level students and 61 of whom were high school level. In 1944 Richard Ishmael McKinney, a Yale Ph.D., became the first black president at Storer, and two years later the West Virginia Board of Education accredited the Storer B.A. degree in education.[31] After being an elementary school, high school, industrial school, normal school, and junior college for most of its existence, Storer College was finally living up to its name by becoming a four-year college.

Returning veterans using the G.I. Bill swelled the ranks of students at Storer College in the late 1940s as they did at most other colleges. In the halcyon days following World War II, Storer established a full college football schedule, and the basketball schedule was expanded for both men and women. But, in the 1950s, the college began to face severe financial difficulties; enrollment in West Virginia's black colleges declined as the black population in the state declined. The decreasing number of students again made it difficult to put winning teams on the field. The *Storer Record* reported that the 1952 Homecoming football game was lost to Miner Teachers College because of a "shortage of available men." Even the basketball teams began to suffer. In 1953, the boys' basketball team played a limited schedule of nine games. The girls' basketball team played only a seven-game schedule.[32]

Continuing financial problems prompted the college to sell off land, mortgage buildings, and even rent rooms to tourists in the summer. Nothing helped. Diminished support from the American Baptist Church and increasing competition from other colleges caused Storer to amass a debt estimated at $14,000 by the early 1950s.[33]

Storer College began the 1953–54 academic year with only 71 students and a faculty of seven full-time and four part-time teachers.[34] The following year the enrollment grew, but to only 88 students. In 1954 the West Virginia Board of Education notified Storer that it would no longer receive funds for teaching local black high school or teacher training students because integrated schools were available to them. The Storer College Board of Trustees voted on April 13, 1955, to suspend operation of Storer College for the 1955–56 academic year,[35] which proved to be its death knell. Without the state subsidy, heavily in debt, and believing it would not be able to compete for students after integration, Storer College never reopened.[36]

* * *

In 1891, the West Virginia legislature established the West Virginia Colored Institute, one of 17 black land grant colleges established under the Second Morrill Act of 1890. The original Morrill Act had used money from the sale of public lands to build state land grant universities, including West Virginia University. Similarly, the Second Morrill Act used the sale of public lands to build public black colleges, which were also designated as land grant colleges. This designation and the federal funds that followed were major factors in the growth of what ultimately became West Virginia State University. Located a short distance from the state capital of Charleston and between Huntington and Charleston, that became the state's two largest cities, gave West Virginia State huge political clout and access to a significant segment of the state's black population. Those were big advantages in gaining state funding and recruiting West Virginia students.

The West Virginia Colored Institute opened its doors to students in 1892. Originally established as a school for industrial training, it soon developed an academy program for high school students. But from the beginning the emphasis was on a normal program to train teachers.[37]

President Byrd Prillerman (1909–1919) strengthened the academic programs and the West Virginia Legislature changed the school's name in 1915 to the West Virginia Collegiate Institute. College level courses were added to the curriculum. Under the leadership of President John W. Davis (1919–1953), the school continued to grow. In 1927, the enrollment reached 661 students, 381 of whom were at the college level. That same year, the North Central Association of Secondary Schools and Colleges accredited the Institute, making it the first black land grant college in the United States to receive regional accreditation.[38] In 1929, the school was renamed West Virginia State College. The name was changed again in 2004 to West Virginia State University. Often the university is simply referred to as "State."

West Virginia State, the largest and best funded of West Virginia's black schools, consistently had the best athletic program. Its athletic program began in 1901 when coach John C. Gilmer started a football team that played its first game in October against the Parkersburg Colored Athletic Club. State won 11–5. Later that season, State beat the Charleston Athletic Club, 15–5. The final game of the season was the Thanksgiving Day game against Storer College. Ex-governor G.W. Atkinson attended the game and cheered for State. The Yellow Jackets came away with a resounding 18–2 victory. Both West

Virginia State and Storer were considered college teams, but like West Virginia's smaller white colleges of that era, they liberally played students who were enrolled in the industrial program and the high school or academy programs on their campuses, along with the college students.[39] For the next 54 years, State continued to play football against a schedule composed only of other segregated black colleges.

In 1922, West Virginia State hired Adolph P. Hamblin as biology professor and the coach of all sports teams. Hamblin, the namesake of the science building on the campus, had been an outstanding athlete at Galesburg (Illinois) High School and at Knox College in Galesburg, where he had an exceptional college athletic career and earned 16 letters, four each in football, basketball, baseball, and track. The versatile and talented Hamblin was All-State both as an end on the football team and as a guard on the basketball team. In addition, he batted over .400 for the baseball team during his junior and senior years.[40]

West Virginia State developed a strong football program from the beginning under Coach Hamblin. The Yellow Jackets went undefeated in 1922, Hamblin's first year as coach. The Yellow Jackets won the Midwest Athletic Association (MAA) championship and claimed to be the national black college champions. However, the *Pittsburgh Courier* awarded the national championship title to Hampton Institute, even though Hampton Institute's 6–1 record

Adolph Hamblin was hired by West Virginia State to teach biology and coach all sports in 1922. West Virginia State had excellent football teams under Hamblin who coached football until 1945. The science building at West Virginia State is named Hamblin Hall in his honor (courtesy West Virginia State University Archives and Special Collections).

was not as good as West Virginia State's undefeated record. The black weekly newspapers, particularly the *Pittsburgh Courier* and *Chicago Defender*, carried extensive coverage of black college sports. Both circulated widely in the South and both named national football champions. Hampton was named national black college champions over West Virginia State because they were an established football power among the black colleges and had won the prestigious Colored Intercollegiate Athletic Association (CIAA) football championship that year.

Hamblin was fortunate to have team captain Mark "Foxy" Cardwell, who was nicknamed "The Fox" because he was such an elusive running back. Growing up on a farm south of Columbus, Ohio, Cardwell attended integrated Columbus East High School, where he was a football star in the same backfield as Chic Harley, who went on to become Ohio State University's first All-American. Cardwell chose to attend segregated West Virginia State, where he became an All-American football player, and was well known throughout black communities in West Virginia. Cardwell stayed in West Virginia after graduation to coach at Clarksburg's Kelly Miller High School and later returned as coach at West Virginia State.

The featured game of the 1924 season with Wilberforce College of Ohio was played in Columbus, Cardwell's hometown. Three thousand fans attended the game, including the mayor of Columbus, attesting to Cardwell's popularity there. The game ended in a tie.[41]

The West Virginia State football team was beginning to draw national attention in the ranks of black college teams. The Yellow Jackets, led by All-American quarterback Elbert Turner, had another undefeated team in 1925 with a 6–0–1 record. West Virginia State was scored on only once during that entire season, in a 7–3 win over Wilberforce. In the highlight game of the season, State battled Howard University to a 0–0 tie. At the end of the season, Howard (6–0–2) and Tuskegee Institute (8–0–1) were named national champions. Howard, which withdrew from the CIAA over an ineligible player controversy, was successful playing an independent schedule and Hampton claimed the championship of the South. West Virginia State was recognized only as being one of the "other" top teams.[42] The Yellow Jackets went undefeated again in 1936 (8–0) under Coach Hamblin. This time they were named National Negro Co-Champions, along with Virginia State, by the *Pittsburgh Courier.*

Basketball drew much less interest than football on the West Virginia State campus. The basketball team was begun 18 years after football was started. In its first season, 1918–19, State played, and defeated, both Wilberforce College and the Columbus (Ohio) YMCA. The early home games were played in the small gym in the E.B. White Trades Building, but the team often practiced out of doors. Hamblin was the basketball coach from 1922 to 1933.

MEET ME AT THE ARMORY Charleston, W. Va. Saturday March 26, 1921 8: p. m.
Wilberforce University vs West Virginia Collegiate Institute.
Roller skating after the game. An evening of entertainment. Bring a friend.

West Virginia State's 1921 basketball team. Despite the excitement of contests with schools like Wilberforce from Ohio, it was necessary to add roller skating to increase attendance at games during the school's third year to have basketball (courtesy West Virginia State University Archives and Special Collections).

In the 1930s, West Virginia State was a member of the Midwest Athletic Association which included Kentucky State, Wilberforce, Virginia State, and Lincoln University. The Yellow Jackets basketball team won the MAA championships in 1935, 1938, and 1940, under three different coaches.[43]

The "Golden Age" of West Virginia State sports began in the 1940s. In December 1941, West Virginia State joined the CIAA. In 1942 Fleming Hall, a new and modern gymnasium, was completed with an excellent basketball court, one of the best in the CIAA, as well as a swimming pool. Hamblin retired from coaching football after 23 years in 1945, to be replaced by his former star player, Mark Cardwell.[44] Coach Cardwell was able to build on the solid foundation that Coach Hamblin had laid, the new conference affiliation, and the new facilities to create an athletic powerhouse. Combining the returning service veterans from World War II with the new recruits from both in-state and out-of-state high schools, Cardwell created a two-sport juggernaut. In 1948, West Virginia State won the CIAA football, regular season basketball, and basketball tournament championships and was recognized as the national Negro college basketball champions. In 1949, State again won the CIAA regular season and tournament basketball championships. In 1950,

West Virginia State won the CIAA regular season basketball championship and was runner-up in the CIAA tournament. And, in 1951, State won the CIAA football championship. One national and seven conference championships were an astounding achievement for Coach Cardwell.

* * *

The Bluefield Colored Institute (now Bluefield State College) was the third college established for African Americans in West Virginia. The city of Bluefield, which barely exceeded 20,000 people, was the biggest city in a largely rural region of southern West Virginia. While Bluefield was within 100 miles of 50,000 of West Virginia's 117,745 African Americans, Bluefield State historically had difficulty recruiting students, particularly against West Virginia State. Bluefield State was the poor relative of the West Virginia black colleges because it was poorly funded by the legislature; it was without the federal funding that West Virginia State received; and it did not receive church funding, as had Storer College.

Bluefield State opened in 1895 with 18 students and offered class work extending down to the elementary school level. The teacher training or normal diploma program grew slowly. By 1901, only three graduates had received two-year normal diplomas.

In 1913–14, the black colleges in West Virginia received 18 percent of the state's funding for colleges, yet African Americans represented only 5.3 percent of the population. Part of the reason for the disproportionately high amount of funding was the black colleges' role in educating a larger number of high school and elementary students when compared with white colleges. Many of the local county school systems sent black children to the colleges instead of establishing a "separate but equal" school program. This was particularly true at both Bluefield State and Storer. In 1914–15, the Bluefield State College catalog reported that 169 students were enrolled in the elementary or high school programs, while only 45 students were enrolled in the college teacher training program.[45]

Despite these low numbers, in 1914 Bluefield State fielded its first football team. As at many colleges, the athletic program was discontinued during World War I because of the lack of men on campus and the influenza epidemic that swept the nation. In the first game following World War I, Bluefield suffered a humiliating 73–0 loss to West Virginia State. Even as late as 1924, the Bluefield State football team consisted mostly of boys in the Bluefield State high school program, and the team played a schedule of area black high school teams.[46]

In the 1920s, interest in football surged at black colleges nationwide, similar to what was occurring at white colleges. Many black colleges increased the quality of football play by hiring experienced coaches and improving the football facilities. In 1920, the *Pittsburgh Courier*, which circulated in West Virginia began to cover black college football. This coverage, in part, increased interest in black college football. By 1926 Cleveland Abbott, the highly successful coach at Tuskegee in Alabama, noted that the public was more interested in the games among black colleges and that more students were coming out for the teams.[47]

In 1925, Bluefield State, following the lead of other black colleges, moved to strengthen its athletic program. The Bluefield State football team had previously played at the County Fair Grounds, but in 1925 excavation began on an on-campus football stadium. Harry R. "Big Jeff" Jefferson was hired as the athletic director and football coach, and by default he was also the basketball coach. Jefferson had played at Parkersburg Sumner High School and West Virginia State before transferring to Ohio University in 1920; at that time West Virginia State did not grant four-year degrees. He received his undergraduate degree from Ohio University in 1922 and coached at Wilberforce College in Ohio before moving back to West Virginia.[48]

In 1926, the struggling Bluefield State added collegiate level classes in education, business administration, and home economics to the existing teacher training classes in a move to upgrade the academic programs to the college level and become a four-year college. Bluefield State had grown to 338 students, but many of the students were in the sub-college level classes and almost all of them were local residents from McDowell or Mercer counties in West Virginia or from nearby Tazewell County, Virginia.[49]

By 1926, Bluefield State played a full football schedule of five college teams for the first time. The Blues posted a 3–2 record defeating Morristown (TN) Normal and Industrial College, Storer College, and Virginia Seminary. Wilberforce defeated Bluefield 16–0 and, in the in-state rivalry game, West Virginia State easily beat Bluefield State, 24–7. Jefferson was not particularly interested in coaching basketball except that it helped him recruit future players for the football team. That winter the Bluefield State basketball team played a schedule that included college teams such as Howard University, Lincoln University, and Storer College, but Bluefield State also played Huntington Douglass, Clarksburg Kelly Miller, London Washington, Charleston Garnet, and Parkersburg Sumner high schools. Playing high school teams was a smart recruiting tactic for Coach Jefferson, as it gave him a chance to scout the state for athletic talent. The Bluefield State yearbook reported, "It is rumored that several of the high school stars will cast their lot with the Big Blues next season."[50]

By 1927, the Big Blues, as they were being called in honor of their coach "Big Jeff," were ready for high level football competition even with a small team of fewer than 30 players. The turning point in the season was the traditional game against West Virginia State. The game was played in front of an estimated crowd of 5,000 fans at Lakin Field in Institute. The Yellow Jackets jumped off to a 6–0 lead in the first quarter, but Bluefield State came back to score three touchdowns, securing an 18–6 victory. In a post-game story, William Nunn, the sports editor for the *Pittsburgh Courier*, wrote, "Coach Jefferson [is] the most sought-after man in college circles. From nothing three years ago he has welded together a machine today which stands at the peak of offensive football."[51]

The 1927 Big Blues had performed the near impossible feat of going from a 3–2 record to an 8–0–1 record in only their second season of college competition and against strong college teams. The *Pittsburgh Courier* named Bluefield State the 1927 co-national champions along with Tuskegee Institute. The 1927 season was an unprecedented achievement for a team that was so new to playing college football.

In 1928 Bluefield State had another strong team. The Blues won their first three games of the season. The next game against the traditionally strong Howard University was played at Bluefield on a miserable day when rain and snow fell intermittently. The wet field proved to be difficult for both teams and the game ended in a 0–0 tie.

The traditional Homecoming game played against West Virginia State matched two undefeated teams. Bluefield State had tied the Howard Bison while West Virginia State had defeated them. Bluefield State's strategy was to punt the ball frequently and rely on a strong defensive line to play for breaks. The strategy was successful, leading to a 13–0 victory for Bluefield State.[52]

Two more wins pushed the Big Blues' record to 6–0–1. The final game was the Columbus Shrine Club's Thanksgiving Day game played in Columbus, Ohio. The Shrine Club traditionally invited two of the best black college teams in the country to play a Thanksgiving Day game as the featured event of their holiday week activities. This game was one of the highlights of the black college football season in the 1920s. The appeal of this game was that it matched Bluefield State, the defending national champions, with Morehouse College of Atlanta. Morehouse had a strong football tradition, having claimed four "southern championships" in 12 years under the coaching of B.T. Harvey. The game was a mismatch from the beginning. The Big Blues dominated the first half, scoring 34 points and holding Morehouse to no first downs. In the second half Bluefield State coasted to an easy 40–0 win before a big crowd of 7,000 fans.[53]

The *Pittsburgh Courier* again named Bluefield State the Co-National Negro Champions along with Wiley College of Texas. Both teams had an 8–0–1 record. A post-season game was scheduled between Bluefield State and Wiley to be played in Marshall, Texas, which would determine the national champion, but a last-minute financial disagreement caused the game to be canceled.[54]

Bluefield State's back-to-back national football championships in 1927 and 1928 were a great accomplishment for the Big Blues, considering they had been playing a full college schedule only since 1926. In addition, Bluefield State had a small enrollment and very limited funding for the college and the athletic program. During that two-year span Bluefield State posted an undefeated 18-0-2 record. Quarterback Fred Buford, fullback Artis Graves, and tackle Ted Gallion were named to the *Chicago Defender* black college All-American team.[55]

Coach Jefferson left Bluefield State in 1930 to coach at North Carolina A&T College. He returned to Bluefield State in 1932, though, and led the Blues to an 8-0-1 record that season, before moving on to Virginia State in 1934. Jefferson was again extremely successful at Virginia State, where he led the Trojans to CIAA championships in 1936, 1938, 1939, and 1945. In addition, Virginia State was also named co-national champions in 1936 with West Virginia State. Jefferson then moved to Hampton Institute, where he was highly successful from 1949 to 1957. In 1961 he was hired as the first full-time CIAA Commissioner, and, in recognition of his successful coaching and administrative career, Jefferson was named to the NAIA Hall of Fame in 1961 and the American Football Coaches Hall of Fame in 2010. He died in 1966.[56]

In 1929 Bluefield State moved to becoming a full college with a name change to Bluefield State Teachers College. In 1930 Bluefield State's enrollment was 293 students, but only 70 were enrolled in the college program, and of those, 54 (mostly women) were enrolled in the normal diploma program. Women continued to outnumber male students in the normal program at an almost two-to-one ratio. The high school program was discontinued in 1933 and the name was changed again in 1943 to Bluefield State College.[57]

Harry "Big Jeff" Jefferson, a graduate of Parkersburg Sumner High School, who attended West Virginia State and graduated from Ohio University. Big Jeff coached the Bluefield State football team to back to back national football co-championships in 1926 and 1927. After coaching at four CIAA colleges, he was named the first CIAA commissioner in 1961 (courtesy Bluefield State College Archives).

Despite the low number of male students, in 1932 Bluefield State joined the CIAA, one of the oldest and most prestigious of the African American college conferences. Founded in 1912 at a meeting at Hampton Institute, the CIAA was the third oldest athletic conference after the white Big Ten (1896) and the white Missouri Valley Conference (1907).

The purpose of the conference was to control excesses in college athletics by setting standards for officials, scheduling, and championship play. But the conference had a higher calling in the eyes of the founders. "To the founders, the new athletic organization would represent the very best sport could offer—characterized by strict adherence to rules, sportsmanship, fiscal transparency and impeccable organizational structure ... and by extension combat the deeply entrenched stereotypes of black inferiority and moral degradation," wrote historians David K. Wiggins and Chris Elzey.[58]

The founding members of the CIAA—Hampton Institute, Shaw University, Howard University, Lincoln University, and Virginia Union University—were among the leading black colleges of the time. The CIAA served as a model for other African American athletic conferences and, by 1932, it had expanded to 12 members. Winning a championship in the CIAA was considered the highest honor an African American college could achieve, and the conference champions were often considered the "National Negro Champions."[59] Most of the CIAA colleges were located in Virginia and North Carolina, making it easier for Bluefield State, located in the extreme southern part of West Virginia, to create an athletic schedule.

The post–World War II years were good for Bluefield State. In 1946–47 more than 150 veterans enrolled under the G.I. Bill, straining Bluefield State's capacity, and in 1949 a record 63 students graduated. That year Bluefield State received accreditation from the North Central Association of Colleges and Schools.

Even with the glut of veterans after World War II, Bluefield State never reached an enrollment level of more than 1,000 students before integration, largely because of West Virginia's small black population. In addition, Bluefield State offered many of the same academic programs as West Virginia State, which was only 125 miles away. Bluefield State continually lost the battle for West Virginia's African American students because it never reached the funding level or prestige that State had achieved. Located on a steep hillside overlooking the railroad yards, the Bluefield State campus suffered in comparison with that of West Virginia State, where the buildings are spread over an attractive, level campus set along the banks of the Kanawha River. Bluefield State held little appeal to out-of-state African American students.

The potential pool of students was further depleted when the African American population in southern West Virginia began to decline during the Great Depression, when black miners were the first to be laid off. The percentage of black miners in the labor force fell from more than 22 percent in 1930 to about 17 percent in 1940. "The Depression and World War II also unleashed forces that transformed the coal industry, and stimulated massive out-migration in the post war years," wrote historian Joe William Trotter, Jr.[60] With the black population declining, Bluefield State suffered significant enrollment problems except during the immediate post–World War II period when veterans used the G.I. Bill.

While the West Virginia State-Bluefield State football game had remained a heated rivalry through the 1930s and 1940s, West Virginia State began to dominate the rivalry following their 1936 national championship season. During World War II, State continued their strong athletic program by using military personnel who were training on the Institute campus. In the post-war years both colleges grew to record enrollments from returning veterans using the G.I. Bill to attend college. West Virginia State remained larger and the football and basketball teams profited from the returning military personnel, winning every game in the in-state rivalry from 1942 through the end of the decade.

In 1950 Bluefield State had a good team and the West Virginia State game was being played in Bluefield. More than 8,000 fans filled Mitchell Stadium on a beautiful fall day perfect for the Bluefield State Homecoming festivities. The Blues were led by Ergie Smith, a halfback who had been a star athlete at the black Keystone (WV) High School.[61]

The game was high scoring but closely contested. A record-setting 108-yard kickoff return by Bluefield State's Pete Oldham gave the Blues the lead. But late in the game West Virginia State scored to take a 32–30 lead. With four minutes remaining, Bluefield State had the ball on its own 30-yard line. In the daily newspaper the *Bluefield Telegraph*, sports editor Stubby Currance wrote, "But just as it looked as if the sun set on the chances of the Big Blue victory Halfback Ergie Smith broke loose through the right side, cut back and sprinted seventy yards into pay dirt and victory for Bluefield State.... Only four minutes of play remained when the Kimball youth waltzed himself into the Big Blue Hall of Fame and earned himself a place among other Bluefield State gridiron immortals."[62] Bluefield State students celebrated a 36–32 victory during the Homecoming dance that evening.

Bluefield State had a successful football team that year, posting an 8–2 record in addition to defeating West Virginia State in the annual in-state rivalry game. "That game against West Virginia State was our big game every year. When it was in Bluefield we would play them at Mitchell Field and draw between 10,000 and 12,000 fans, because everyone would want to see that game," recalled Ergie Smith.[63] Mitchell Field, the biggest stadium in Bluefield, was the home of Bluefield Park Central, the black high school, which played on Thursday nights; Bluefield High School, the white high school, which played on Friday nights; and Bluefield State College, which played on Saturday afternoons.

In 1951 Bluefield State had another good team, matching 4–1 records with West Virginia State going into the Homecoming game to be played in Institute. The pre-game article in the *Charleston Daily-Mail* touted Bluefield's Ergie Smith and West Virginia State's lineman Herb Henderson as players to watch. State was favored despite Bluefield's winning the previous year's game. The article mentioned that Bluefield State had not won in Institute since 1941.[64]

The West Virginia State Homecoming game was played in front of 4,000 fans at State's Lakin Field. Bluefield State looked good early in the game by scoring first on a short pass to take a 7–0 lead. But West Virginia State stormed back to score the next 17 points and pull out a 17–7 homecoming win.[65] Bluefield State's Ergie Smith was well defended in that game and was not able to provide the heroics of the previous season's game.

Ergie Smith, a graduate of Kimball High School. While at Bluefield State Smith was named to the All-CIAA football team and to the *Chicago Defender* and *Pittsburgh Courier* All-American teams in 1951. He became a very successful basketball coach at both black and integrated high schools in West Virginia (courtesy Bluefield State College Archives).

Smith recalled, "They had a 'spy' [defensive player assigned to guard him] on me but everyone did that season. They just had a better team and we did not play as well."[66] That victory was West Virginia State's revenge for the Bluefield State upset win the previous season.

However, Bluefield State went on to an outstanding 7–3 season record. With the homecoming victory, West Virginia State went on to win the CIAA championship, their second football title in coach Mark Cardwell's first six years. Ergie Smith had a great 1951 season for Bluefield State. He was named to the All-CIAA Team and the All-American teams named by the *Pittsburgh*

Courier and the *Chicago Defender*. Smith had an offer of a try-out with the New York Giants, but instead took a teaching and coaching position at the black Gary District High School. "I had to make the team with the Giants. That was a risk and pro football was not big-time then like it is now. I had a guaranteed job at Gary so I took it," said Smith.[67] Smith made the right choice because he went on to a stellar high school coaching career, first as a co-head coach at segregated Gary District High School, later at integrated Gary High School, and finally at the consolidated Mount View High School. He coached state championship basketball teams at all three schools and was later elected to the board of education.[68]

In the fall of 1955, Bluefield State left the CIAA and joined the West Virginia Intercollegiate Athletic Conference (WVIAC). Integration soon followed as white students began to enroll at Bluefield State. Through the first 60 years of its existence, Bluefield State had been overshadowed by the much larger, better funded, and more prestigious West Virginia State, except on the football field. During the glory years of the mid–1920s, when "Big Jeff" roamed the sidelines and the Big Blues won two national Negro football championships and again in 1950, Bluefield State was able to compete with West Virginia State on the football field and basketball court. For Bluefield State, the college that was the equivalent of the poor relative in the state, the national championships and athletic success were major bragging points in an otherwise uneven struggle for supremacy between the state's two black public colleges.

* * *

The three black colleges in West Virginia represented three very different types of colleges during the first half of the 20th century. Storer College, founded shortly after the Civil War to educate the newly freed slaves, struggled throughout its existence. Storer was a private church college that was founded by, but that received little financial support from, the Freewill Baptist Church. It survived financially only due to subsidies provided by the state of West Virginia to teach black high school students, there being no local black high school. Located on the margin of the state in the Eastern Panhandle, Storer had few ties to West Virginia. Recruiting students proved difficult and in most years the high school students at Storer College outnumbered the college students.

Because of the low enrollment of college students, the Storer athletic program was never successful. For most of its existence, Storer played a schedule of black teams from high schools, industrial schools, and club teams with an occasional college game in the mix. When West Virginia withdrew the state subsidy following the *Brown* decision, heavy debt and low enrollment forced the college to close.

West Virginia State was a land grant college founded by the West Virginia legislature in 1891 under the Second Morrill Act. West Virginia State had the advantage of being centrally located, near Charleston, the state capital. Well-funded by the state government, West Virginia State was the most prosperous of the state's three black colleges. In 1922 Adolph Hamblin, hired as a science instructor and coach, built an athletic program that played at the highest level of black college football, competing for black national championships and being named co-champions in 1936. Joining the CIAA in 1941 and hiring Mark Cardwell in 1945 took State to the apex of athletic power in black college sports in both football and basketball.

Bluefield State, though it did not have funding or enrollment comparable to West Virginia State, became a black college football power against all odds in the 1920s. Under the leadership of coach Harry "Big Jeff" Jefferson, the "Big Blues" were named national black college football co-champions in 1927 and co-champions in 1928. In 1936 West Virginia State was named co-national champion, with a 7-0-1 record under coach Adolph Hamblin. A friendly rivalry had developed between the two black state colleges, and their annual football game became a centerpiece of life for educated black West Virginians.

West Virginia's three black colleges were important to the growing African American community in the state in the first half of the 20th century. They provided an educated middle class and teachers for the growing segregated school system. They produced people who were leaders and role models in the small scattered African American communities. The college athletic teams demonstrated success and instilled pride by playing at the very top of black college sports and by being named national champions. From the turn of the century through World War II, football was the most popular and successful sport at West Virginia's black colleges. Big football games provided social events for alumni, and successful seasons publicized the colleges in the black weekly newspapers. The football team and, to a lesser extent, the other sports were a way to get the college's name before the public and were used to attract badly needed students. The black colleges demonstrated a pathway to leadership and success in a very segregated world.

3

The First Black State
High School Basketball
Tournament in the United States,
1925–1944

On Thursday, March 19, 1925, 11 of West Virginia's 24 black high school basketball teams gathered at the tiny West Virginia Collegiate Institute gym in Institute, West Virginia, for the inaugural West Virginia Athletic Union (WVAU) state basketball tournament. The *Pittsburgh Courier* referred to the event as "[t]he first of its kind staged in West Virginia among Negro schools and one of the first ever held in any Negro school in the country."[1] The tournament, a double elimination affair, required 18 games over a three-day period to reduce the field to the championship finalists.

"My players were really excited about going to that first tournament, but they didn't know much about basketball," recalled Andrew Calloway, coach at DuBois High School in Mount Hope. "We had just played playground basketball. You see, we didn't have a gym and had to practice outside at a basket that hung on a pole."[2] The inexperience of the DuBois players was evident as they lost their first two games, 21–14 to Montgomery Simmons and 20–8 to Gary District, which had started its basketball team several years before the 1925 tournament.

Mount Hope DuBois and Gary District were typical of the small black high schools found in nearly half of West Virginia's 55 counties. The schools' size reflected the small African American population in the state. These small high schools were located in the state's small towns and coal camps; the few exceptions (Charleston Garnet, Huntington Douglass, Fairmont Dunbar, Clarksburg Kelly Miller, and Wheeling Lincoln) were located in cities. Most of the black high schools were isolated from each other by long distances and bad mountain roads, and they had few amenities such as gymnasiums, theaters, and typewriters.

In 1911, the Gary District, located in the southern West Virginia coalfields,

42

had four elementary schools for black children. Junior high school classes were added in 1913; high school classes began in 1922 and the first high school class graduated from Gary Negro High School in 1923. After the building that housed the high school was destroyed by fire, a new brick building with 10 classrooms was opened in the fall of 1926, which housed all 12 grades. The improved high school was called Gary District High School to distinguish it from the white high school, which was known by its nickname, "Gary High School Coal Diggers."[3]

Watching Gary District in the first state tournament was a thrill for James Wilkerson, a 1924 graduate who had been on the school's first basketball team. He had a front-row seat for the action on and off the court.

"I was a student at West Virginia State at the time and they drafted a bunch of us to be hosts to the different teams," recalled Wilkerson. "They played day and night because it was double elimination, and we had to be there the whole time we weren't in class. In those early tournaments at West Virginia State, everyone slept on army cots in the gym. They set up army cots and assigned teams to different parts of the room. It was very noisy and there were a lot of distractions. Later, when the new gym was built, they put the teams in rooms below the gym, but that was hard on the teams that won because if you were in with teams that had been eliminated, they wanted to horse around."[4]

When he attended college, Wilkerson's ties with basketball were primarily through the tournament. "At West Virginia State, I didn't play on the basketball team. I tried out for it, but I really didn't have much talent for basketball. I did help some in football. I had a little bit of speed and an ability to remember plays." But after graduation in 1928, he returned home and followed a familiar career path. "I took a job as an elementary school principal in McDowell County. I was an elementary school teacher and principal for four years. In 1932, they offered me the teaching and coaching job at Gary District High School, and I took it. I coached at Gary District High School from 1932 to 1965 when they closed and merged it with Gary Coal Diggers High School."[5]

After two and a half days of hard basketball, McDowell County's Kimball High School reached the winner-take-all championship game against Wheeling Lincoln High School. Kimball had defeated Wheeling Lincoln (9–7) earlier in the tournament. On the surface, the championship game seemed to be a mismatch because Wheeling, located on the Ohio River in the Northern Panhandle of the state, was the largest city in the state with a population approaching 30,000. Kimball was a small town of around 1,500 people in the southern coal fields. Wheeling Lincoln, founded in 1866, was one of the oldest black high schools in West Virginia and one of the first public schools for African Americans in the United States. A high school program began at

Lincoln School in 1900, and in 1914, when J.H. Rainbow was appointed principal, he established an athletic program and served as coach. By the 1920s the enrollment in all 12 grades grew to 450 students with 20 teachers.

Despite being the largest city in West Virginia in 1925, Wheeling had a small black population, with only 4 or 5 percent of the total population. Because the city had been a hotbed of abolition and statehood during the Civil War, there were only 100 slaves in all of Ohio County in 1860. In fact, the 125 free blacks outnumbered the slaves; Ohio was one of two counties in West Virginia to have more free blacks than slaves.

By 1925, Wheeling had a strong black professional class with a black doctor, dentist, undertaker, attorney, and, of course, the teachers at Lincoln School, which housed grades one through 12. Since Wheeling was an urban area, African Americans also found employment in service occupations, working as waiters, bartenders, domestics, and janitors. In addition, some African Americans worked for the Valley Camp Coal Company. Wheeling served as a cultural and business hub for African Americans not only in the Northern Panhandle of West Virginia, but also in the Ohio River towns of eastern Ohio.

Kimball is a small coal town located in McDowell County on the extreme southern end of the state. Ironically, McDowell County, which had no slaves or free blacks in 1860, grew to have the largest concentration of African Americans in West Virginia when the coal companies began recruiting large numbers of African Americans as labor in the coal mines after the turn of the century. The new workers came primarily from the nearby states of Virginia and Kentucky.

Kimball may have been a small town, but it had about as many African American high school students as Wheeling Lincoln. "About forty percent of the Kimball population were black," said Ergie Smith, a Kimball High School graduate. "The high school in Kimball was for black students and the white kids in Kimball went to either Welch or Northfork High Schools. Plus, Kimball drew black students from that end of McDowell County from towns like Welch, Keystone, Yeager, Bradshaw, and the small coal camps. Kimball was a good-sized high school for the time. In addition to having a large number of students, Kimball had the best gym of any black high school in the district and an excellent coach in H. Smith Jones," added Smith.[6]

Kimball had beaten Wheeling Lincoln 9–7 in a low scoring contest earlier in the tournament and, true to form, took an 11–6 half-time lead. In the second half, however, the Kimball players had difficulty making foul shots. Wheeling Lincoln was able to stage a comeback, pulling out a narrow 25–24 win and the first state WVAU championship. Approximately 175 fans watched the game that the *Pittsburgh Courier* pronounced a "huge success."[7]

That championship game and the 1925 WVAU State Basketball tourna-

The First State High School Champions - 1925

Lincoln High School — Wheeling, W. Va.
First Row: J. H. Rainbow, Principal and Coach; L. Berry, H. Dennis, L. Campbell, L. Spriggs; Back Row: W. Riley, W. Kinney, C. Earley, J. Woods, O. Shannon. C. Hunter.

Wheeling Lincoln High School basketball team, winner of the first West Virginia Athletic Union State Basketball Tournament held in 1925. Wheeling defeated Kimball 25–24 in the championship game of the inaugural eleven team double elimination tournament (courtesy West Virginia State University Archives and Special Collections).

ment were events of historic importance because West Virginia was the first state to hold a statewide high school basketball championship tournament for African American high schools. In 1925 the West Virginia Athletic Union was formed at West Virginia State College under the leadership of Adolph Hamblin, State's coach and athletic director. As sport historian Robert Pruter wrote in *The Rise of American High School Sports and the Search for Control: 1880–1930*, "In the 1920s, basketball was played by more high schools than any other sport, and it was often the genesis of many state high school athletic associations, many of which were formed to regulate basketball."[8] A 1924 survey of 399 high schools nationwide found that basketball was the most popular sport in high schools, with 98 percent of the high schools surveyed sponsoring a basketball team. According to the same survey, 91 percent sponsored football, 64 percent sponsored baseball, and 44 percent sponsored a track and field team.[9] The percentages of teams in West Virginia high schools would have been very similar to the national study, particularly because of the growth in the number of small high schools in West Virginia during the period from 1910 through 1930. Many small white high schools such as Sand Fork, Jane Lew, Bethany, and West Liberty were too small to field football

Kimball High School basketball team, runner-up in the 1925 WVAU Basketball Tournament. Although Kimball had defeated Wheeling Lincoln 7–5 early in the double elimination tournament, Kimball lost to Lincoln in the finals. Kimball High School was the strongest team in early WVAU basketball tournaments winning four of the first nine state championships between 1925 and 1933 (courtesy West Virginia State University Archives and Special Collections).

teams but did have basketball teams. The 1925 white West Virginia Secondary Schools Athletic Commission (WVSSAC) state boys' basketball tournament drew 72 teams to Buckhannon and the 1924 girls' tournament drew 24 teams to the championship finals held in Spencer.[10]

As in many other states, the formation of the West Virginia Athletic Union in 1925 led to the first statewide tournament for black high schools. The WVAU went on to regulate other sports when in 1933 a track and field championship was held at West Virginia State and later a state football champion was named.[11] However, the state basketball tournament remained the centerpiece of black high school sports in West Virginia.

According to Pruter, the experience of African Americans in the creation of African American interscholastic sports varied depending on the section of the country. In the Deep South, the white establishment kept the black schools impoverished. States such as Mississippi, Alabama, and Georgia lagged far behind white schools in the South and black schools in other parts of the country. In the border region between the north and south, economic support for black high schools was not comparable to that of the white high schools, but was still far superior to the economic support given to black high schools in the Deep South, and black high school sports thrived in the border states in the 1920s despite being rigidly segregated.[12]

The founding of the first high school basketball tournament for African American high schools put West Virginia in the forefront of basketball among black high schools in the United States. Pruter added, "The border states were where we find the origin of interscholastic sports for the black high schools, namely West Virginia, Virginia, Kentucky, Missouri, Kansas, as well as in Washington, D.C. and southern Illinois."[13] In addition, both Indiana and Illinois had some legal segregation.

Early on, Washington, D.C., held a four-high school basketball tournament that was clearly not on the level of the West Virginia tournament. Illinois also held a basketball tournament for black schools in 1925 in the southern part of the state. The Illinois tournament was only a regional and not a state-wide tournament like West Virginia's.[14]

In 1925 West Virginia founded the first state black high school association and held the first black "statewide" basketball championship tournament. Most of the other segregated states did not form black state athletic associations until the 1930s, when they began to hold statewide tournaments, according to Pruter.[15]

The histories of segregated high school basketball tournaments in many states are incomplete, but there are records of segregated school basketball state tournaments beginning in 1928 in North Carolina and Virginia. In Florida, Lincoln Park Academy of Fort Pierce won the inaugural black tournament in 1930. In 1931, Oklahoma organized an association and the following year in Kentucky, Louisville Central defeated Free High School of Marysville to win the first Kentucky black tournament. In 1934 Tennessee initiated a tournament for black high schools and Texas followed in 1938.[16] Other states also initiated black high school tournaments in the 1930s; however, little information is available. But all were begun later than the West Virginia black tournament.

West Virginia may seem an unlikely state to be the site of the first state-wide black high school basketball tournament in part because of the small population of African Americans, which was little more than 6 percent of the state population, and the difficulty of travel over the rugged, mountainous land. But West Virginia had a number of advantages over the other segregated southern and border states. It had an established black school system in 1865 and in the late 1800s and into the early 1900s state laws required the establishment of schools for black children. African Americans were able

to leverage their power as workers and their voting power to encourage mine owners, industrial leaders, and the Republican Party to build schools and colleges and to provide protection from violence, although West Virginia remained tightly segregated in most areas of life.[17]

* * *

In 10 of its first 12 years, the WVAU tournament was played on West Virginia State's home court in the E B. White Trades Building, an industrial arts building with two gyms. "I grew up playing in the E.B. White Building," said Warne Ferguson, a native of Institute and later a player for West Virginia State. "There were actually two small gyms in that building. The bigger of the two was still small with the out-of-bounds line on the sides right up against the wall. There were small bleachers on each end and people could sit in a small balcony running track," Ferguson added.[18] Even the E.B. White Trades Building on the West Virginia State campus with its tiny court, uneven surface, and lack of seating seemed luxurious to many of the black high school teams that did not have gyms of any kind and practiced on outdoor dirt courts.

During the 1920s and 1930s, the WVAU tournament grew steadily, along with the popularity of basketball and an increase in the number of black high schools in the state. The black basketball tournament was the centerpiece of the athletic year for the black high schools because even the smallest schools that could not field football teams could put a five-player basketball team on the court.

Seventeen teams entered the 1928 WVAU tournament and 22 teams played in the 1930 tournament. Eventually, there were too many teams, making it unwieldy and too expensive to bring everyone to the state tournament. A number of schools, the northern schools in particular, strongly advocated having regional tournaments to qualify teams for the state tournament. In 1929, the northern high schools held their own separate tournament in Fairmont where Clarksburg Kelly Miller defeated Wheeling Lincoln in the championship game 23–13. The advocates of regional tournaments prevailed and by 1932 the state was divided into the regions of north, south, east, and west, with the regional champions and runners-up advancing to an eight-team, single elimination state tournament.[19] West Virginia was holding four regional tournaments before many states were even holding state championship tournaments.

The Southern Region, with eight teams including the five McDowell

Opposite: **The 1927 WVAU basketball tournament players and coaches. London Washington defeated Kimball 26–24 in the championship game (courtesy West Virginia State University Archives and Special Collections).**

County teams, was the largest in the state. With the state event hosting only eight teams after 1932, many contended that the Southern tournament surpassed the state event in importance. "I remember the regional tournament as being a lot more exciting and fun than the state tournament," said Elizabeth Scobell, a former Gary District cheerleader who became a reference librarian at West Virginia State and later was named the head of the library. "There were a lot of rivalries, competition, and school spirit because there were so many close friendships between the people in the different communities. Charleston was a long drive away then, and West Virginia State, where they held most of the state tournaments, seemed remote to us. We felt McDowell County was the black center of the state. It was just more fun to cheer against, and in front of, people you knew."[20]

The Southern Regional was just as exciting from a coach's perspective. "We had seven or eight teams: Gary, Bramwell, Kimball, Elkhorn, Excelsior, and Northfork from McDowell County; Liberty from Williamson; and, of course, Bluefield's Park Central [named Genoa until 1947]," said coach Elhanier Willis. A graduate from an integrated high school in Pittsburgh, Willis was recruited to play at segregated Bluefield State College. Willis remained in Bluefield after graduation to coach at Bluefield Park Central High School from 1947 until 1969, when Park Central closed. "When the season started, everyone wanted to know when the regional tournament would be. When we held the tournament at the old Elkhorn gym, or in the Northfork gym, all the railroads and mines closed down. We would put Liberty up in a hotel for three days and pay for that, and all the teams would take home between $2,000 and $2,500 from the gate. The state tournament never handled that kind of money."

The Southern Regional tournament lasted three days and each team brought their cheerleaders and their "Miss." The "Miss" for every school was the girl who raised the most money in a fundraising contest over the summer. She represented the school at all of the athletic contests during the school year. After the final game, the host school held a dance. "One reason the Southern Regional was so big was that there wasn't anything for black people to do after working. There weren't any clubs or social activities except what the churches and schools provided. The tournament was the key social event for black people in southern West Virginia. If you didn't see people there, or at the West Virginia State-Bluefield State football game, you just didn't see them," said Coach Willis.[21]

"Another reason the Southern Regional tournament was so important," Willis continued, "was that the schools had been playing each other so long that a lot of rivalries had developed. Playing in that tournament meant everything to our kids. It was something that they could brag about and kid their friends about for the rest of their lives." Willis smiled, obviously relishing the memory: "Win a ball game ... so what? But to win the tournament—it wasn't anything monetary—but the mouth and the whoop ... that were it!"[22]

During the 1920s and early 1930s, teams from the Southern Regional—primarily Kimball—dominated the state tournament. After placing second in 1925, Kimball defeated Lincoln 30–12 in the 1926 championship game. Kimball proceeded to win a championship in 1929, defeating Genoa of Bluefield, 28–17, in an all-southern region final. Likewise, Kimball beat McDowell County rivals Excelsior of War, 29–28, in 1932, and Gary District, 29–28, in 1933. Kimball won four of the first nine championships. In the first nine tournaments, 10 of 18 teams that played in the final championship games were teams from the Southern Regional, and five of those teams won championships.[23]

Many people attributed the early success of Kimball and other southern teams to the heavy concentration of African Americans in the southern coalfields, particularly in McDowell County.[24] This gave the southern schools a much larger pool of talent from which to choose players. John Mackey, the longtime coach at War Excelsior High School, disagreed. "H. Smith Jones, the coach at Kimball, was just smarter and knew more basketball than the rest of us."[25]

Coach Mackey spoke from experience. In 1932, Mackey's Excelsior team made it to the championship game against Coach Jones' Kimball team. While Kimball High School had tournament experience from the beginning of the WVAU tournament in 1925, Excelsior High School, located in War, West Virginia, was relatively new in 1932. The school began in the early 1920s but did not graduate its first class of two students until 1926. Coach Mackey, who had graduated from Storer College's high school branch and from Lincoln University in Pennsylvania, had begun coaching at Excelsior in 1929.

Coach Mackey recalled the 1932 tournament: "That was my first tournament as a coach and five or six of my former teammates from Storer College were students at West Virginia State. They said, 'Pete, you just bring your team into the dorm and stay with us.' That really helped because our kids were not mixed up with the kids staying in the gym talking and messing around. Those kids from Storer were like assistant coaches, because when I told my players to stay in their rooms, those boys from Storer saw that they stayed in the rooms."

"We got put in the tough bracket for some reason and had to play three games on the last day. We played Parkersburg Sumner in the morning and State High [West Virginia State High School] in the afternoon, both of whom had excellent teams. We bumped them off and played Kimball that night for the championship. We had that game won, but I still think the timer sandbagged me, and I never will believe otherwise. We had an eight-point lead with a minute and some seconds left to play, and the game kept going on and on. My guard took it upon himself to freeze the ball, but [Kimball's] Hinge Johnson and Bus Thompson cornered him up in that little gym and just kept taking the ball away. We played well, but they beat us 29–28. There was no sense in losing that game, but it was just one of those things."[26]

* * *

The popularity of basketball increased during the 1920s and 1930s as national high school basketball tournaments sprang up around the country. The national basketball tournaments as well as many state tournaments were sponsored by colleges as a way to publicize the colleges and recruit students and athletes. The public high school national tournament was a fixture at the University of Chicago from 1917 to 1929, the Catholic high school national tournament was held at Loyola University in Chicago from 1924 to 1941, and the girls' national high school tournament was held at various sites through 1928.

The segregated schools in the South and border states were excluded from participation in the track and field meets being sponsored by major white universities, the national white high school basketball tournaments, and the state white high school basketball tournaments. To provide post-season events for black high schools, black colleges followed the pattern set by white colleges and began to sponsor track meets and basketball tournaments for black high schools.

In 1929 the National Interscholastic Basketball Tournament (NIBT) for black high schools was begun at Hampton Institute to promote basketball in the black high schools and provide a post-season event. That first tournament drew 10 teams. West Virginia's black schools participated and were very successful from the first tournament. Huntington Douglass, which lost in the semi-final of the WVAU Tournament, fared better in the national event. Douglass advanced to the tournament final, where it lost a close 22–19 game to Armstrong Technical High School in Washington, D.C. The following year, 1930, Huntington Douglass lost in the final game of the WVAU Tournament to Gary District, 21–20, and again advanced to the finals of the national tournament only to lose again to Armstrong, 32–23. West Virginia schools continued to be successful with Genoa of Bluefield (1931) and Kelly Miller (1935 and 1936) finishing as runners-up. Although the tournament had the word "National" in the title, almost all of the teams came from the East throughout the history of the event.[27] The West Virginia teams were successful in the early tournament because of the experiences they had playing in the West Virginia regional and state tournaments, while tournaments in other states were just beginning.

However, one of the most memorable national tournaments for West Virginia's black high schools was the 1940 event. By then the National Invitational Basketball Tournament (NIBT) tournament had moved to Fayetteville, North Carolina, and was in competition with the post-season Southern Interscholastic Basketball Tournament held at Tuskegee Institute. In 1940, coach James Wilkerson's Gary District team advanced to the finals of the WVAU tournament only to lose to Charleston Garnet, 26–24. But the NIBT invited both the state champions and runners-up to play in the 10-team national tournament. The trip was exciting for the Gary District players and coaches, most of whom had never been out of West Virginia. "We drove the team down there to Fayetteville, and it was like going to California or someplace the players had never been before," said Coach Wilkerson. "We were surprised to see black people living in nice brick houses."[28] The Gary team played well and even defeated Garnet in an early tournament game. On the last day of the tournament, Gary District advanced to the national championship finals to play Gary Roosevelt High School, a large high school from Gary, Indiana. The game was close in the first half, but Roosevelt pulled away to win, 37–24. "We ended up runner-up in the state tournament in West Virginia, and runner-up in the national tournament," recalled Coach Wilkerson.[29]

In 1935, Tuskegee Institute in Alabama began the Southern Interscholastic Basketball Tournament (SIBT). The tournament drew 25 boys' teams in 1939. By 1941, the name of the event was changed to the National Invitational Interscholastic Basketball Tournament (NIIBT) and drew 18 boys' teams and 16 girls' teams from 12 states. Teams from Oklahoma, where most of the black high schools were named for Booker T. Washington, made a strong showing. However, both the eastern and southern tournaments ended in 1942 because of World War II.[30]

The National Invitational High School Basketball Tournament (NI-HSBT) was begun in 1945 in Nashville and ran for 20 years under the sponsorship of Tennessee A & I State College (now Tennessee State University). Tennessee A & I was a basketball power during that era. It was the first black college to win the NAIA national tournament in 1957 and won the next two championships.[31]

By that time the small black West Virginia high schools had a difficult time competing against the large city high schools like St. Elizabeth in Chicago, Louisville Central, and Nashville's Pearl High School. Elkhorn was the only West Virginia school to make the finals, losing a close 36–33 game to Oklahoma City Douglass in 1945. The tournament that year drew 13 teams from five states.[32]

Sport historian Robert Pruter wrote, "In 1957 West Virginia, one of the founding states in the national tournament and with a rich tournament history ended its tournament participation ... so by March of 1957 the West Virginia Athletic Union held its last state tournament sending Park Central High of Bluefield to the national tournament before disbanding."[33] The last

Nashville tournament was held in 1967. The tournament ended because the black high schools were either being closed by integration or were increasingly playing in the formerly all-white state association tournaments, both of which had occurred in West Virginia.

* * *

All of the first 12 WVAU tournaments were played at West Virginia State except for the 1931 event, which was played in Charleston, and the 1933 tournament held in Clarksburg to placate northern schools. At West Virginia State the teams either slept on cots in the gymnasium in the E.B. White Trades Building or in the dormitory rooms of friends. The communal living arrangements were a major contributor to establishing one of the tournament's longstanding traditions—the long underwear vs. short underwear basketball game. Almost every coach told the same story. The tradition began when players from teams that had been eliminated from the tournament decided to play games against each other. The teams were divided between the boys from the country, who wore long underwear, and the boys from the cities, who wore short underwear. Knute Burroughs played for Clarksburg's Kelly Miller in the early 1930s, graduated from West Virginia State, and later coached at Accoville Buffalo High School. "When I was a player and a coach, that game was one of the most exciting things about the tournament," said Burroughs. "The teams that had been eliminated would slip over to the gym, turn on the lights, and play what we called the long underwear-short underwear midnight classic. You could really see basketball come out of an individual then because there weren't any coaches or referees, and the kids just played natural fun basketball."[34]

From 1934 through 1944, the WVAU tournament was played at four different sites. In the three years from 1934 through 1936, the tournament returned to West Virginia State. Newer gyms were being built that were nicer than the tiny gym in the E.B. White Trades Building. From 1937 through 1944 the tournament was played at Charleston Garnet High School, Bluefield State, and Clarksburg Kelly Miller.

During that time, Clarksburg Kelly Miller High School became the power team in black high school basketball in West Virginia. Clarksburg, a historic city founded in 1785, is located in the north-central part of the state. By 1900 Clarksburg, on the B&O Railroad line, had a population of 4,050. The city had a large enough African American population to warrant building the segregated Water Street School. By 1920 the total population had exploded to 27,869 with the development of numerous industries, including chemical plants, potteries, glass plants, and foundries. In 1920 Water Street School was renamed for Kelly Miller, a professor and the dean of arts and sciences at Howard University. Miller, a well-known civil rights speaker and author with nationally circulated newspaper columns, came to Clarksburg to speak that year. The Clarksburg community was so impressed by Miller that they renamed the school in his honor.

In 1929, the Clarksburg Board of Education funded a major expansion to Kelly Miller High School, adding a gymnasium, swimming pool, home economics rooms, library, and an auditorium seating 825. All of those changes marked Kelly Miller as one of the leading African American high schools, if not one of the leading high schools, in the state.[35]

Bob Wilson, a basketball star at Kelly Miller in the early 1940s who went on to play at West Virginia State, believed that Kelly Miller became an excellent high school because of the strength of the black community in Clarksburg. African Americans in Clarksburg worked at a variety of occupations including the glass plants, as waiters in the hotels, as domestics, janitors, or chauffeurs. "E.B. Saunders, the principal at Kelly Miller for decades, provided strong leadership and race relations were good in Clarksburg," said Wilson.[36]

To ensure that Kelly Miller would become an athletic success, Mark Cardwell was hired to coach all sports. Cardwell was well known in the black communities in the state because he had been an All-American football player at West Virginia State.[37] When the new gymnasium was completed at Kelly Miller in 1929 and with Cardwell on the job, all of the pieces were in place for a strong athletic program at Kelly Miller.

"Cardwell was a good coach—he worked at it—but he was also a recruiter," said Knute Burroughs, who had played for Cardwell at Kelly Miller in the 1930s. "He got a kid out of Columbus named Walls and Bo Spearman out of Pittsburgh. He would move them in and find someone related to them in the area, and they were good."[38]

Led by Bob Wilson, Cardwell's best teams at Kelly Miller played in the early 1940s. At six feet, four inches, Wilson was tall for that era. He was also heavy enough to be an All-State end in football. He had the size to be an excellent rebounder, but also had a soft shooting touch. "I started playing in eighth grade and by the time I was a sophomore we had a great team," recalled Wilson. Kelly Miller ran off a string of three straight state championships from 1942 through 1944 and Wilson was named the tournament's Most Valuable Player each year. "We had good teams and lost very few games in that stretch. We secretly scrimmaged against some of the white high schools in Clarksburg, particularly St. Mary's, the Catholic school. We also traveled to Homestead, Pennsylvania and played some integrated high schools just to get some better competition," said Wilson.[39] Games and even scrimmages between black and white high schools were seldom if ever played.

The 1944 tournament was the end of an era for Kelly Miller High School. Immediately after graduation Wilson was drafted into the army. Earlier in 1945 Adolph Hamblin at West Virginia State retired from coaching and was succeeded by Mark Cardwell, who had been immensely successful at Kelly Miller High School, having won six WVAU football and five WVAU basketball championships in 20 years. His basketball team posted a 307–46 record.[40]

* * *

The first WVAU tournament in 1925 and the subsequent events were not so much about basketball as about the excitement of traveling to West Virginia State and being part of an overarching African American experience unparalleled in West Virginia at the time. Scores and game accounts cannot capture the excitement generated by that first tournament and the 32 that followed. The WVAU tournament represented more than just playing a few basketball games. It became an annual reunion for hundreds of African American students, athletes, coaches, and community members. Coming from small, isolated black communities within a larger, white world, they faced segregation and discrimination in every aspect of life, although the adversity often tended to create a milieu of cultural unity. The WVAU was a reflection of those positive feelings of oneness. Unfortunately, many of the records, accomplishments, and even memories of the tournament and that era at large have faded in an integrated America.

Strong leadership in the black community in both the political and athletic areas from people such as presidents Byrd Prillerman and John W. Davis and coach/professor Adolph Hamblin and Dean Ancella Bickley at West Virginia State; Dr. Anthony Major and James Wares in Weirton; Robert Simmons in Parkersburg; W.B. Saunders, and Mark Cardwell in Clarksburg; Horace Belmear in Fairmont; Jim Jarrett in Charleston; Lacy Smith in Logan; James Wilkerson and Ergie Smith in Gary; H. Smith Jones in Kimball; Knute Burrows in Accoville; Ed Starling in Williamson; Elhanier Willis in Bluefield; J.H. Rainbow and John Wilkes Kinney in Wheeling; and Z.L. Davis in Huntington fostered the development of a strong educational system and the establishment of the WVAU tournament in 1925 as the first statewide black high school basketball tournament in the United States. The continuation of the tournament through the 1950s was a strong unifying force for black West Virginia.

4

Earl Lloyd and the Golden Age of West Virginia State University Basketball, 1945–1954

By 1940, West Virginia State College had weathered the effects of the Depression and had reached an enrollment of 936 students. The president was John W. Davis, who began his tenure in 1919. Football coach Adolph Hamblin, who was also the head of the Biology Department, continued to roam the sidelines and to conduct biology lectures and labs much as he had since 1922. However, Hamblin had given up coaching the basketball team in 1933. Five men had coached the basketball team between 1933 and 1945.

Funding for West Virginia State remained stable and was adequate even during the Depression because West Virginia State was a land grant college. In addition, West Virginia's governors and legislators were always looking for visible ways to help West Virginia State as a means to court the black vote. But changes, both from internal decisions made by the West Virginia State College administration and also from a changing racial situation in the United States, would come swiftly and dramatically to West Virginia State in the two decades between 1940 and 1960.

* * *

The first major change occurred in December 1941: West Virginia State joined the Colored Intercollegiate Athletic Association. The CIAA was the most prestigious African American college athletic conference with members that included leaders in academic and athletic programs in the Southeast and Mid-Atlantic regions. The CIAA conference champions were often considered the National Negro Champions.[1] West Virginia State was more than competitive; it won several CIAA championships in football and basketball during the 1940s.

West Virginia State had several advantages, particularly during the war

Location of the 18 colleges in the Colored (later Central) Intercollegiate Athletic Association in 1950. Founded in 1918, the CIAA was the most prestigious of the African American athletic conferences; its conference champions were often considered national champions. Bluefield State joined in 1932 and West Virginia State became a member in 1942 (map by James Atkinson).

years. The school had excellent facilities including Fleming Hall, a modern gymnasium that was completed in 1942. It was considered one of the best basketball facilities in the CIAA. In addition, West Virginia State's athletic teams were able to use men in the military training programs housed on campus. In addition to having ROTC, in 1939 the college had become the first of six African American colleges to develop an aviation program under the Civilian Aeronautics Authority (CAA). The college played an important part in the war effort as many men from its aviation program became fighter pilots and more than 600 students and alumni from West Virginia State served in the war. While these men were on campus, their participation enabled West Virginia State to maintain an athletic program during the war, albeit on a limited basis.[2] Wartime restrictions made scheduling and travel difficult. Other colleges without military programs often did not have enough men on campus to field teams. In addition, gasoline rationing and the military being given preference on rail travel made it difficult for teams to travel. In 1943, the Yellow Jackets were only able to play an abbreviated football schedule of two games.

* * *

With the end of the war, the Golden Age of West Virginia State athletics began. The college had long been a Mecca for aspiring African American students. As the land grant black college in West Virginia, it attracted students from African American communities throughout the state who regarded it as "the" state college, in much the same way that white students viewed West Virginia University. Moreover, its excellent academic reputation attracted the children of black professionals from other states in the East, South, and Midwest.

A glimpse of campus would be enough to convince some students to enroll. Set in a tiny village of a few houses, a small grocery store and a post office, the grounds were a picture of a traditional campus. A long sweeping tree-lined lawn ran through the middle of campus. "An Administration building that housed offices, science labs, classrooms, and the library [was] at one end, and the newly constructed Fleming Hall gymnasium at the other end. On the sides were the three dormitories for men and three for women, the president's house, a house for unmarried faculty, the Home Economics House [where the Home Economics students lived], and the E.B. White Trades Building. It was a beautiful setting," said Caroline Mathews, a 1951 graduate.[3]

Enrollment grew from 936 in 1940 to 1,785 in 1947–48, almost doubling the campus population. "The campus was crowded with students, mainly because of the veterans coming to school. Single veterans lived in temporary Quonset huts, and the married students lived in trailers," said Ancella Bickley, a student during the late 1940s who later became the school's dean of academic affairs.[4] Although the school was growing, Bickley found everyone to be friendly, speaking to everyone was the norm. State maintained the atmosphere of a small protected community. "President Davis was like a father figure who knew every student by name. He had strict rules against drinking and staying out late. The girls had to be in the dorms by 9:00, a little later on weekends, and girls never smoked in public," said Carolyn Matthews. "But the veterans were adult men. So Dr. Davis loosened up some of the rules when they got to campus. But even then, if someone drank openly or was drunk on campus, they were sent home."[5]

Academics remained a priority at West Virginia State. "Dr. Davis, the president, was a strong leader who ran a tight ship," said Bob Wilson, the star basketball player from Clarksburg and a World War II veteran. "The faculty and the staff took a personal interest in the growth of the students."[6] Teammate Earl Lloyd agreed: "The faculty cared if you learned, and the other students were serious. Anyone who went there and wanted an education could graduate."[7]

Once on campus, students were immersed in an African American community unlike anything most of them had previously experienced. For out-of-state students coming from integrated school systems, it was the first time many had black teachers, coaches and administrators. For students from the small, isolated black neighborhoods in West Virginia it was the first time many had experienced opportunities for social activities like those at the college with its fraternities and sororities, intramurals, dances and sports teams. For all students, it was a refuge from the racism that existed outside the campus.

West Virginia State was a place where students felt they could be themselves and celebrate being African American. "There was a lot of racism back then; West Virginia State served as a safe house. We barely left campus, only for basketball trips," recalled Earl Lloyd, the college's most famous basketball player.[8] There was little reason to leave since, as Lloyd continued, "there were dances and the campus had a great intramural life. We also had active fraternities and sororities." Travel to surrounding towns was not easy. "Charleston was like 1,000 miles away to us. On the bus with all of those stops, it took forever," said Lloyd. And once off campus, students faced racism, even having to sit in a roped-off area if they went to see a movie in nearby Nitro, West Virginia. Most would agree with Lloyd's assessment that "State was a place where you felt as if you belonged."[9]

There were the beginnings of a desire for change even in this idyllic setting.

Veterans who entered West Virginia State on the G.I. Bill had fought for their country and seen different cultures in other parts of the United States, as well as in Europe and Asia. They had experienced some loosening of segregation in the armed forces and returned home expecting that race relations would be improved and segregation lessened.

In the late 1946 and 1947, there were signs that those expectations were realistic. After being segregated since 1934, professional football became integrated again in the fall of 1946 when Kenny Washington and Woody Strode joined the Los Angeles Rams of the National Football League and Marion Motley and Bill Willis signed with the Cleveland Browns of the All-American Football Conference. In the spring of 1947, Jackie Robinson played for the Brooklyn Dodgers, reintegrating major league baseball, a game that had been segregated since the 1890s.

Changes were also enacted by the federal government. In 1947 President Harry Truman established the President's Council on Civil Rights, which recommended laws that would guarantee voting rights and equal employment. In 1948, President Truman issued Executive Order 9981, which abolished racial discrimination and segregation in the United States Armed Services. These were hopeful signs of a fully integrated future.[10] The West Virginia State students were beginning to realize that they would have an additional responsibility—to lead their African American communities through an increasingly desegregating American society. "It was an exciting time to be alive on the Institute campus," said Ancella Bickley.[11] It was the dawning of a Golden Age.

* * *

Two individuals played key roles in State's Golden Age of athletics—coach Mark Caldwell and basketball star Earl Lloyd. The era began when Adolph Hamblin retired from coaching football in 1945 and was succeeded by Mark Cardwell who took the reins of all sports teams. Cardwell was a popular choice to serve as football and basketball coach at State. More than one coach has claimed that the West Virginia's black coaches signed a petition to nominate Cardwell for the position at West Virginia State. Many said the reason for the petition was that Cardwell beat them so often. The college job would get him out of the ranks of high school coaching so they would not have to face his teams anymore.

Cardwell was just as successful as a college coach as he had been as a high school coach. In 1945 his first football team finished the year with a 6–0–2 (4–0–2 CIAA) record. In 1948, the Yellow Jackets, had a 5–2–2 record overall and won the CIAA championship with a 5–1 league record. In 1949, the team had an impressive 8–0–1 record but were second in the CIAA behind Morgan State whose team was undefeated and untied. Cardwell's Yellow Jackets again won the conference championship in 1951 with an overall record of 6–2–1 and 5–0–1 in the CIAA. Coaching success continued and when he retired from coaching football in 1958, Cardwell had a record of 71 wins, 53 losses, and 14 ties for an excellent 57 percent winning percentage.[12]

"I think that the main reason my father gave up football was that by 1958 white colleges were beginning to recruit black athletes. Dad realized that it was going to become more difficult and time-consuming to recruit enough good football players to produce a winning team. He felt that he had a better chance of recruiting basketball players and did not need as many," said Mark Cardwell, Jr.[13]

His son's explanation is consistent with the historical record. By 1958 small colleges in West Virginia, as well as Marshall College in Huntington, were recruiting black athletes. Although the number of black athletes being recruited was limited, it was becoming increasingly clear that West Virginia State and Bluefield State would no longer have an unchallenged pick of black football players in West Virginia.

Partly due to the multiple coaching changes from 1933 to 1945, the basketball program was in disarray in 1945 when Cardwell took the reins. Cardwell quickly began to strengthen the program by recruiting. His prize recruit in 1946 was Earl Lloyd, a six-foot, six-inch center from Parker-Grey High School in Alexandria, Virginia. (During integration, Parker-Grey merged with T.C. Williams High School in 1965; the school's 1971 championship season is portrayed in the movie *Remember the Titans*.)

Earl Lloyd had grown up in the projects in a tough section of Alexandria in what he calls the cradle of segregation. The Lloyds were working poor— his mother was a domestic and his father worked in a coal yard shoveling coal on and off trucks, a low paying job with work hours that often kept him from seeing Earl's games. But education was important to his family. Like the teachers, who were all from the community and cared for the students as if they were their own children, "they looked at the way things were and were dedicated to one proposition: you're going to get an education, and no one can ever take that away from you." Fortunately, Lloyd was a good student, even skipping a grade in elementary school.[14]

Even though he was younger than his classmates, Lloyd grew to be an excellent basketball player and a strong (but wild) baseball pitcher at Parker-Grey. The limited facilities at Parker-Grey with no gymnasium, baseball field or track mattered less than a revered and inspirational coach, Louis Johnson, and the teams and Lloyd enjoyed considerable success. While at Parker-Grey, Lloyd was a three-time All-South Atlantic Conference basketball player, and he was twice named to the All-State basketball team in the segregated Virginia Interscholastic Conference.

When Lloyd graduated from high school in the spring of 1946, college recruiting had not returned to its peacetime procedures. World War II had ended only nine months earlier and many coaches as well as prospective and former players were in the process of being discharged from the armed services. Consequently, recruiting was somewhat disorganized and graduating seniors did not always receive the usual amount of attention. This was especially true for black athletes whose opportunities were very limited in any event because most colleges in the South accepted only white students and most integrated colleges in the North signed only a few African American players. There were some exceptions. The "color line" had been recently broken in the Big Ten, and eastern colleges such as Columbia, Princeton, CCNY, Yale, and Long Island had had African Americans on their teams. UCLA had had two of the most famous black college basketball players in six-foot, five-inch Don Barksdale and Jackie Robinson, who had led the Pacific Coast Conference in scoring in both 1941 and 1942.[15]

Although Lloyd faced many recruiting limitations, he talked with coaches from Howard and North Carolina A&T, as well as West Virginia State. Nevertheless "there was no question where I was going," said Lloyd.[16]

As he pondered his decision, his mother simply asked, "What did Coach Johnson say?" Johnson was a graduate of West Virginia State and had been a teammate of Mark Cardwell. That gave Cardwell the inside track to persuade Lloyd to commit to the Yellow Jackets and get on the train for Institute.

In the fall of 1946, Lloyd arrived at campus to begin what he considered the most memorable time of his life. During his first week at school, he was initiated like every other freshman by being given silly jobs to perform in what would be the first step in creating lasting bonds from shared experiences. "Because I was so tall, I was given the job of fixing the moon. When guys had dates, they would want the moon to be in a romantic place in the sky. They would come to me and tell me where they wanted the moon placed and I was supposed to reach up and fix the moon. The nickname 'Moonfixer' stuck," said Lloyd.[17]

The basketball team was a little thin during Lloyd's freshman year with predominantly young players, because many men were still in the military and would not be discharged in time to join the team. "I was a freshman, just a baby. But Coach Cardwell told me that I was the biggest player he had, so I had to play a lot because we did not have anybody else to play. I grew up pretty fast that season," said Lloyd.[18] Despite the lack of veteran players, the team finished with a 17–4 record for the 1946–47 season.

Coach Cardwell had more time to recruit and a larger field of potential players as veterans returned in time to join the 1947–48 team. He mined the surrounding states as well as West Virginia for talent, signing Frank Enty, who had played at the integrated Westinghouse High School in Pittsburgh, Pennsylvania. The team gained an excellent defensive player when Joe Gilliam, from Steubenville, Ohio, just across the Ohio River from West Virginia's Northern Panhandle, transferred from Indiana University. But Cardwell's prize recruit was Bob Wilson, Jr., an army veteran who had played for him at Clarksburg's Kelly Miller High School. At six feet, four inches, Wilson was big enough and strong enough to play under the basket. With these three players joining Lloyd, the nucleus of the Yellow Jackets for the next three seasons was complete.[19]

Military veterans gave the team a mature edge because most of them were in their early to mid-20s, older than most graduating seniors. There was some potential for discord, however. "They were good basketball players, but they also had a huge advantage with the girls. They were on the G.I. bill and had money coming in every month. They could take girls out for steak dinners. The rest of us were lucky if we could buy girls hot dogs," recalled Lloyd.[20] Bob Wilson laughed when he heard the hot dog story. "I had money from the G.I. Bill, but I also worked as a waiter at some of the hotels in Charleston on weekends and when I was going to summer school. I never had to ask West Virginia State for money because I always had my own," said Wilson.[21]

Despite differences in age, maturity and economic resources, Cardwell's leadership brought the disparate group together. "He was like a father figure to us, and we were like a family," Lloyd later said.[22] Wilson explained that Cardwell set a high moral standard: "He led by example. In all of the years that I played for him, I never heard him curse."[23]

During the 1947–48 season, Coach Cardwell's approach was tested in the opening game. The game was one that Earl Lloyd remembered vividly as he wrote, "We knew we were supposed to be pretty good, but Tuskegee came into our gym for the first game ready to go, and we almost blew it." The game went into overtime. With State leading by one point, Tuskegee had the ball for a final shot. "It hit the rim and came off, and we thought, 'Oh man, are we lucky.' If we had played another minute, we might not have won it."[24] The game set the tone for the rest of the season. Not only did West Virginia State defeat teams from the traditional basketball strongholds at Virginia Union, Howard, and North Carolina College for Negros (later named North Carolina College and then North Carolina Central University), the Yellow Jackets went on to win 20 straight games for an undefeated season. They won the CIAA regular season championship, which the CIAA called the "Visitation Championship." Although Visitation Championship is an unusual name, it was appropriate because the visiting team stayed overnight on the home team's campus and ate their meals in their opponent's cafeteria. The "visitation" saved money for the visiting team and allowed them to avoid the difficulties of finding hotels and restaurants that would serve African Americans in the segregated states where the CIAA colleges were located.

To achieve an undefeated season, the Yellow Jackets had to overcome the challenges of playing on the road as well as defeating all opposing teams. Fortunately, Coach Cardwell developed a successful strategy for meeting the challenges that his team would face while traveling in the segregated South. "Because we were on the fringe of the conference geographically, we made trips where we would play four or five games in a row. We traveled in two big DeSoto Touring cars because we had an incident where we had to ride in the back of the bus in North Carolina. Coach Cardwell didn't like that, so he bought us our own team cars," said Lloyd. Being on the road was difficult because few restaurants and hotels accepted black customers. "We ate a big meal before we left on the trip, then we would have a packed lunch. We would stop and eat on the hood of the cars while we were traveling. We ate dinner in

Opposite: **Earl Lloyd, a six-foot, six-inch center from Alexandria, Virginia, who led the West Virginia State College Yellow Jackets to two national championships, three CIAA regular season championships, and two CIAA tournament championships between 1947 and 1950. In 1950, Lloyd became the first African American to play in a National Basketball Association game. Photograph dated 1950 (courtesy West Virginia State University Archives and Special Collections).**

the other teams' dining hall. They put us up for the night and fed us all of our meals," said Lloyd. "The gyms were small and cramped, difficult for visiting teams to adjust to. Fleming Hall on the West Virginia State campus was a palace compared to most of the conference gyms. But Coach Cardwell said not to worry because both teams are playing on the same court," recalled Lloyd.[25]

As winners of the CIAA Visitation Season, West Virginia State was guaranteed another road trip, this time to Turner's Arena in Washington, D.C., where the CIAA conference championship tournament would be played. The championship, one of the earliest post-season tournaments to be established in the United States, had been begun in 1946, partly as a money-making venture. Conference representatives had mixed feelings about establishing the event, but the deciding factor was that the conference had only $165.75 in the bank and some of the colleges were having difficulty paying the conference dues. The top eight teams of the conference's 18 teams (the CIAA had expanded to 18 colleges in 1945) were invited to Turner's Arena, a small 2,000-seat venue used mostly for professional wrestling. The major advantage of having the tournament in Turner's Arena was that it was only two blocks from the famous U Street, Washington's "Black Broadway." To save money, the teams slept on cots on the arena floor. West Virginia State had participated in the first CIAA tournament. They were seeded fourth but were upset 60–56 by North Carolina College in the first round. Although the inaugural tournament was not a success for the Yellow Jackets, it was a financial success for the CIAA, generating a profit of almost $934. The tournament continued to be financially successful and after the next two tournaments the CIAA banked $1,566 and $1,300, respectively, putting the conference on a sound financial basis.[26]

When the top eight teams from the 18 team CIAA conference gathered at Turner's Arena on March 11, 1948, to open the third CIAA tournament, West Virginia State was not the favorite. The defending champions, Virginia State College, had failed to make the top eight was not present to defend its title. West Virginia State had beaten everyone in the regular season. Why then were the Yellow Jackets not the favorites? The *Pittsburgh Courier* called it the "tourney jinx" pointing out that no team had ever won both the visitation title and the tournament. The *Courier* picked the Virginia Union Panthers to win, even though West Virginia State had given Union its only loss in the regular season, when the Yellow Jackets had defeated the Panthers 46–40.[27]

The tourney jinx was not in evidence as Yellow Jackets won the opening round of the tournament by defeating Johnson C. Smith College 58–24. In the semi-finals, West Virginia State won by 65–60 over North Carolina College, a team they had defeated twice during the season. The heavily favored Virginia Union team was upset by Howard 58–43 in the other semi-final game.

The championship contest between West Virginia State and Howard began as a low scoring, defensive battle. At the half, the Yellow Jackets had only an 11–10 lead. But State had an advantage which would become apparent during the second half. As the *Pittsburgh Courier* noted, West Virginia State, with six-foot, seven-inch Earl Lloyd (he had grown an inch since high school), six-foot, four-inch Bob Wilson, and six-foot, three-inch Clarence Clark, was an exceptionally tall basketball team. In the second half, the taller and heavier West Virginia State players began to wear down the Howard Bison. Then in the fourth quarter, the Yellow Jackets forward Joe Gilliam caught fire and scored 14 points to help State pull away for a 42–31 victory. Gilliam was the high scorer for the Yellow Jackets, with 14 points, followed by Lloyd with 13. West Virginia State forward Clarence Clark, who scored two points in the final game, was named the most valuable player in the tournament.[28] The Yellow Jackets had beaten the "tourney jinx" to win the CIAA Visitation Season and the CIAA Tournament and to complete a 23–0 season.

Rumors soon surfaced that State might be invited to play in the National Invitational Tournament (NIT) at Madison Square Garden, but no invitation

The 1947–48 West Virginia State College basketball team was undefeated with a 23–0 record. The Yellow Jackets won the CIAA regular season and tournament championships and declared themselves the "National Negro College Champion" (courtesy West Virginia State University Archives and Special Collections).

was forthcoming. Earl Lloyd later suggested State was not invited because southern teams like Kentucky would have objected to playing against a black team and might have withdrawn from the tournament.[29] Marketing factors might also have played a role since promoters knew that fans would come to see white teams play, but there was no evidence that black teams would draw as well since none had been in either the NIT or NCAA tournaments and few games had been played between black and white teams. With no additional post-season tournaments in the offing, West Virginia State contented themselves with their undefeated record and claimed the title of National Negro Basketball Champions while the Negro Associated Press named Coach Cardwell Coach of the Year.

* * *

The 1948–49 season opened with expectations that the Yellow Jackets would extend their 23-game winning streak and win another championship. A veteran team was returning led by 1947–48's leading scorer Bob Wilson, leading rebounder Earl Lloyd, CIAA tournament MVP Clarence Clark, and forwards Joe Gilliam, Douglas Rockhold and Frank Enty. The only 1947 team members missing were three-time captain Bill Nunn, Jr., and back-up guard Wallace Simms who had both graduated. State began the season as expected with a 65–37 win over Shaw College of North Carolina in the home opener at Fleming Hall. Win followed win, including a decisive 50–31 defeat of Howard, the team State had defeated in the 1948 CIAA finals. Soon the Yellow Jackets had a 9–0 record and a 32-game win streak.

To add to the season's excitement, a four-game tour had been scheduled against white colleges in Nevada and California in February. According to Herman Hill, a sportswriter for the *Pittsburgh Courier*, Frank Walsh, the flamboyant basketball promoter for San Francisco's Cow Palace arena, had approached him about the possibility of bringing West Virginia State to California for a series of games. Walsh had been impressed by State's undefeated record in 1947–48. He also was informed that black teams had been shut out of playing at Madison Square Garden. Walsh said that he was "determined to wipe out that injustice" and invited West Virginia State to play at the Cow Palace.[30]

Built in 1941 with 11,000 seats, the Cow Palace was home to sports events and stock shows, hence the name. To fill the arena for college basketball games, Walsh used the double header format (four college teams played two games in one session) that had become so popular at Madison Square Garden in New York. Occasionally, Walsh brought teams from as far away as the Midwest to fill some of his events.[31] West Virginia State would be the first black college to be invited to play there.

The invitation Walsh extended to West Virginia State in 1948 was a bold move on his part because much of the United States was locked into various levels of racial segregation. Charles Martin in *Benching Jim Crow* wrote that Southern states such as South Carolina, Georgia, Florida, Alabama, and Louisiana had either local or state laws banning interracial athletic competition. Major college teams from those states refused to play against northern teams with black players. Even the Big Ten conference in the Midwest banned black players from basketball teams (despite having black football players and track athletes) through the early 1940s and later enforced a quota system into the 1950s that limited the number of black players on basketball teams.[32]

Not only would the State's games be among the few played between black and white colleges, the significance of the contests was increased by the press coverage. In *Separate Games,* sport historians David K. Wiggins and Chris Elzey cite the effusive praise that the West Coast sportswriters heaped on West Virginia State in pre-game stories. The Yellow Jackets were hailed as the "National Negro Intercollegiate Champion" and "the best Negro team in the country." The team's 32-game win streak was frequently mentioned.[33] West Virginia State was viewed as the *de facto* representative of black college basketball.

It was in this atmosphere of heightened excitement that Coach Cardwell, the team manager, and 10 players left for California on February 5, 1949. West Virginia Governor Okey L. Patteson had sent a letter congratulating the team and wishing them good luck.[34] Thirty-four individuals and organizations in the West Virginia State community had made contributions of $1.00 to $14.29 for a total of $175 as a gift for the team. "A little extra money with which to buy a souvenir or stamps for letters to their wives, sweethearts, or friends," wrote the college president, John W. Davis, to the school treasurer.[35] Then came four days of train travel to be followed immediately by the Cow Palace double header.

In the first game of the double bill at the Cow Palace, an excellent crowd of 5,216, almost 1,000 spectators larger than the arena's average basketball crowd, watched Bradley University play the University of San Francisco. The travel-weary West Virginia State team took the floor against St. Mary's College in the second game. The hot-shooting St. Mary's Gaels took the lead immediately and at the half led 31–20. Earl Lloyd scored 16 points, and Bob Wilson added 12 points, but it was not enough. St. Mary's defeated West Virginia State, 66–52.[36]

The Yellow Jackets fared better in their second game in San Francisco, easily beating the Broncos of Santa Clara College, 57–44. State then traveled to Los Angeles, where they lost to Loyola University, 65–58. The following night, in Reno, the University of Nevada led 38–22 at halftime and played their reserves during most of the second half to beat the Yellow Jackets, 74–66.[37]

In discussing the three losses, Earl Lloyd explained that while the teams

OFFICIAL PROGRAM 25c

West View Hospital Benefit

Basketball - 1949

© W.D.P.

West Virginia State College vs. Loyola
Oakland Bittners vs. San Francisco Y. M. I.
(Broadcast by Tide Water Associated Oil Co.)

Shrine Auditorium — Monday, Feb. 14, 1949
Los Angeles, California

This game program, with Walt Disney cartoon characters on the cover, is from the 1949 West Coast tour of California. West Virginia State lost the game to Loyola College 65–58. West Virginia State won one and lost three games on the trip (courtesy West Virginia State University Archives and Special Collections).

that beat them were good, "they were playing with a chip on their shoulders because they felt like they didn't get much respect from Eastern teams. And the style of play in the West was really rough. We weren't used to the style of officiating, but it was fair because the calls went the same way for both teams. But the hardest thing for us was that we had to ride on the train for four days without a chance to practice or even run." Nevertheless, Lloyd concluded that "at the end of the trip, we felt good because we knew that we could play with those teams in spite of losing three of four games."[38]

Despite the losses, the team took their role, as the first black college basketball team to play on the West Coast, seriously. "We kept reading that we were 'Ambassadors of good will,'" said Bob Wilson (42). In this respect the team received praise from Herman Hill, who wrote in the *Pittsburgh Courier*, "Their sportsmanship and conduct was highly commendable."[39] Moreover, race relations in California provided an eye-opening experience for the State players. "California was a good racial situation. We saw white people and black people in the restaurants. I felt as if I could go into any place and would not be turned away," said Wilson.[40]

After their return home, West Virginia State had only one loss, to North Carolina College, in the eight remaining games of the CIAA visitation season. "It was different to play against white teams in front of white crowds in California. It felt good to be back home and playing in familiar territory," recalled Lloyd.[41] State won the CIAA Visitation Championship and ended the season with a 16–4 record.

C. I. A. A. Champions – 1948-49

West Virginia State's 1948–49 basketball team was the CIAA regular season and CIAA tournament champions for the second consecutive season (courtesy West Virginia State University Archives and Special Collections).

Even though West Virginia State had won the regular season champion-ship, North Carolina College was favored to win the CIAA tournament be-cause of their regular season win over State. The Yellow Jackets had a strong beginning in the tournament, defeating Morgan State of Baltimore, Mary-land, in the opening round. They went on to an overtime 53–50 victory over Virginia Union in the semifinal game. As expected, West Virginia State and North Carolina college met in the championship game. Initially, predictions of a North Carolina College victory seemed accurate as North Carolina led 31–26 at halftime. West Virginia State fought back to tie the score at 43, then North Carolina College was able to gain a four-point lead with four minutes to play. In a thrilling conclusion, Clarence Clark led a State rally in the final minutes of the game for a 60–53 win and their second consecutive CIAA tournament championship. With 16 points Frank Enty was State's leading scorer, followed by Earl Lloyd, with 13. After winning the CIAA Visitation Championship and the CIAA tournament championship, State claimed an-other national Negro championship.[42]

* * *

In the 1949–50 season, the West Virginia State team returned with their powerful nucleus from the previous two years, but the rest of the CIAA was beginning to catch up by recruiting more veterans to blend with recent high school graduates. After four easy victories to start the season, West Virginia met Virginia Union at a neutral site in Norfolk, Virginia. The game was closely officiated, and starters Earl Lloyd, Clarence Clark, and Joe Gilliam fouled out with 10 minutes to play. Without the star players, Virginia Union was able to upset the Yellow Jackets, winning 69–42. The following night, the Yellow Jackets got revenge with a victory over the same Virginia Union team on its home floor in Richmond.[43]

West Virginia State had accepted a second invitation from Frank Walsh to play in the Cow Palace and planned another trip to the West Coast during the 1949–50 season. The team had a 12–1 season record as the 10-player travel-ing squad boarded a train to head west on January 28, 1950. Warne Ferguson, an Army veteran from Institute, who was the only freshman on the traveling squad, has not forgotten the instructions given to the team. "Coach Cardwell told us to be on our best behavior because he did not want us to do anything to embarrass our race. But he really didn't need to say anything. None of the guys on our team drank or smoked. In fact, if anyone was caught smoking on the State campus, they were sent home," recalled Ferguson.[44]

This year, Coach Cardwell decided to break up the long train trip so that the team would not be stale and travel weary when they arrived in California. They stopped in Dubuque, Iowa, for a game against Loras College, who they trounced 74–50. On February 5, eight days after leaving West Virginia, State faced San Jose State College at the massive Cow Palace in San Francisco. Playing before a disappointingly small crowd of 2,217 spectators, West Virginia State trailed from the opening minutes of the game and was behind 32–23 at halftime. State was able to close the gap in the second half, only to go down to defeat by 52–50.

California governor Earl Warren was so impressed with the West Virginia State team that he arranged for the Yellow Jackets to play against the San Quentin State Prison basketball team. "Governor Earl Warren met with our team for more than an hour. He joked with us about how we could get rich in the stock market. I think that he arranged the game because he had just appointed a black man as the head of the California prison system. He was trying to improve race relations," said Bob Wilson.[45] Warren later did even more for race relations as chief justice of the Supreme Court.

After the West Virginia State team toured the prison, the game was played on a makeshift court in the prison dining hall. "Right before the center jump, their center said to our center, 'Don't outjump me because I am in here for murder,'" recalled Ferguson.[46] The West Virginia State team was not intimidated by the San Quentin center or the 1,500 prisoners who were allowed to watch the game, as the Yellow Jackets easily won, 65–37. Bob Wilson led State in scoring, with 23 points.[47] The game received little attention. Prison teams occasionally played teams from the "outside" during that era.

In *They Cleared the Lane: The NBA's Black Pioneers*, Ron Thomas described the impact that the game and a tour of the prison had on Earl Lloyd. "Not that I had any inclination toward being a crook, but I learned what I didn't want to be. You take a young black guy into a maximum-security prison, it scared the hell out of me," said Lloyd.[48]

West Virginia State began the final leg of the tour by losing to the national AAU Champions, the Oakland Blue n' Gold, 73–68. At the next stop in the California state capital, they redeemed themselves by crushing Sacramento State College, 57–36. In the last game of the tour in Denver Colorado, they lost in overtime to Regis College, 49–44.[49]

The Yellow Jackets quickly put their losses during the Western trip behind them as they defeated Bluefield State, 103–54 and the Mexican National Team, which was on a national tour of the United States, 87–57. Then the team began another tour, this time to the South where they met CIAA foes. A string of victories followed with wins over Winston-Salem, Shaw, and St. Augustine in North Carolina, and Virginia State and Howard in Virginia. This tour was followed by a home court victory over Wilberforce, giving West Virginia State a 24–4 record and another CIAA Visitation Championship.

Then it was on to the CIAA tournament in Washington, D.C. In 1950 the tournament site was moved from Turner's Arena to the larger Uline Arena, which had become the home of the Washington Capitols in 1949–50, the season that the Basketball Association of America took in the remaining teams in the National Basketball League and took a new name, the National Basketball Association. Uline could seat 9,000 fans, and the move from the 2,000 seat Turner's Arena to a much larger venue clearly indicated the powerful draw that the CIAA tournament had become. Many well-educated African Americans lived in Washington where they could obtain civil service jobs commensurate with their education and the CIAA Tournament had become an important social, as well as sports, event for them. The Washington residents were joined by prosperous out-of-town alumni of the CIAA colleges who felt comfortable in coming to Washington where hotel accommodations and restaurants that would serve them could be easily found. In fact, for the first time, the State team did not have to sleep on cots in the arena. Instead they were able to stay at the all-black Dunbar Hotel.

West Virginia State was the top seed in what was expected to be a very competitive CIAA Tournament. The more than 5,000 fans who flocked to the Uline Arena for each of the three days of the tournament would not be disappointed. All of the teams had a strong contingent of military veterans going to school under the G.I. bill and many of the teams had reached a sophisticated level of play. These eight teams appeared capable of continuing the history of upsets in the tournament. Nevertheless, West Virginia State defeated Johnson C. Smith College, and Lincoln University of Pennsylvania to reach the final game of the tournament for the third straight year.[50]

In the final game West Virginia State met North Carolina College, led by point guard Harold Hunter, and coached by their veteran coach, John McLendon. State had beaten them twice during the visitation season and the Yellow Jackets were favored to win their third straight championship. However, the Saturday afternoon game remained close with West Virginia State holding only a one-point lead to end the half at 37–36. The lead changed hands 29 times in a back and forth contest. The game was tied at 70–70 in the closing seconds. Then North Carolina hit a basket and two foul shots to win the game and the championship with a final score of 74–70. The "tourney jinx" had struck again.

"That game absolutely broke my heart. Sometimes the basket just seems smaller. We didn't play our best, but that afternoon North Carolina was equal to the task," recalled Lloyd.[51] North Carolina's Harold Hunter was named the Most Outstanding Player in the tournament and later was selected in the 11th round of the 1950 NBA Draft by the Washington Capitols.[52] West Virginia State forward Bob Wilson set a tournament record by scoring 72 points, and coach Mark Cardwell was named the outstanding coach in the tournament, but these honors provided little consolation.[53]

The Charleston Gazette called the final game of the regular season the "climax of an era."[54] During three years, the State fans had never seen their team lose at home. In those three seasons, the team had won more than 60 games, three CIAA Visitation championships, two CIAA tournament championships and had claimed two National Negro Basketball championships. "Those were great teams at State because we were so close. We did not care who scored, and we did not have one or two superstars. We thought we had five or six superstars," said Bob Wilson.[55] Indeed, an era had ended on the basketball court with the graduation of six exceptional West Virginia State basketball players: Earl Lloyd, Bob Wilson, Joe Gilliam, Douglas Rockhold, Clarence Clark, and Frank Enty.

* * *

As one era ended for the West Virginia State team, another era was beginning in professional basketball. It was announced unceremoniously to Earl Lloyd when a State student yelled, "Moon! I just heard your name on the radio! You've just been drafted to play for some team called the Washington Capitols."[56] It was true. The Capitols had scouted Lloyd while he had played on their home court in the CIAA tournament and liked what they saw well enough to draft him in the ninth round of the NBA draft.

If Lloyd had graduated a year earlier, he would not have had this chance.

Previously, professional opportunities for African American basketball players had largely been limited to black touring teams like the Harlem Globetrotters and New York Rens. In addition to exhibition games, both these teams had played in Chicago's World Professional Tournament against white professional teams. A previous attempt had been made to integrate the National Basketball League (NBL). In 1948, the black New York Rens became the Dayton Rens and joined the NBL, one of two major professional basketball leagues at the time. However, the city of Dayton never fully supported the Rens and the experiment lasted only one season and was not successful.[57]

In 1949 The Basketball Association of America (BAA) absorbed the remaining teams of the NBL to form the National Basketball Association (NBA). In the 1950 NBA draft, the Boston Celtics drafted Chuck Cooper, an African American, in the second round, which opened the door for NBA integration. Earl Lloyd walked through that door as a ninth-round draft choice. Joining the Capitols was a unique experience for him: "I'd never even been in a locker room with white guys before, and now I'm in an NBA training camp," he wrote.[58]

Although he was a ninth-round choice, Lloyd made the Washington Capitols, which was located near his hometown of Alexandria, Virginia. On October 31, 1951, he stepped onto the floor for a game against the Rochester Royals, making him the first African American to play in an NBA game. He scored six points and pulled down 10 rebounds. Shortly thereafter, African

Americans Chuck Cooper of the Boston Celtics and Nat "Sweetwater" Clifton of the New York Knicks made their NBA debuts.

Two of the six African American players in the NBA before 1952 were from West Virginia State. After playing a summer with the Harlem Globetrotters, Lloyd's State teammate, Bob Wilson, joined the NBA in 1951. Wilson played a season with the Milwaukee Hawks before a knee injury cut short his NBA career.

Lloyd's initial career with the Capitols was also cut short when he was drafted into the U.S. Army shortly after joining the team. Following his discharge from a two-year tour, he played six seasons with the Syracuse Nationals and two with the Detroit Pistons. In 1971 he became the first African American to be named head coach of the Detroit Pistons. Lloyd coached the Pistons in 1971–72 and part of the 1972–73 season. He was inducted into the Naismith Memorial Basketball Hall of Fame in 2003.

* * *

West Virginia State had not only performed at an outstanding level on the court against other black colleges, but also proved to be pioneers in scheduling the West Coast games. Coach Cardwell had defied segregationist policy and scheduled white college teams. In front of predominantly white audiences on the West Coast tours, his team played with both skill and sportsmanship. The game with San Quentin Prison provided an historic connection. California Governor Earl Warren, who was so impressed by the West Virginia State team that he met and talked with the players before the game, was soon to become the Chief Justice of the United States Supreme Court. In 1954, the Warren court handed down a decision in *Brown v. Board of Education* that would radically change life at West Virginia State and race relations in the United States.

5

The Legacy of Black
High School Basketball

World War II had a dramatic impact on African Americans nationwide and in West Virginia. More than 11,000 of West Virginia's African Americans had served bravely and skillfully in the armed services. At least three of the veterans had been high school students who had enlisted. When they came back from the war, they re-enrolled in high school and played in the WVAU state basketball tournament. Brothers Bob and William Trice joined the Navy while in high school, and at the end of the war they both returned to Weirton Dunbar to finish high school. Likewise, James Henshaw joined the Navy while a student at Morgantown Monongalia High School, returning after the war to Monongalia to finish his class work. All three led their team to the WVAU state basketball championship game in the late 1940s. There may have been more, but they were the only three athletes who were identified as veterans, either black or white, who returned to play high school sports.

When the veterans came home from the war, they returned to a state with worsening economic conditions. A rapid decline in coal mining jobs, even when coal was selling well, occurred because of increasing mechanization in the mines. In 1947, there were 125,000 coal miners in West Virginia, but by 1960 that number had fallen to 49,000. The counties in the southern part of the state were particularly hard hit by the loss of coal jobs. The overall population of West Virginia declined by 7.2 percent between 1950 and 1960, causing the population to fall from over two million to a little more than 1.8 million. Much of the population decline was due to former miners migrating to other states in search of work. African Americans left West Virginia in greater numbers than whites. The number of African Americans in West Virginia was at a high of 117,700 in 1940 but declined to 65,000 in 1980. In 1940, blacks made up 6 percent of the state's population, but that number was reduced to only 3 percent by 1980.[1]

In 1954, school integration brought a completely new set of civil rights issues to many communities in West Virginia when the United States Supreme

Court handed down the *Brown v. Board of Education* decision that mandated the integration of public schools in the United States. The immediate issues no longer revolved around receiving separate but equal treatment, but instead became issues of access to and equal treatment within an integrated system. From the fall of 1954 through 1969 the process of the closing of black schools and sending black students to integrated high schools unfolded in West Virginia.

* * *

Major changes also occurred in the WVAU basketball tournament. The first was that West Virginia State College became the favored place to host the tournament in large part because of the new gymnasium, Fleming Hall, completed in 1942. In addition, not only was Institute centrally located in the state, but West Virginia State was the center of black education and culture in West Virginia, as well as the alma mater of many high school coaches and teachers. State hosted the tournament nine out of the 12 years from 1946 through 1957.

The elevation of Mark Cardwell from the coach of Kelly Miller High

Fleming Hall on the West Virginia State campus in Institute was completed in 1942. The building has an excellent basketball court, swimming pool, offices and classrooms. Fleming Hall was not only the home court for West Virginia State, but became the most popular site for the West Virginia Athletic Union's annual high school basketball championship tournament (courtesy West Virginia State University Archives and Special Collections).

School to the head basketball coaching position at West Virginia State solidified the basketball program at State, which had been under the leadership of a number of basketball coaches in the 1930s and 1940s. Cardwell actively encouraged the tournament move to West Virginia State so that he would have an opportunity to recruit outstanding high school players.

The WVAU tournament continued throughout the war. The high schools could still field teams because high school boys were not being drafted, although a few high school boys did enlist. The first post–World War II tournament in 1946 had a surprising result. The traditional powers like Kelly Miller, West Virginia State High School, and Elkhorn qualified for the tournament, but a surprise entry was Morgantown Monongalia High School. Monongalia was one of the smallest black high schools in West Virginia, despite drawing students from the entire Monongalia County and parts of Preston County. Ken Blue, a former student at Monongalia, recalled, "Our classes were small. In seventh grade we had maybe 20 students but by high school we would be down to the teens. We did field a football team, although I think some of the football players came out of the coal mines to play in games."[2]

In 1946, Monongalia was playing in the WVAU state tournament for only the second time in the 21-year history of the tournament. The Bulldogs, under veteran coach John Edwards, had an excellent season, losing only two regular season games, one of which was to Clarksburg Kelly Miller High School. They lost again to Kelly Miller in the championship game of the northern region tournament, but both the regional winners and runners-up from each of the four regions advanced to the WVAU Tournament.[3]

Kelly Miller and Monongalia were placed in opposite sides of the state tournament bracket. Both won their first-round games on Friday. Kelly Miller defeated Huntington Douglass, 46–31, and Monongalia defeated heavily favored West Virginia State High School, 30–28. "We were a small school. I only had 15 in my graduating class," said William Dunlap, a guard on the Monongalia team. "State was favored to beat us easily. The game was close but we pulled it out."[4]

"The reason that Monongalia was so good was that they had a player named James Henshaw who came out of the Navy to play. He was really good," claimed Warne Ferguson, who played for State in that game.[5] "I don't know how long James was in the Navy but he was only a year older than we were," countered Dunlap.[6]

The black high schools were not as strict as white schools regarding players' age and age documentation. The prevailing practice at the black schools seemed to be that if a student was attending school he could play on the school's teams. The black schools seemed more interested in keeping students in school than keeping them off teams.[7]

Kelly Miller won its Saturday afternoon semi-final game, 73–40, over

Bluefield Genoa, and Monongalia upset heavily favored Elkhorn, 29–21, to set up a Saturday rematch between the two Northern Region teams for the state championship. Everything seemed to be in Kelly Miller's favor for the championship game. Kelly Miller was larger with 167 students (grades 7–12) compared with Monongalia's 127 (grades 7–12). Kelly Miller had had a modern school and gymnasium since 1929, while the Monongalia High School gym had only been built as a Depression relief project in the early 1940s. Kelly Miller had the basketball tradition with five state championship teams, while Monongalia had qualified for the tournament only twice. And Kelly Miller had beaten Monongalia the week before in the regional championship.

True to form, Kelly Miller increased a tight 25–24 halftime edge into a 38–34 lead to end the third quarter. But Mike Denson, who had been the leading scorer for Monongalia all year, could not miss. On the other side, the Kelly Miller shooters could not find the basket. An astounding 14–1 run in the fourth quarter earned Monongalia a 48–39 victory and the state championship. Denson finished the game with 28 points, while Navy veteran James Henshaw scored only two points.[8] Monongalia qualified for the WVAU state championship tournament twice more before integrating with Morgantown High School in 1954, but never again made it out of the first round of the state tournament.

* * *

Travel to tournaments and games was expensive for many high schools, but the black high schools in West Virginia financed their athletic teams through strong fan support from the black community and some creative fundraising. Gary District High School under coach James Wilkerson was one of the most successful fundraisers. "We didn't have to raise money from the community," Wilkerson explained. "We financed our trips out of the school treasury. We had socials and dances after the games, a Miss Gary contest, and, of course, gate receipts. We always took Miss Gary, the cheerleaders, and a chaperone to all the games and tournaments."[9] Almost all of the black high schools had a "Miss" contest. The girls nominated for the contest would have fundraisers and the girl who raised the most money would represent the school as the "Miss" for the school year.

Arintha Poe Hairston, the 1956 Miss Gary, raised $200 to win the title. "That was a lot of money then," she said. "My family helped me by having bake sales and hot dog sales and donating things to sell in the summer. I was so excited when I won, I was on cloud nine. I was excited for my parents because they worked so hard for me and they were so proud. The high point was getting to ride in the convertible on the field at a football game," Hairston added.[10]

* * *

The 1947 WVAU Tournament also provided a couple of firsts. Fairmont Dunbar, which had often been runner-up to the ever-powerful Kelly, Miller upset Kelly Miller to win the Northern regional tournament. But, in 1947, Weirton Dunbar, with its best team in the history of the school, also upset heavily favored Kelly Miller to qualify as the other team from the Northern Region. (Both Dunbar High Schools had been named for the African American poet Paul Lawrence Dunbar.)

As predicted, Genoa, Fairmont Dunbar, and Kimball won first round games and moved into the semi-finals along with Weirton Dunbar, who upset heavily favored Montgomery Simmons in a tight 46–44 game. In the semi-final games both Dunbar teams won again, with Fairmont defeating Genoa, 42–37, led by center Bob Echols with 12 points, and Weirton edging Kimball, 45–44, led by 18 points from Charles Rice and 13 by center Bob Trice.

The championship game was a reprise of the Northern Regional championship game of the previous week. Weirton Dunbar, located in Hancock County in the Northern Panhandle of the state, was the most northern of the West Virginia black high schools. Weirton was a heavily ethnic city with large Greek, Italian, and Eastern European communities. The Weirton Steel Company, then the largest employer in West Virginia, was desperate for workers to fill their expanding steel operation and actively recruited African Americans and foreign nationals through the early 20th century. By 1913, Weirton Steel employed enough African Americans that Weirton opened a segregated elementary school. Later, in 1932, Weirton opened Dunbar High School for 40 students who had in previous years been bused across the Ohio River to the integrated high school in Steubenville, Ohio. Dunbar remained small, growing to only 121 students in grades seven through 12 by 1947. Anthony Major, who had earned a doctoral degree at the University of Pittsburgh, was the principal at Dunbar from 1932 until his death in 1949. In 1934 James T. Wares, a former All-American football player at West Virginia State, was hired as the all-sports coach at Dunbar. A three-story brick building was built in 1939 as a federal New Deal work project to house Dunbar High School (grades 7–12), but the new school, like many of the black schools in West Virginia, did not have a gymnasium until 1954.[11]

"Dunbar was allowed three days a week to either practice or play games in the integrated Weirton Christian Center," recalled Bob Kelley, who attended Dunbar through junior high school. "The Christian Center had a small gym floor with the end line right against the wall. The bleachers were in a small balcony above the floor. When Dunbar played games there the seating was crowed and it was really hot and humid."[12] The football situation was no better. Dunbar practiced and played most games on the top of a steep hill next to the power station.

A major factor in the success of the Weirton team that year was the Trice

"One of Dunbar's Best Basketball Teams"
State Championship Runner Up 1947

Tournament held on Campus of West Virginia State College

Front row kneeling Left to Right
Robert "Sugarhead" Young (deceased), James "Taxi" Strong (deceased)
Herbert Veal, James P. Miller, John Baines

Standing Left to Right
Belche Casterlow (deceased), Orlidge Byrom (deceased), Charles Rice,
Robert Trice (deceased), Shelly Trice, Edward Miller (deceased)
Mr. James Wares, Coach (deceased)

The Weirton Dunbar 1947 basketball team was the school's most successful basketball team. They were runners-up in the WVAU state tournament, losing 44–36 to Fairmont Dunbar. In the back row, Bob and Shelly Trice are fourth and fifth from the left and Coach James "Ham" Wares is sixth from the left (courtesy of the Weirton [WV] Area Museum and Cultural Center).

brothers: Bob and William "Shelly." Both had dropped out of Dunbar to join the Navy during World War II and, after returning from the service, they re-enrolled at Dunbar. Shelly Trice, who played guard, had been in the Navy for 10 months and was only 18 years old that season. Bob Trice, a dominating six-foot, three-inch center on the Dunbar team, was 20 years old and a tremendous athlete.[13]

Fairmont Dunbar was more than twice the size of Weirton Dunbar with 278 (grades 7–12) students. While the population of the towns was similar at about 20,000, Fairmont had twice as many African American citizens, most of whom were employed in the coal mines. The African Americans in Weirton worked at Weirton Steel.

Fairmont, coached by Horace "Happy" Belmear, had a narrow 20–18 lead at halftime. In the third quarter, Fairmont opened a 10-point lead and never looked back, winning the WVAU state championship, 44–38. George Thomas and Bob Echols led Fairmont with 16 and 15 points, respectively. The

BOB TRICE pitcher *KANSAS CITY ATHLETICS*

Bob Trice, a Weirton Dunbar athlete and Navy veteran, played professional baseball as a pitcher starting with the Negro League's Homestead Greys. His best season was in 1953 when he went 21–10 for Ottawa in the International League. In 1953 he integrated the Philadelphia Athletics (later Kansas City Athletics) of the American League. He played parts of three seasons with the Athletics before finishing his career in the Mexican League. Photograph dated 1955 (baseball card courtesy Weirton [WV] Area Museum and Cultural Center).

Trice brothers paced Weirton. Bob Trice led all scorers with 17 points and his brother Shelly chipped in with seven points.[14]

Bob Trice was also an outstanding baseball pitcher. He had a successful career in the minor leagues where he won 21 games in 1953 for the Ottawa, Canada, A's in the International League. Trice was brought up by the American League Philadelphia Athletics as a 27-year-old rookie late in the 1953 season, and on September 13, 1953, became the first African American to play in a game for the Athletics. He pitched for the Philadelphia and, later, Kansas City Athletics from 1953 through 1955. His career record was nine wins and nine losses. He was also a good hitter, carrying a lifetime major league batting average of .288.

After the Trice brothers graduated, Weirton Dunbar was never as strong as they were in 1947. Weirton played in the state tournament again in 1955, the last year of the school's existence, but was eliminated in the first round. Fairmont fared better, playing in four more WVAU tournaments and making the semifinal round in both 1951 and 1954.

* * *

While Clarksburg Kelly Miller, Charleston Garnet, Kimball, Wheeling Lincoln, Gary District, and Huntington Douglass were establishing dynasties in WVAU basketball and winning multiple championships, there were many more teams, mostly from smaller high schools, who, like Weirton Dunbar and Morgantown Monongalia, played only for brief moments of glory. The four schools profiled below stand as examples of the many other black high schools in West Virginia.

Parkersburg Sumner, founded in 1862, was the first black school for African Americans in West Virginia as well as the first black high school in the state, graduating a class of four students in 1887. Despite being established early in the history of West Virginia, and housing grades 1 through 12, Sumner was always a small school. Early in the 20th century, Parkersburg, which is on the Ohio River, was a center for transportation, oil, and gas, but those industries recruited few black workers. By 1950, Parkersburg had a population of almost 30,000, but the high school classes at Sumner consisted of 15 to 20 students. Sumner drew from the entire Wood County, but of the 13,914 students in the county, less than 1 percent was black. "Sumner never was very big because the black population in Parkersburg and Wood County was small. There was nothing to draw African Americans to Parkersburg," said Tim Swarr, the former superintendent of Wood County schools.[15]

Sumner qualified for the WVAU basketball tournament on seven occasions but only twice advanced to the semi-finals. The golden age of Sumner basketball was in the 1949 and 1950 seasons. In 1949, the Golden Knights won the Northern Regional tournament. In the WVAU state tournament they lost, 59–42, to a strong Huntington Douglass team led by Hal Greer's older brothers. Sumner returned to the WVAU tournament the following year and crushed Byrd Prillerman, 65–37, in the opening round, only to lose, 47–26, to eventual state champion Douglass.[16] Parkersburg Sumner High School closed in 1955.

Buckhannon Victoria High School, located in Upshur County, showed promise in the early WVAU tournaments. In 1920 the population of Buckhannon was little more than 3,700 people, but with enough African Americans to build the segregated Victoria High School. In 1926, Victoria played in the second WVAU tournament, and, in 1928, they were strong enough to win three of five tournament games. Victoria reached the zenith of their athletic accomplishment in 1929 when they made the semi-finals of the WVAU state tournament. However, over the next 20 years, Buckhannon grew by fewer than 700 people and the black population declined significantly. After 1931, when the regional tournaments were instituted, Victoria qualified for the eight-team WVAU tournament only in 1943. By the late 1940s, the small school became even smaller when African Americans left Upshur County in search of jobs. In 1948, Victoria High School was closed and the remaining high school students were bused 35 miles to Kelly Miller High School in Clarksburg, the closest black high school. In the fall of 1954, Upshur County's two black students integrated Buckhannon Upshur High School.[17]

Black education began in Beckley in 1907 when Rock Quarry Elementary School was opened to teach the children of Beckley's 10 black families. As the black population in Beckley grew, Stratton High School was established in 1921 and graduated its first class in 1925. A new brick building to house Stratton High School was built in 1939 with a gymnasium added in 1950. Stratton quickly fielded athletic teams and began playing in the WVAU basketball tournament as early as 1929. In the 1950s, Stratton had their best basketball teams. In 1952, Stratton advanced to the WVAU state semi-finals; two years later they won the 1954 WVAU state championship, beating Byrd Prillerman, 65–55, in the championship game. The next year Stratton finished as runner-up to Charleston Garnet. The football team won WVAU football championships in 1937 and 1949.[18]

In 1957 Stratton began to play in the formerly all-white WVSSAC state basketball tournament and continued in that tournament until the school closed in 1967. After having little success in the first eight years, in 1965 and 1966 Stratton was the sectional champion in Class AA (there were three classes) and advanced to finish as regional runners-up only one game from the state tournament. In 1968 the integrated Beckley Woodrow Wilson basketball team finished as runner-up in the WVSSAC state basketball tournament.[19]

The closing of Stratton High School in 1967, 13 years after the *Brown* decision, was painful for Beckley's black community because of the pride they felt for their school and the way integration was handled. An article in the *West Virginia All Black Schools Sports and Academic Hall of Fame Program* expressed that bitterness: "In 1967 when Stratton was forced to integrate.... It was the end of an era. Unfortunately, the written history and other tangible artifacts of history were destroyed by the county board of education.... Many who had been principals in the all black schools were offered assistant principal in integrated schools and refused to accept the position and be demoted."[20] The former Stratton High School building is now Beckley-Stratton Middle School.

Lewisburg Bolling High School drew students from Greenbrier County, a largely rural county in the southeast corner of West Virginia bordering Virginia. Before the Civil War, Greenbrier County had one of the largest concentrations of slaves of any county in what became the state of West Virginia. Black education began in Greenbrier County as early as 1877. The first principal was Edward Bolling, for whom the high school was later named. Through the 1920s, Bolling Junior High and Elementary School taught students first through ninth grades. Students from Greenbrier County who wanted a high school education traveled a long distance to enroll in either Storer College or Bluefield State College's high school programs, where they had to live on campus. Finally, Bolling became a high school in 1935. Students were bused to Bolling High School from all of Greenbrier County, the second largest county in West Virginia in area, necessitating long bus rides for many of the students from outlying towns.

The Lewisburg Bolling High School athletic teams faced insurmountable challenges. Bolling High School quickly established an athletic program, but facilities were a problem. The football team practiced on a rocky pasture next to the school and the basketball team practiced and played at Lewisburg High School, but only when the gym was not in use by the white students. The enrollment at Bolling was small. In 1954, the school enrollment in Greenbrier County was 9,489, of whom fewer than 5 percent were black. In addition, busing was a problem. A professor at West Virginia University, Dr. Floyd Jones' mother, Opal Jones, graduated from Bolling in 1950 and talked with Floyd about her experiences there. "She often told me that the athletes had to ride the bus home with the other students so they did not have much practice time. There were good athletes, but just not many of them because the school was so small. It was hard for Bolling to compete with the bigger schools," recalled Floyd Jones.[21] Despite the disadvantages of being a small school that drew from a large geographical area, with a borrowed gym and hand-me-down equipment, Bolling persevered. Bolling qualified only once for the WVAU basketball tournament. In the last tournament in 1957 the powerful Gary District team easily defeated Bolling, 82–37. But, in 1959, Bolling began to play in the WVSSAC sectional tournament. In 1960 Bolling

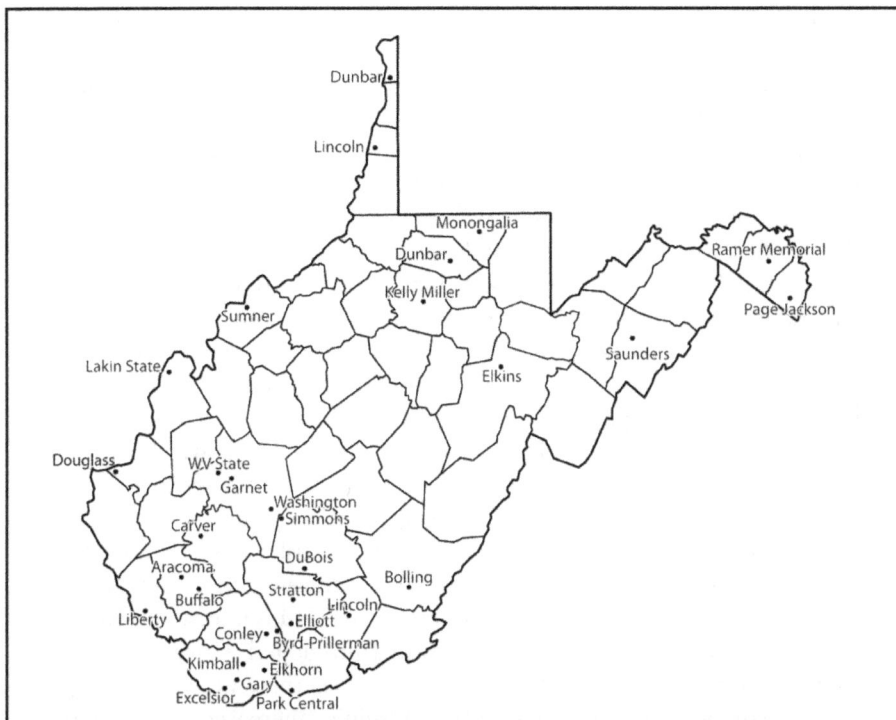

This map shows the location of the black high schools in West Virginia in 1950. The black high schools were concentrated in the southern coal region of the state. The other black high schools were spread thinly throughout the state making scheduling difficult. The schools in the eastern panhandle played black high schools from Virginia, Maryland, and the District of Columbia (map by James Atkinson).

defeated Renick High School, 47–33, in the sectional tournament their only winning game in the WVSSAC tournament. Bolling closed in the spring of 1961 and the students were integrated into white high schools in Greenbrier County.[22]

* * *

Traveling to the WVAU state tournament, regional tournaments, and even games during the season sometimes required overnight trips. Traveling in segregated West Virginia was difficult for the black high school teams because most hotels and restaurants refused to serve African Americans. But those necessary overnight basketball trips became a strong unifying force for African Americans in West Virginia.

"When the teams came to play at Wheeling Lincoln it was an event," said Wilkes Kinney, the son of John Wilkes Kinney, Lincoln's basketball coach in the 1940s and 1950s. "The players from the visiting school would stay with the families of the Lincoln players. My family would sometimes house the other team's coach, but we never took in players because I had five sisters and my mom did not want those boys running around our house. The games were played at the CRC, Colored Recreation Center, because Lincoln did not have a gym. We would have a band and after the game we had a dance for the visiting team. When the teams were from places like Huntington or Bluefield the families, they stayed with would pack lunches and the team would load the bus and drive all night. Those were long trips in the days before interstates and because of segregation there was no place for the team to stop."[23]

Travel was often long and difficult for the black high school athletic teams. The 40 black high schools were spread through West Virginia, creating long trips by black high school teams in school buses or cars over mountain roads. Segregation made travel even more difficult. The players usually ate cold packed lunches because there were few restaurants that would accommodate black patrons. Roadside bathroom stops were frequent and embarrassing because most gas stations had rest rooms for white customers only. Sometimes in the back of the minds of African Americans traveling in unfamiliar territory was the fear of getting lost and stumbling on a sunset or sundown town. Those towns often had laws or customs that prohibited African Americans from being in their town under threat of violence. There were rumors of the existence of those kinds of towns in West Virginia. There were also rumors of black travelers leaving for a trip and never being heard from again.[24]

The lack of integrated facilities contributed to the development of strong relationships among the state's black communities. Lacy Smith, former coach at Logan Aracoma High School, said, "When we had games at Weirton Dunbar, Parkersburg Sumner, or Fairmont Dunbar, we would eat in the school cafeteria and stay overnight with the players and coaches from the other team. Then, when they came here, we would do the same for them. So, when we got to the state tournament, our players already had some strong friendships with players on most of the other teams."[25]

When the WVAU Tournament was held on the Bluefield State or West Virginia State campus, the teams slept on cots in the gym or in dormitory rooms. But when the tournament was held at Garnet High School in Charleston or at Kelly Miller High School in Clarksburg, the teams stayed in people's homes. "The closeness and the friendships at the tournament were what made everything so nice," said Ruth Jarrett, a student at Garnet in the late 1930s and, later, wife of Garnet coach Jim Jarrett. "When they had the tournaments at the high schools, the people in the community took the players and coaches into their homes and the teams were fed in the school cafeteria. You see, there wasn't but the Ferguson Hotel for black people to stay in and nobody stayed there. Everything else was segregated. The people that took the teams into their homes came to the tournament—that was our people and they supported the school."[26]

* * *

By the 1950s, Huntington Douglass and Charleston Garnet, located in the largest cities in the state, emerged as the power teams in the black high school ranks. Public education for Huntington's black children began as early as the 1870s. Huntington Douglass High School, a two-story, six-room brick building with a basement, was opened in 1891 as a grades 1 to 12 school. The first class graduated from high school in 1893. Three years later, in 1896, Carter G. Woodson graduated from Douglass. He returned as a teacher at Douglass and served as the principal from 1901 through 1903. Woodson went on to earn a Ph.D. from Harvard University in 1912. Founding the Association for the Study of Negro Life and History, which published the *Journal of Negro History*, Woodson is recognized as the "father of black history."[27]

In 1924, the black school enrollment in Huntington had grown to 600, necessitating the building of a new three-story school, Douglass High School, to house grades seven through 12. Through the 1930s and 1940s, Douglass High School established a well-rounded academic program as well as a strong music program under director Revella Hughes, a Broadway performer who returned to Huntington to care for her ill mother and to teach at Douglass. The athletic program blossomed under coach Z.L. Davis in the 1940s. Douglass won its first state championship in 1941.[28]

By 1950, Huntington had grown to a population of more than 86,000, making it the largest city in the state. The African American population was 4,500, larger than most towns in West Virginia. Huntington had a thriving black community with dentists, doctors, a black hospital, and numerous black-owned businesses. Many members of Huntington's black community worked as porters for the railroad, which was considered a good job at the time. Others worked as waiters or service staff at one of Huntington's many hotels. Some worked as domestics.

In 1948, chinks were developing in the armor of segregation. Earlier in the decade Clarksburg Kelly Miller High School had scrimmaged with Clarksburg St. Mary's, the Catholic high school, and had played against integrated high schools in Pennsylvania. But a huge step came in December 19, 1948, when Huntington St. Joseph High School (usually called St. Joe) announced its basketball schedule. On that schedule were home and away games with Huntington Douglass. Huntington's *Herald-Dispatch* proclaimed, "The meeting between St. Josephs and Douglass will be the first time in the history of Huntington that teams of the two races have met."[29] The *Huntington Advertiser* claimed that the game was "West Virginia's first between Negro and White high school teams."[30] This was the first known game played in

West Virginia between black and white high schools. There appears to have been no written rules or laws in West Virginia prohibiting interracial play as there were in many states. The lack of interracial high school sports seems to have been by custom rather than by law. In addition, St. Joe, as a Catholic school, was not a member of the WVSSAC and did not have to follow either their rules or customs. A high school so small it did not have enough boys for a football team, St. Joe prided itself on the basketball team that annually played a schedule that included Catholic and public high schools. The Fighting Irish played the large schools in the area, including Huntington High School and Huntington East High School, and more than held their own. Douglass played only other black high schools, so, to the white fans, Douglass was an enigma.

The only public reaction to the game seemed to be positive because on the day before the game Father Sylvester Staud, a priest at St. Joe and the basketball coach, announced that the game would be moved from the tiny St. Joe gym to the Huntington East High School Gym to accommodate the expected crowd. St. Joe had a 4–6 record and Douglass sported a 2–0 record including a victory over Charleston Garnet.[31]

The game drew a standing room only crowd evenly divided between fans of both teams. St. Joe jumped out to a 19–16 halftime lead and stretched it into a 29–22 advantage at the end of the third quarter. The Douglass Wildcats came within two points, but after missing two shots in the final seconds of the game, St. Joe came away with a 31–27 victory. In the *Herald-Dispatch* game story, sportswriter Fred Burns wrote, "the most important thing was that a couple of basketball teams from different races met for the first time in the sports history of Huntington and resulted in nothing more than a hard-fought athletic contest between groups of high school boys. In fact, the game was a lot cleaner and much more interesting than many others we have seen between teams of the same race."[32]

The second game of the series, a Douglass home game, was moved from the Douglass gym to Huntington's Radio Center arena, home of the Marshall College basketball team, to accommodate the crowd. No one was disappointed in the game. Douglass raced to a 26–18 halftime lead. But St. Joe fought back in the second half and, with the score tied at 44–44 with 10 seconds left in the game, St. Joe's Bud Powers hit a foul shot to win the game, 45–44, for the Irish.[33]

St. Joe finished the season with a 38–33 loss to Fairmont St. Peter's in the first round of the West Virginia Catholic Tournament. Douglass was more fortunate. The Wildcats beat Parkersburg Sumner, 59–42, in the first round of the WVAU Tournament and nosed out Williamson Liberty, 59–57, in the semi-final game. Garnet won the state championship, beating Douglass in the two teams' third match up of the season.[34]

The series between St. Joe and Douglass, which continued until the closing of Douglass in 1961, demonstrated the power of sports in the desegregation movement. There were never any negative reactions to the game reported in the press and the large crowds that attended the games demonstrated that even before the *Brown* decision in 1954 there were people in Huntington who wanted to schedule and watch games between black and white high schools. The St. Joe–Douglass games were hard fought, cleanly played, and very well attended.

* * *

From 1949 through 1953, Douglass advanced to the WVAU state championship game four of five years. In 1950, Douglass won its first ever WVAU basketball championship, beating Mullins Conley 50–36. The following year a slender freshman, Hal Greer, led the Wildcats to a second straight championship with a 55–53 game victory over Garnet. Greer was the youngest of the six Greer brothers who were mainstays on the Douglass teams in the late 1940s and into the 1950s. J.D. Greer, the best of the Greer brothers before Hal, had gone on to play football and basketball for Elizabeth City State College in North Carolina. But Hal proved to be even better. A three-sport star at Douglass, Hal was best at basketball. He would become the most famous alumnus from the WVAU Tournament. Greer, however, did not dominate the tournament as might be expected from someone who quickly became a star in integrated college and professional basketball.

After leading the Wildcats to the 1951 championship as a freshman, in Greer's sophomore year Douglass lost in the opening round of the 1952 WVAU Tournament to Kelly Miller High School, 47–42. However, 1953 proved to be Greer's best season. Douglass and Garnet battled throughout the season, splitting the regular season games, but Douglass won the regional championship game between the two teams. In the first round of the WVAU State Tournament Greer hit for 29 points as Douglass beat Fairmont Dunbar, 58–43. In the semi-final game Douglass defeated Amigo Byrd Prillerman, 52–41.[35] The 1953 championship game was the fourth game of the season between Douglass and Garnet. Douglass prevailed in a rough foul-marred game when the Wildcats made 36 out of 44 free throws, while Garnet hit on only 24 free throws. Douglass won a close 56–52 game. Hal Greer and Valmore Hill were named to the All-Tournament team, and Greer was named to the All-State team.[36] In an astounding turn of events during Greer's senior season, Douglass lost in the opening round of the 1954 WVAU tournament to Byrd Prillerman by 46–43. Greer was only named an "honorable mention" All-State selection.[37]

The 1954 *Brown v. Board of Education* decision, which mandated the integration of public schools in the United States, had an immediate impact

Twenty-Fifth Annual

STATE BASKETBALL TOURNAMENT

March 16, 17, & 18, 1950

West Virginia State College
Institute, W. Va.

3 SESSIONS

1st -- 6:00 P. M. -- March 16
2nd -- 7:00 P. M. -- March 17
3rd -- 8:00 P. M. -- March 18

25th Anniversary
SOUVENIR PROGRAM
15c

Compliments of—

THE FERGUSON HOTEL
1006 E. Washington Street

...AND...

THE FERGUSON THEATER
WHOLESOME ENTERTAINMENT
1004 E. Washington Street

Charleston, West Virginia

The players on the 1950 West Virginia Athletic Union state basketball tournament program look very white. The printer must not have had any covers with black players (courtesy West Virginia State University Archives and Special Collections).

on Hal Greer, because Marshall College offered Greer a basketball scholarship. He accepted the offer from coach Cam Henderson, and in the 1954–55 basketball season he became one of the pioneers who integrated West Virginia college sports. After 1954, students in Huntington had a choice of attending either Huntington High School or Huntington Douglass. The coaches at

Huntington High School began to recruit black athletes to transfer from Douglass. Yet Douglass remained in operation until 1961 despite an ever-shrinking student population during the nine years after the *Brown* decision. This was so in part because the black community did not want to lose their school and also because some parents did not want to send their children into the sometimes-hostile environment of integrated schools.

* * *

Charleston Garnet was the other power team in the WVAU during the 1950s. Charleston Garnet High School, named for the abolitionist minister Henry Highland Garnet, was established in 1900 to educate the 12 African American students in Charleston who had passed the high school entrance examination. A new Garnet High School, built in 1929 to house the expanding number of black high school students, was an educational showplace with an auditorium, gymnasium, science labs, a domestic science room, and printing training. By the 1935–36 school year the booming population in Kanawha County helped Garnet become the largest black high school in West Virginia with 264 students in grades 9 through 12. In addition to strong athletic teams, Garnet boasted a popular men's speech choir, the famous Hancock Singing Group, and a full array of extracurricular clubs and activities.[38]

By 1950, Charleston had grown to a population of more than 73,000 and was the second largest city in the state behind Huntington. Garnet was the largest of the three black high schools in Kanawha County, drawing students from Charleston, South Charleston, and vocational students from the entire county.

Garnet had a long and excellent basketball tradition, winning championships in 1928, 1931, 1938, and 1940. In 1948, Garnet further strengthened its athletic program with the hiring of Jim Jarrett as the coach of all sports. A Charleston native, Jarrett had been a senior on Garnet's 1931 state championship team and went on to play football at prestigious Howard University in Washington, D.C. After graduation he returned to coach at Boyd Junior High School in Charleston from 1935 to 1942.

Jarrett was successful immediately at Garnet. His teams won the 1949 and 1950 WVAU football championships. Garnet won the 1949 basketball championship, defeating Douglass, 48–34, in the championship game, and Garnet won again in 1952, defeating Bluefield Park Central, 64–38.

The 1954–1955 WVAU regional and state tournaments had an air of drama in part because of the exciting games on the floor, but more importantly because of the uncertainty of the future of the black high schools caused by the *Brown* decision of the previous spring. Knute Burroughs, the coach of Accoville Buffalo High School, vividly remembered the 1955 regional tournament. "Jim Jarrett was an excellent coach, and he was slick," said Burroughs.

"I had my best team ever in 1955, but we blew it. We were playing Garnet in the western regional semifinal and we were beating them by a couple points near the end of the game. I had a kid named Ernest Williams who could handle the ball and dribble as good as any Globetrotter. When Ernest had the ball, wasn't anybody who could take it away. I told Ernest to control the ball and not to take anything but the good shot. So, Ernest was dribbling the ball and all at once Jarrett jumps up and yells, 'He's out of bounds.' The referee got flustered and blew his whistle. Ernest picked up the ball, looked, and he was three feet from the out of bounds. He just slammed the ball down, and you know what that is? Technical foul! That gave Garnet a foul shot, the ball, and they beat us."[39] "Jim Jarrett was one of the finest basketball coaches I have seen at any level of the game," said Ed Starling, who later became an assistant basketball coach at Marshall University and then associate athletic director.[40] Jarrett compiled a 170–40 basketball record in eight seasons at Garnet.

The 1955 tournament was the beginning of the end of the black state tournament in West Virginia. The *Brown* decision began to reduce the number of black schools in West Virginia. In the autumn of 1954, Monongalia and Randolph counties completely integrated their schools, causing Morgantown Monongalia and Elkins Riverside to close. Part of the ease of integrating both schools was that they were small schools with graduating classes numbering in the teens. "The 1955 tournament was a tough time for a lot of the coaches," said Horace Belmear, the coach at Fairmont Dunbar. "We thought maybe it was our last show. A lot of them didn't know where they would be the next year, or what was going to happen to the black schools. At the coaches' meeting [James] 'Ham' Wares, the coach at Weirton Dunbar, gave a brief talk about what athletics and the coaches had meant to the black communities. He talked about how we had tried to instill a strong sense of pride and character in the students. He was afraid that the black kids would lose sight of the game—and the meaning of the game—and get caught in the big money syndrome. A lot of what he said has come true. Ham was a real orator and tears were evident all over that room."[41]

The 1955 tournament was the last for Coach Belmear. Growing up in Louisville, Kentucky, he loved the WVAU tournament, believing it was more exciting and more popular than the black state tournament in Kentucky. After graduation from West Virginia State and military service in World War II, he became the basketball coach at Fairmont Dunbar High School until the fall of 1955, when Fairmont integrated its schools. Belmear was offered only a junior high school coaching position, which he held for a few years before taking a job at Fairmont State College. He later worked at West Virginia University, and for the federal government in Pittsburgh.

For the players it was a different story. "Most of the players on the Garnet team were seniors so we were not going to be back anyway. We never even thought about integration because it was not going to affect us," said Claude "Buster" Harvey, a player on the 1955 Garnet team. "It was different for the coaches because they could not be sure if they would have a job next year," he added.[42]

* * *

School integration proceeded at a very uneven rate across the state. In 1953–54 there were 451,991 children enrolled in West Virginia's public schools, of whom 25, 646 were African American, 6 percent of the school population.[43] Despite the small number of minority students, integration took 15 years in West Virginia. In the larger cities of the northern and central part of the state, integration occurred very quickly. In addition to the closing of Morgantown Monongalia and Elkins Riverside in 1954, within three years Weirton Dunbar, Wheeling Lincoln, Clarksburg Kelly Miller, Fairmont Dunbar, Charleston Garnet, Moorefield Saunders, and London Washington were all closed, their students integrating the white high schools. In the eastern and southern counties there was strong opposition to integration, and the process dragged on in some areas into the late 1960s.

The WVAU Basketball Tournament continued for three more years after the *Brown* decision, despite the declining number of teams. Not only had many of the black schools closed, but some of the remaining black schools began playing in the West Virginia Secondary Schools Activities Commission (WVSSAC) tournament. The 1956 WVAU Tournament was played at West Virginia State and drew eight teams. Byrd Prillerman High School defeated Knute Burroughs' Buffalo High School team 69–66 for the championship. The last West Virginia Athletic Union basketball tournament was held in March 1957 at Bluefield Park Central High School with 12 schools participating. The other schools had either been integrated or had joined the WVSSAC.[44]

It was the first and last time that Page Jackson High School ever played in the tournament. Located in Jefferson County in the Eastern Panhandle of West Virginia, Page Jackson was established in 1938. The first class graduated in 1941, but the school did not start an athletic program because many of the boys volunteered for World War II. In 1946, after World War II, the school played six-man football for one season, and the following year a full football and basketball team were organized.

The Appalachian Mountains separated the Eastern Panhandle from most of the rest of West Virginia, making travel into the rest of the state difficult. "We played a schedule of black high school teams from the Virginia and Maryland counties close to us, plus we played the big high schools in Washington," said James Taylor, the Page Jackson coach from 1959 until the closing of the school in 1965. "We did not play in the WVAU Tournament for that reason. It took a whole day just to get to Charleston."[45] Travel to Bluefield was even more difficult, but the team made the trip to play in the last WVAU event. Unfortunately, Page Jackson lost 65–58 to Williamson Liberty in the opening round of the 12-team tournament. Page Jackson closed in 1965.

Park Central advanced to the final game to meet defending champion Byrd Prillerman. Park Central was heavily favored because they had beaten Byrd Prillerman twice before and had won the Southern Regional Tournament the previous week. The Park Central Thundering Herd jumped out to a 30–25 halftime lead and hung on to win 62–54 behind a balanced scoring attack where all of the starting team scored in the double figures.[46]

That same evening, Douglass, which had withdrawn from the WVAU and did not play in the final black tournament, lost to Burch High School, 62–54, in the, formerly all-white WVSSAC area tournament finals. Had Douglass won that game, they would have been the first all-black high school to qualify for the WVSSAC state tournament.[47] Accoville Buffalo, West Virginia State High School, Beckley Stratton, and Logan Aracoma also participated in the 1957 WVSSAC tournament.[48] The WVAU disbanded after that final state tournament in 1957, and the remaining black high schools were absorbed by the WVSSAC.

* * *

"What made the black tournament so unique was the closeness of the people," said Ruth Jarrett. "My sons played in the tournament for Charleston High School after it was integrated, but the teams all stayed in motels spread all over town. It just wasn't the same feeling. For black people in Charleston, the First Baptist Church and Garnet High School were the centers of social life. When Garnet hosted the tournament, everyone supported it."[49] Ed Starling remembered, "There was a feeling of genuine camaraderie among the coaches. That doesn't mean they wouldn't try to beat your brains out on the floor, but when the game was over, the host coach would invite the other coaches out to his home for a social hour or dinner." Starling explained that this tradition did not die with the black tournament. Until his death in 1981, Jim Jarrett would invite all the black coaches to his home for breakfast whenever a tournament was held in Charleston.[50] "You should have been here," added Ruth Jarrett. "They would sit around and talk and argue and laugh about games and tournaments as if they happened yesterday and nothing had changed."[51]

* * *

For both blacks and whites in West Virginia, small town high schools and churches represented the focal points of community life. Segregation tended to tighten that focus for African Americans. Though a community may have had a number of black churches, there was only one black high school, and the high schools sponsored many social and cultural activities which reached out to the community. The high school athletic programs, however, and basketball in particular, reached beyond the limits of the local community, establishing both regional and statewide ties. In West Virginia's small, isolated black communities, the WVAU State Tournament represented one of the few opportunities to reinforce a sense of black pride. As coach James Wilkerson said, "Our kids and fans just lived for that tournament."[52]

PART II

The Integration
of West Virginia's
High Schools and Colleges,
1954–1964

It was not until 1954 that the "separate-but-equal" doctrine established by *Plessy v. Ferguson* was successfully challenged. In that year, the U.S. Supreme Court, in the *Brown v. Topeka Board of Education* decision, ruled that separate schools are inherently unequal, thus setting the stage for desegregation of American schools. Although the Brown decision ruled against school segregation, desegregation progressed slowly for nearly a decade. Despite the slow progress of school integration, the Court's decision triggered a new wave of activism that battled for desegregation and changed race relations in America. African Americans sought equal educational, employment, and economic opportunities in an integrated country. The challenges to discrimination against African Americans led to passage of the 1964 Civil Rights Act and the sweeping civil rights legislation in the mid–1960s. Throughout this period, African Americans sought equal opportunities in sport and once the playing field was leveled, they found increasing success.

6

Integrating Small Colleges

A member of the West Virginia legislature once boasted that there was a college within commuting distance of every citizen in the state. In May 1954, on the eve of the *Brown* Supreme Court decision, West Virginia was home to 19 colleges, a large number for a state with a population of only two million. They included West Virginia University, the state's flagship university, mid-sized Marshall College (now Marshall University), three black colleges, six small state colleges, six private church-affiliated colleges, and two junior colleges.

African American students were attending or had attended some of West Virginia's white colleges before 1954 based on two Supreme Court decisions, *Missouri ex rel. Gaines v. Canada* (1938) and *Sweatt v. Painter* (1950), and a 1948 decision by the West Virginia attorney general. In the Missouri decision, the court said that if any state college offered an academic program for white students, it also had to provide the same program for black students. Rather than developing parallel programs for African Americans, West Virginia opened the graduate and professional schools at West Virginia University to black students, which saved the state the expense of establishing separate programs. In 1948, the West Virginia attorney general ruled that state laws did not prohibit whites and African Americans from attending private schools for nursing, and that judgment was also interpreted as meaning that all private and church-related colleges in West Virginia could admit African American students. After 1948, Alderson Broaddus, West Virginia Wesleyan, Bethany, and Davis & Elkins began to admit African American students. The 1950, Sweatt Supreme Court decision said that the University of Texas had to admit an African American to its law school because the law school that Texas was establishing for African Americans would not be equal to the University of Texas Law School. That year, Marshall College opened its graduate school to black students.[1]

West Virginia's colleges integrated quickly following the June 1954 *Brown v. Board of Education* decision. In the fall semester of 1954, only months after *Brown*, all of West Virginia's state-supported colleges, except Glenville State, were integrated. Also, West Virginia State, Bluefield State, and Storer College, the three former black colleges which that fall semester enrolled white students. In addition, six of the eight private colleges were integrated.[2]

W. W. Trent, the state superintendent of schools, which included the state-supported colleges, contended that all of the colleges in West Virginia were integrated before the summer of 1955.[3] Trent was referring to all of the state-supported colleges. But Trent was not far wrong, as 17 of the 19 colleges in West Virginia were integrated before or during the 1954–55 school year. Salem College integrated in 1955–56. There is no record of when Beckley Junior College integrated.

The apparent ease of integration occurred in part because of the support of Governor William C. Marland, Attorney General John G. Fox, and W. W. Trent, the state superintendent of schools, who had oversight of all public colleges in West Virginia except WVU. Each of those state officials took positive steps to promote integration. A second and more important reason was that students in West Virginia, both black and white, saw the *Brown* decision as an opportunity to pursue a college education close to home. White students who enrolled at the black colleges, West Virginia State and Bluefield State, demonstrated a desire for an education regardless of the race of the teacher or the race of the other students sitting beside them in class, as well as a respect for the black colleges in the state. African American, students who enrolled at previously all-white colleges were taking a courageous step since they did not know what kind of reception to expect.

Even as African American students gained entrance to college campuses, they were not ensured access to residence halls or participation on various college athletic teams. The student cultures of white campuses were barely prepared to engage integration and were not prepared or equipped to fully understand the social condition surrounding the integration process. Those issues were not as much of a problem for the white students who attended the black colleges, all of whom lived at home and commuted to college.

The most startling integration case was the "reverse integration" of West Virginia State. West Virginia State was located in Institute, which was home to a small number of black families. In the fall 1954 semester, 182 white students registered for class at West Virginia State. By the end of the spring semester, 268 white students were enrolled in the student body of 983.[4] Within one year of integration, 26 percent of the student body at West Virginia State was white, all of whom were commuters from Kanawha County and nearby Putnam County, who wanted to take advantage of the opportunity to live at home and enroll in a state college that had low in-state tuition. Similarly, African American students who integrated the white colleges were mostly commuters in search of an inexpensive education.

This trend could be found throughout the state. The easy integration of

West Virginia's colleges and public schools in 1954 is all the more impressive when compared to the University of Mississippi, which was not integrated until James Meredith registered with the help of the National Guard in 1962. According to Sam F. Stack, Jr., the 17 Jim Crow states varied in response to the 1954 *Brown* ruling. Responses ranged from "wait and see" to outright defiance.[5]

Within two years of *Brown*, seven of the 18 colleges (Storer College closed in 1955) in the state had integrated their intercollegiate athletic programs. By 1964, all of the athletic programs had been integrated. The number of black athletes on teams during that era usually ranged between one to five on the football team and one or two on the basketball team. More black athletes on a team were an exception. Little recruiting of athletes was done by the coaches in the small colleges who were usually overworked, coaching three sports, and also teaching classes. Some of the pioneer black athletes in West Virginia's small colleges took part in campus life, but most lived at home, played sports, and went to class. As West Liberty State athlete Bob Douglas said, "Black athletes then did not have a social life. If you wanted a social life you went home for it."[6] In essence, the African American athletes were usually enrolled "invisibly" among the various campuses, largely leading to "lives at home" or "lives alone" which was de facto segregation. The situation was much more an isolated existence for black athletes at WVU and at Marshall, since they were recruited mostly from out of the area and lived on campus.

* * *

While the formal integration of West Virginia's colleges was impressive, access to athletic teams, and the social and political conditions on campus and in the communities where games were played, were important factors in both the academic and athletic success of African American athletes in the 1950s and 1960s. African American athletes faced many problems once they were on campus, including racial stereotyping, position stacking, and quotas. One of the recurring patterns of discrimination in collegiate athletics at that time was known as stacking. It was a common form of spatial segregation and refers to the disproportionate concentration (i.e., stacking) of ethnic minorities—particularly blacks—in specific team positions such as left halfback or tackle. Positions such as center and quarterback were reserved for whites. Black athletes were in effect, denied access to other team roles and it limited the number of black athletes who could be on the field at one time. Consequently, intra-team competition was often between players of the same race.

* * *

Five of the small colleges in West Virginia and Marshall integrated their athletic teams in the first academic year after the *Brown* decision (the small colleges were members of the West Virginia Intercollegiate Athletic Conference [WVIAC] which was conducive to athletic integration). Fourteen of West Virginia's 19 colleges in 1954 belonged to the WVIAC, and most schools in the conference played athletic schedules against other conference teams. There were fewer travel problems for integrated teams in West Virginia than in southern and border states, and after a season or two, the coaches knew which restaurants and hotels would serve integrated teams. For the most part, fans were not hostile to black athletes, who were well known in the state, at least by reputation.

* * *

West Virginia was one of the first states with a segregated school system to integrate intercollegiate athletic teams. In the academic year immediately following *Brown*, five West Virginia's small colleges (Concord, Potomac State, Fairmont, Alderson Broaddus, Wesleyan and Marshall) had at least one integrated team. Two additional colleges had a mixed-race player and an African American player prior to 1954.

In 1921 fullback Walter Jean played on the 1921 Bethany College football team. Jean was born in Chillicothe, Ohio, in 1898 to a black father and white mother. Because he was of mixed race at times, he was considered black and at other times to be white. For example, in the 1900 census he is listed as black. In the 1910 and 1920 censuses he is listed as mulatto, and the 1930 and 1940 censuses he is listed as white. His 1917 Draft Card lists him as being white but the list of Ohio's World War I soldiers lists him as colored. He was also recognized by the Green Bay Packer team historian Cliff Christi, as the first black Packer. To add to the confusion, he sometimes went by the name Walter LeJean.

Jean's college football career is not very clear either. He claimed to have played for West Virginia University, University of Missouri, Heidelberg College and Bethany College. That was not uncommon in the age of "tramp athletes" when many colleges filled their football rosters with players who were not students and were only on campus during football season. WVU and Missouri have no records of his participation. According to Bethany College's Associate Registrar, Maureen Golick, Walter Jean was a student in 1921 for at least one semester. Jean went on to play in the National Football League for the Akron Pros (1922 and 1923), Milwaukee Badgers (1924), and the Green Bay Packers (1925 and 1926).[7]

The first recognized African American athlete to play for a white collegiate team in the state during the 1950s was William Reape, who was a member of the West Virginia Wesleyan College basketball team during the 1950 season. Wesleyan was founded in 1890 by the Methodist Episcopal Church in Buckhannon in the north central part of West Virginia. Wesleyan had very successful football and basketball teams under coach Cebe Ross from 1925 through the early 1940s, often playing major colleges. Following the 1948 West Virginia Attorney General's opinion that African Americans could attend private nursing schools, the West Virginia Wesleyan Board of Trustees voted to "admit to West Virginia Wesleyan College qualified Negroes as regular students pursuing courses leading to a degree," wrote Kenneth Plummer in *A History of West Virginia Wesleyan College: 75 Years in the Service of Christian Higher Education 1890–1965*.[8] The motion was met with some apprehension regarding the role of the church in integration. Nonetheless, the Board of Trustees defeated a motion to rescind the decision of the administration committee, and Wesleyan moved to integrate.[9]

Four African American students enrolled in the fall of 1949. Then, in 1950, William Reape, a freshman from the Bronx, New York, joined the basketball team. Though Reape is in the yearbook picture of the Wesleyan basketball team, he is not mentioned in the yearbook season summary. Reape withdrew from Wesleyan after his freshman year, and Wesleyan has no alumni information about Reape.[10] Luvall Wilson was a member of the Wesleyan track team in 1955 and 1956, but he did not go beyond his sophomore year and, like Reape, is not listed in any of the Wesleyan alumni directories.[11] The first known black, female college athlete in West Virginia was Jo Ellen Flagg, who joined Wesleyan's 1956 field hockey team during her junior year. In 1956, the team was undefeated in a four-game schedule. Field hockey was the only intercollegiate team for women at Wesleyan and at most colleges in the 1950s; it was identified as a woman's sport and neither the NCAA nor NAIA recognized the sport. Flagg, from Charleston, was active in campus life as a member of the Women's Recreation Association, the Psychology Club, and Kappa Phi. She graduated in 1958 with a degree in library science. There were no other black athletes at Wesleyan until after 1960, though there were black students enrolled.[12]

* * *

One of the first colleges in West Virginia to integrate following *Brown* was Concord College (now Concord University). Concord Normal School opened to students on May 10, 1875. Located in Mercer County, Concord was the most southern white public college in West Virginia. In 1954, Billy Owens became the first African American to enroll at Concord and the college's first black athlete. Owens grew up in the coalfield community of Grotto, located in Mercer County, West Virginia, and attended segregated Bluestone High School, where he played on the football team. After high school, Owens enlisted in the U.S. Air Force and fought in the Korean War. Returning home from the Air Force, Owens enrolled at Concord on the G.I. Bill.[13]

During the 1954 and 1955 seasons Concord football coach Joe Friedl, Sr., asked Owens to join the team. Owens played offense, defensive back, and returned kickoffs. In a 2013 interview, Owens talked about two travel situations that exemplified the racism facing black athletes in the era of integration. Owens refused to travel with the team to a game in Tennessee: "I told the coach, I'm not going. I figured it was a little bad here, but I knew it would be much worse there."[14] An incident occurred on the trip to his final game with the team. "We had to stay overnight…. We went to the hotel…. The person in charge there told us that I couldn't stay," said Owens. "That's when Coach Joe Friedl spoke up and said, 'Well, if he don't stay, we won't stay.'" But Owens was eventually provided lodging at "an all-black place in the city's downtown."[15] Owens attended three years at Concord College, majoring in biology and physical education. He did not complete his degree from Concord College but spent most of his professional career working at Long Beach Memorial Hospital in New York. In October 2013, Billy Owens attended a football game between Concord and Fairmont on the Concord campus, where he was named honorary team captain.

* * *

Potomac State College is located in Keyser, West Virginia, a town that in 1950 had about 6,000 people and is in northeastern West Virginia along the Maryland border. In 1901 Keyser Preparatory Branch of West Virginia University was founded. The school soon became Potomac State College, a junior college to prepare students to enroll at West Virginia University.[16] Potomac State College moved quickly to integrate its athletic teams following *Brown*. Robert Smith, a five-foot, eight-inch, 170-pound Arts and Sciences major from Keyser, played running back on the 1954 and 1955 football teams. William Perry, an accounting student from nearby Piedmont, played on the baseball team in 1955.[17]

The following year, Perry played on both the basketball and baseball teams. Raymond Coleman, a pre-law major, and David Coleman, both from Piedmont, joined him on the baseball team. The Potomac State baseball team was one of the first college teams in West Virginia to have more than one African American player, and it had a more than respectable 8–3 record against four-year colleges.[18]

* * *

Fairmont State (now Fairmont State University) was founded in 1865 in Fairmont, located in central West Virginia. One of the larger cities in the state, Fairmont had a population of almost 30,000 in 1950. Marion County had a large enough African American population to support Fairmont Dunbar High School, one of the biggest black high schools in the state.

Fairmont State integrated its football team immediately following

Brown. Nevertheless, the experience proved difficult. Three African Americans—Roy Meeks, John Smith, and Sam Garrison—reported for football practice in the fall of 1954. They were included in the football team picture in the 1955 *Mound,* the Fairmont State yearbook. Meeks chose Fairmont State over Southern University in Louisiana because his mother and his pastor, afraid that he might get hurt, convinced him that race relations were dangerous in the South. Unfortunately, within two weeks, Meeks and the other two black players were no longer on the team. "Coach Duvall threw them off the team," said Mike Arcure, a lifelong resident of Marion County, a former Fairmont State coach, and the longtime chairperson of the Fairmont Athletic Hall of Fame Committee. "Coach Duvall told me, 'They would not do anything.' When we ran drills, they just stood off by themselves. We could not have that so after a while I dismissed them from the team. I was afraid the NAACP would come after me, but we could not have that."[19] The following year, 1955–1956, no black players were on any of the Fairmont State athletic teams.

However, in 1956–57, two black athletes played on teams at Fairmont State. Ernestine Knox, from the nearby village of Four States, was a member of the field hockey team. She remained on the team through 1959 when she graduated with a degree in elementary education. Knox was also active on campus as a member of the Student National Education Association and the Physical Education Majors Club.[20] The other black athlete, Moses Guin, began his legendary four-year Hall of Fame career on the 1956 football team.

Guin had attended Fairmont Dunbar until the Marion County schools integrated just before his senior year. He attended and helped integrate Barrackville High School in his senior year. "There was not much discrimination at Barrackville. It was a small town and we all knew each other," said Guin. "I went to Fairmont State and lived at home because it was close and all that I could afford. I went out for the football team and made the team," continued Guin.[21] That season the Fairmont State football team posted an outstanding 7–1 record and were second in WVIAC football. Guin was also on the track and wrestling teams.

During the 1957–1958 academic year, the number of black students on the Fairmont campus increased. Moses' younger brother Curtis joined him on the football team and was in the starting line-up on the basketball team. African American Roy Johnson was also on the basketball team and Knox was on the field hockey team. In addition, African American students were active in campus life as members of the debate team and the yearbook staff. The Fairmont State football team went 7–0 and won the WVIAC football championship with the Guin brothers playing important roles.[22] "I really did not have much to do with campus life. I did not have time. I played three sports and worked on campus for buildings and grounds cutting grass, raking leaves, and shoveling snow. I was well taken care of by buildings and grounds and by Coach Duvall. I kept my mouth shut and did what I was told. If I didn't, I would have to answer to my mother when I got home," said Moses Guin.[23]

In 1958–1959, African American participation more than doubled. Five African Americans were on the football team, four on the wrestling team, two on the basketball team, and one each on the field hockey and track teams.[24] That number remained about the same in 1959–1960.

The 1959 football team was one of the greatest in Fairmont State history. The team had five African American players led by the Guin brothers, with strong support from Roy Meeks, who had returned from the military, Eugene Beasley and Milton Jackson Fairmont State rolled to a perfect 8–0 record and the WVIAC football championship. Black players played an important role in many of the victories. Moses and Curtis Guin both scored touchdowns in Fairmont State's 26–6 win over Concord College. Eugene Beasley scored on a 35-yard pass interception for the winning touchdown in Fairmont State's 19–12 win over West Virginia Tech. Curtis Guin caught the winning touchdown pass in the 7–0 victory over Glenville State, and Moses Guin scored two touchdowns in Fairmont State's season final 25–13 victory over West Liberty State. Moses led the football team in rushing in 1958 and 1959 and total offense in 1959 and was named to the WVIAC All-Conference football team in 1958.[25]

By 1960 African Americans had become an important part of the athletic program at Fairmont State. Moses Guin recalls that he did have some problems at the college and when playing in the Southern part of the state.[26] "Nine out of ten times when I played, we stayed in private homes," said Guin. "I liked that because the food was better than the restaurant food that the white guys had to eat. There was a lot of name-calling at different games. Not so much of the 'N' word, but for some reason I was called the 'black dog' a lot of the time," said Moses Guin.[27] Following graduation from Fairmont State, Guin had a career in YMCA work in New Kensington, Pennsylvania. "There were some hard times, but black people were proud of our schools and we had people to look up to. I would not trade the life I had for anything," said Guin in a 2016 interview.[28]

Moses Guin was inducted into the Fairmont Athletic Hall of Fame in 2001. He was a four-year letterman in football, and outstanding on the wrestling and track teams.[29] Roy Meeks, who had been dismissed from the football team during preseason practice in 1954, withdrew from college to enter the military, but returned to Fairmont State and the football team in 1958. Meeks stayed with the team and played his final game for the Falcons in 1960. The game was the long-forgotten West Virginia Bowl. However, in a bravura final performance, Meeks ran for a touchdown and intercepted a pass to be named the Most Outstanding Player six years after he first put on a Fairmont State uniform.[30]

* * *

In the fall of 1955, Shepherd College (now Shepherd University), a state-supported college in the Eastern Panhandle, integrated. William Grant and William Miller, both transfers from Storer College when it closed, integrated the Shepherd basketball team. James Taylor also joined the football team as its first black player. Taylor had a four-year career at Shepherd, playing on both offense and defense. In his senior year, Taylor was All-WVIAC. "I was the only black player on the football team for my first three years at Shepherd. Then in my senior year, another black player joined the team. In fact, I was the only black player on the field in most of the games we played," Taylor said.[31]

Taylor was born in Charles Town, West Virginia, and attended Page Jackson, the black high school. After graduating from high school, Taylor served in the Navy from 1951 to 1955. Following his tour of duty, he enrolled in Shepherd College on the G.I. Bill. Taylor earned both a B.S. and a B.A. degree at Shepherd to teach biological sciences and physical education. He was one of the early African Americans to receive an M.S. degree (1965) from the WVU School of Physical Education. Between 1959 and 1965, Taylor taught general science, biology, and physical education at Page Jackson High School. In addition to those teaching duties, Taylor coached junior high, junior varsity, and varsity sports (football, basketball, and track and field).

Taylor is a dedicated civil rights advocate and historian. In 2000, Taylor and his colleagues (Nathaniel Downy, George Rutherford, and James Tolbert) established the Jefferson County Black Preservation Society Award to recognize the history of African American contributions in Jefferson County, West Virginia. Taylor is the author of two books: *Africans-in-America of the Lower Shenandoah Valley: 1700–1980*, and a *History of Black Education in Jefferson County, West Virginia, 1865–1966*.

* * *

West Liberty State College (now West Liberty University), in the Northern Panhandle of West Virginia, is located near Wheeling in the tiny village of West Liberty (population 650 in 1950). West Liberty State did not experience the racial turmoil during the 1960s as witnessed across America on college campuses. The county school systems in the five counties of the Northern Panhandle of West Virginia had been integrated since the fall of 1955, and the schools in the surrounding states of Ohio and Pennsylvania had always been integrated.

Thus, despite integration, there was only a small contingent of African

American students enrolled through the 1970s. The two most prominent black athletes were Bobby Douglas and Burial "Bo" Holmes. Both student-athletes were excellent multi-sport performers who had attended integrated schools in Ohio. Coach Al Blatnik first recognized Holmes's talent when he was playing football and basketball at Warren Consolidated High School in Tiltonsville, Ohio, and he recruited Holmes to play for West Liberty, integrating its athletic teams in 1958. Blatnik gave a very thoughtful and moving tribute to Holmes when the latter was inducted into the West Liberty Athletic Hall of Fame in 1992, describing some of the racial obstacles Holmes faced in the 1960s while at West Liberty. During the 1960s, West Liberty played football games against WVIAC teams throughout the state.

Coach Blatnik stated, "Traveling south in West Virginia to play football after racial integration was a traumatic event to say the least."[32] Blatnik recalled two specific instances in which Holmes confronted racism on and off the playing field. "A game with Concord College was the cruelest show of racism I had ever seen. The Concord linemen, and particularly one of them, would not even attempt to block 'Bo' Holmes, our only black player, but would swing from their stance with their fists and hit him in the face…. Taunts of the 'N' word rang from the field to the bench and beyond."[33]

Blatnik recalled another racial situation during a trip to play Salem College near Clarksburg. He made reservations for the team to eat at a local restaurant following the game. Blatnik said, "The restaurant owners were unaware that one among us was black. When we entered, the owner of the restaurant came up to inform me that it was against their policy to serve Negroes. I said that if that were the case, we would have to go elsewhere to eat. The owner replied that the 45 meals were already prepared and that Bo could eat in the kitchen." I said, "No, Bo will eat with us in the main dining room, or we are leaving."[34] On a positive note, all of the football players ate in the dining area.

Holmes had an outstanding college football career, resulting in his selection to Second Team All-American. He was also placed in the weight events at the WVIAC track championships. In an effort to meet his college financial obligations, Holmes left college but returned to West Liberty to complete his degree in 1968, later completing an M.S. degree from Youngstown State University. Holmes was hired as an assistant principal at Wheeling High School in 1974. Blatnik said that the West Virginia conference coaches should be applauded for their courage and leadership in promoting and supporting the integration of college sports on their respective campuses.[35]

Holmes was the only black athlete at West Liberty until the fall of 1961, when Bobby Douglas, a thin African American defensive back, joined the football team. Douglas was named to the WVIAC All-Second Team the following year, but football was not his best sport. Instead, the name Bobby

Douglas is synonymous in Ohio and West Virginia with excellence in high school, college, and Olympic wrestling. Douglas graduated from Bridgeport (Ohio) High School, just across the Ohio River from Wheeling, where he was a star on both the football and baseball teams, but he did even better in wrestling. Douglas was a two-time state champion in Ohio, only the second African American to win an Ohio State wrestling championship. "I had scholarship offers but I went to West Liberty because I had the chance to play both football and wrestle. The other offers were just for wrestling. In addition, I followed my high school coach George Kovalick who went there to coach. He actually integrated wrestling in Ohio and West Virginia," said Douglas.[36]

In the 1961–62-year, Coach Kovalick started West Liberty's first wrestling team, which was successful immediately. Douglas went undefeated during his freshman season at West Liberty and won the WVIAC championship. Coach Kovalick took Douglas to the NAIA national championships where, against long odds, Douglas won the national championship. Douglas was the first West Liberty State athlete to win a national championship. In its inaugural season, West Liberty placed 12th in the NAIA. Douglas' championship and the team's top 12 finish were exceptional accomplishments for a first-year coach with a first-year team at a

As a freshman at West Liberty State College, Bobby Douglas was the 1962 WVIAC and NAIA national wrestling champion. He was among the first athletes from the WVIAC to win a national championship. In 1963 he placed second in the NCAA wrestling tournament to become the first NCAA All-American from the WVIAC. Bob transferred to Oklahoma State the next year. He went on to a Wrestling Hall of Fame career as both a college and Olympic athlete and coach. Photograph dated 1965 (courtesy West Liberty University Athletic Department).

college that had never before achieved anything close to that kind of ranking in any sport. That championship was the first NAIA championship for any athlete or team from the WVIAC.

In 1962–63, West Liberty also joined the NCAA for the express purpose of giving Douglas a chance to wrestle in the NCAA Wrestling Tournament. In an astounding performance, Douglas placed second to Mickey Martin from the University of Oklahoma, becoming the first WVIAC athlete to place in any NCAA competition. West Liberty placed 21st in the nation among all colleges in wrestling. Two weeks later, NBC's *Wide World of Sports*, a Saturday afternoon, magazine-style sports program, aired an edited version of the NCAA Wrestling Tournament. The Wide World of Sports showed edited versions of NCAA wrestling every year through the decades of the 1960s and 1970s. One of the featured matches, shown almost in its entirety, was the Douglas-Martin match. That program was the first national television exposure that West Liberty had ever received.[37]

African American athletes on the West Liberty State College campus stayed in the Barracks, a series of four wooden buildings built along the lines of World War II army barracks. Following the war, they were built to house veterans who flooded the campus on the G.I. Bill; Shotwell Hall, the sole men's dormitory, had rooms for only 63 men. The Barracks stood almost empty except for the three or four black athletes who lived there.

"The Barracks were cold in the winter and were overrun by mice, but it was free. I got free lunches by working for housing and I fixed the rest of my meals or brought food from home. I could eat in the cafeteria or student union but that cost money. There were no problems on campus, except if you were black there was no social life; just sports and school. We went home for social life. The only time we had a problem was at a restaurant near Charleston on a football trip. They said that they would not feed the black guys. Therefore, we all got up and left. But every time we stopped it was tense because the black guys knew that there might be an incident," recalled Douglas.[38]

In 1963, Douglas was recruited by and transferred to Oklahoma State University, where he was on full scholarship. Wrestling at the 147-pound weight class, Douglas won the Big Eight Conference title for his weight class and helped to lead Oklahoma State to the 1964 NCAA championship. Douglas was later a five-time national freestyle champion and made the 1964 and 1968 Olympic Teams.[39] He placed fourth in the 1964 games and was named captain of the 1968 Olympic wrestling team.

In 1967, Douglas received his B.S. degree from Oklahoma State and an M.S. degree from Arizona State University in 1981. Becoming a college coach, Douglas led Arizona State to the 1988 NCAA championship. In 1992, he became the head coach at wrestling power Iowa State, where his teams won more than 400 dual meets. In 1992, Douglas was named coach of the

Olympic Freestyle Wrestling Team at the Summer Olympic Games. He was the first African American to hold this title, taking seven amateur freestyle wrestlers on to win gold, silver, and bronze medals. Retiring from coaching at Iowa State in 2006, Douglas is in numerous Halls of Fame and has won every honor in American wrestling. He was inducted into the National Wrestling Hall of Fame in 1987.[40] Bobby Douglas was not only a pioneer as a black athlete at West Liberty, but he was a pioneer in college wrestling, Olympic wrestling, and college and Olympic coaching. Douglas is without question the most outstanding athlete and college coach to have ever played in the WVIAC.

* * *

In 1959–1960, three more of West Virginia's small colleges integrated their athletic programs, bringing the total to seven of the state colleges and three of the five private colleges. Bethany College was founded on March 2, 1840, and is the oldest college in West Virginia. Located in Bethany, West Virginia, a village of little more than 1,000 people in 1950, it is only three miles from West Liberty in West Virginia's Northern Panhandle. Bethany College is a private college affiliated with the Christian Church (Disciples of Christ). Alexander Campbell was also one of the founders of the Christian Church and was the first president and founder of the college.[41] Football (1894), baseball (1892), and basketball teams (1905) were established early on the Bethany campus.[42]

Bethany was a charter member of the WVIAC in 1924, but because of its location in the Northern Panhandle, far from most of the conference colleges, Bethany played only a limited number of conference games. In 1958, Bethany College joined the Presidents' Athletic Conference (PAC), an eight-team conference of private liberal arts colleges located in Pennsylvania. The PAC colleges were located closer to Bethany College than most of the West Virginia colleges and similar in size and mission. The PAC offered more sports than the WVIAC but did not provide athletic scholarships. Bethany participated in the Presidents' Athletic Conference (PAC) and became an example of college athletic success, winning championships in 1962, 1964, 1967, 1968, 1978, 1982, 2001 and 2002. During that time, the college enrollment grew from 620 to a high in 1970 of 1,000.[43] The re-integration of Bethany College's student body was uneventful, and Ellene Marie Kinney of Wheeling, West Virginia, was the first black student to graduate in 1961.

During the 1960s and 1970s two pioneer African American athletes, Lloyd Briscoe and Ernie Whitted, integrated the Bethany College athletic program. Lloyd Briscoe was born and attended high school in West View, Pennsylvania. Briscoe was an outstanding high school athlete, playing three years on the track and basketball teams and two years on the football team.

VARSITY FOOTBALL SQUAD—*Bottom Row, left to right:* J. Compagnone, E. Rosser, D. Bury, R. Fowler, W. Schwarzel, J. Giles, T. Lewis, C. Cox. *Second Row:* Head Coach John J. Knight, R. Streckbine, L. Briscoe, A. Hammond, R. Schmidt, A. Celestin, R. Krieger, D. McNinch, C. Boffo, J. Frankel. *Third Row:* Manager G. Scheller, R. Hack, C. Trosch, W. Young, E. Ostneberg, J. Montaquila, D. Mairs, C. Donaldson, G. Henne, Manager R. Shaffer.

The 1960 Bethany College football team. The team had only one black player: number 27, Lloyd Briscoe (second row, third from left). Enrolled at Bethany in the fall of 1958, Briscoe was the first black athlete at the college. A three-sport athlete, he held school records in three track and field events (courtesy Bethany College Archives).

After graduating from high school in 1958, Briscoe enrolled in Bethany College, where he had an outstanding career. He played football and basketball, but his best sport was track. Briscoe was a four-year track athlete and captain of the track team his senior year. He led the Bethany College track team to conference championships in both the WVIAC (Bethany remained in the conference for track) and PAC. During the 1962 track and field season, Briscoe set school records in three events: the 440 (50.7 seconds), 100-yard dash (9.8 seconds), and the 220-yard dash (21.6 seconds).[44]

After graduating from Bethany College, Briscoe went on to earn an M.S. degree and a doctoral degree in education from the University of Pittsburgh. Dr. Briscoe dedicated a substantial part of his professional career to teaching elementary school, working 30 years in the Pittsburgh public schools. Dr. Briscoe was inducted into Bethany College's Sports Hall of Fame in 1990. He died at the age of 62, on May 21, 2002.[45]

Ernie Whitted remains one of Bethany's most productive and highly acclaimed football players. He is ranked in a number of rushing and scoring categories in Bethany's record books. After sitting out his sophomore season because of injury, he had outstanding years in 1968 and 1969. One of Whitted's most memorable and record-breaking achievements occurred on November 8, 1969, during a football game against Washington and Jefferson. During that game, Whitted set PAC rushing records that stood for 30 years. Byron Sailhalek, a reporter for the Washington, Pennsylvania *Observer-Reporter*, wrote, "Ernie Whitted, brilliant Bethany halfback, showed up on the playing field to destroy the Presidents in their finale, 33–7…. Whitted, former standout at Pittsburgh's Westinghouse High School and rated ninth top ground gainer in the NAIA, raced for a total of 294 yards in 42 carries and scored five touchdowns." During the game Whitted had runs of 53 yards and 33 yards.[46]

* * *

Montgomery, home of West Virginia Tech (now WVU Tech), is located in central West Virginia and had a population of 3,500 in 1950. The original school, called Montgomery Preparatory School, was started in 1895 to prepare students from Fayette County and eastern Kanawha County for college. When high schools were established in that region, the school became a junior college in 1921. The name was changed to New River State School and its primary mission was to train teachers. In 1941, New River became a four-year college. By the 1950s, the college had been renamed the West Virginia Institute of Technology and focused on educating engineering students. Engineering was a popular profession then, and students who wanted to attend a small college or stay close to home flocked to Tech. Enrollment increased to 1,000 students in 1950 and, by 1960, the enrollment had climbed to 2,500.[47]

Neil Baisi was a Tech graduate who became the Tech basketball coach in 1955. During his 12 years as the coach, Baisi developed a high scoring game plan that helped Tech lead the country in scoring and brought national attention to Tech and the WVIAC.[48] One of Baisi's top recruits was William Turner. Turner was born in Smithers, West Virginia in 1940. His father died in 1943, leaving three small sons. The children were farmed out to relatives, and his grandmother in Smithers, West Virginia raised William. Turner began high school at Montgomery Simmons, the all-black high school for Fayette County. When Simmons closed in 1956, Turner went to the newly integrated Montgomery High School for his junior and senior years. Integration went smoothly, according to Turner. "The students got along because we all knew each other from playing together on the playgrounds. But we were surprised that some of the teachers were very prejudiced," said Turner.[49]

"One day, the assistant principal, Mr. Cassell, called me into his office. I thought that I was in big trouble because he never smiled and seemed very grumpy…. He dropped a bombshell. He told me that the coaches at Tech were interested in having me come there to play basketball when I graduated," said Turner. That conversation changed Turner's life forever.[50]

During his senior season at Montgomery High School, Turner led

Montgomery to 22 straight victories before being defeated by Princeton High School, 100–76, in the regional finals. Shortly after the end of the season, Coach Baisi went to Montgomery High School and offered Turner a scholarship to play basketball at West Virginia Tech. Turner was ecstatic. "I always wanted to go to Tech. I followed them on the radio, WMON Montgomery, when I was growing up. Nevertheless, people told me that I could not go there. 'There are no black people there,' they told me. They were right, but I was among the first black students there. It was a dream come true for me," said Turner.[51]

Turner integrated Tech basketball in the fall of 1959. "There were only two incidents that I recall," said Turner. "During my first two years at Tech we had to go in the back door of the hotel in Buckhannon when we played the tournament at Wesleyan, but that ended after two years. The most surprising thing that happened was when the team went to a cafeteria in Charleston and I put my tray down, the woman behind the counter said that they could not serve me. I was surprised and hurt that something like that would happen in my own state capital. However, I put my tray back and walked out the door. When I got outside, I was pleased to see Coach Baisi and the team follow me out the door. They said if I couldn't eat there they wouldn't either."[52] West Virginia Tech fared well in the evenly balanced WVIAC during Turner's years there. In his senior season, Tech had a 15–4 Conference record and won the 1963 WVIAC Tournament.

* * *

Glenville State College in rural West Virginia integrated its teams in 1964–1965. Glenville State was founded as a normal school in 1872 in Glenville (population of 1,700 in 1950), the county seat of Gilmer County. By 1930, Glenville State began granting four-year degrees. Nate Rohrbough was the very successful coach of all sports at Glenville from 1926 through 1943.

Glenville was so remote that early Glenville State athletic teams had to take a riverboat up the Little Kanawha River to Gilmer Station, where they could catch a train to away games. Hard surface roads were finally built in the 1930s, giving the Glenville State College teams better access to the outside world.[53]

Undaunted by size and location, Nate Rohrbough built the Glenville Pioneers into a strong basketball program. He, along with other coaches in the state, proposed a post-season WVIAC basketball tournament. The first WVIAC Tournament was held in 1935 and is among the oldest college basketball tournaments in the country. Rohrbough's Glenville teams won three of the first eight WVIAC tournaments.

Glenville was late to integrate because the college traditionally drew students only from the surrounding mountain counties where few African

Americans lived. Glenville initially integrated the basketball team in 1964–65 under coach Leland Byrd (who became the WVU athletic director from 1972 to 1979). Glenville's first two African American athletes were Bob Minnieweather and Samuel Burns (1963–1964). Minnieweather was born in Clifton Forge, Virginia, but attended White Sulphur Springs High School in West Virginia, and attended college at Glenville between 1963 and 1967, becoming the first African American to graduate from there in 1967. During the 1966 and 1967 WVIAC basketball seasons, Minnieweather was selected to the WVIAC All-Conference First Team. Minnieweather was an excellent basketball rebounder and held school records in rebounding for 35 years. In recognition of his basketball prowess, Minnieweather was awarded Glenville State's prestigious Montrose Award in 2001. His award recognition continued as he was inducted into the Glenville State College Athletic Hall of Fame.[54] Samuel Burns was a sophomore guard in 1965–66 but played only one season.

Jackie Joe Robinson was an outstanding African American student-athlete who attended Glenville State College from 1966 to 1970. As a multiple sport student-athlete, Robinson earned All-Conference honors in football, basketball, and baseball. In 1970, the Glenville Pioneers surprised Morris Harvey College in the WVIAC title game, 71–66, led by tournament MVP Jackie Joe Robinson. The college presented Robinson with the Montrose Award, which was given in recognition for his achievement on and off the field. He graduated in 1970 and later earned an M.S. degree from WVU. He taught and coached at Woodrow Wilson High School in Beckley.[55]

* * *

Morris Harvey College (now the University of Charleston) integrated its basketball team in 1964–65. First called the Barboursville Seminary of the Southern Methodist Church it was established in 1888 and the name was changed to Morris Harvey College in 1901. In 1935, Morris Harvey College moved to Charleston, West Virginia, becoming one of the few urban, small colleges in West Virginia.

Perhaps the most famous athletic alumnus from Morris Harvey was George King. King won the national scoring title in the 1949–50 season with an average of over 31 points per game. King played professional basketball for four seasons and later was the basketball coach at WVU (1961–1965) and Purdue (1966–1972).

Legendary college basketball coach Sonny Moran (who later coached at WVU 1970–1974) is credited with the integration of Morris Harvey's basketball program in the mid–1960s. In a 2010 interview Moran recalled, "Our President came in and told me he thought it was time for us to recruit black athletes. I did not necessarily want a great basketball player, but I wanted a good person. So, I got Gerald Martin from Huntington and he turned out to be one of the few guys that made the All-Tournament (WVIAC) team four years in a row."[56]

Gerald Martin was a leading scorer and rebounder in the WVIAC. "I did not realize that I was integrating Morris Harvey basketball until I got there," said Martin. "There were only seven black students on campus so I was often the only black student in a class. That was difficult in folk dance, but a white girl volunteered to dance with me. She was ostracized for doing that. She hugged me after a basketball game and that created quite a stir," added Martin.[57] Because Martin was from West Virginia, he knew the boundaries of race in the state. "I knew the situation and just assumed that was the way it was supposed to be. However, it really bothered

Gerald Martin is shown chasing a loose ball in a 1968 game against West Virginia Wesleyan. Martin was named to the WVIAC All-Tournament Team each of the four years he played at Morris Harvey, 1965 through 1968 (courtesy University of Charleston Athletic Department).

me when one of the coaches called me into his office before a game with Concord and said, 'Tonight let's show them that our colored boy is better than their colored boy.' That still bothers me today," said Martin.[58] After being named to the WVIAC All-Tournament team each of his four years, Martin graduated in 1968. He was a graduate assistant basketball coach at Marshall and earned his M.S. degree in 1974.

* * *

The integration of 11 of West Virginia's 12 public colleges in the fall semester of 1954 immediately following the May 1954 *Brown* decision was far ahead of the integration of colleges in any of the former slaveholding states. There were few incidents of racial turmoil in the state of West Virginia following *Brown*. For the most part, integration took place without violence, incidents, or the need for the National Guard.

The integration of the athletic teams in the small colleges of West Vir-

Quinn		Ciccarelli	Moore	Meckfessel	Goldstein		Childers
	Null	Mgr.	Asst.Coach	Head Coach	Asst.Mgr.		Plybon
	Martin					Curry	
	Conley					Dawson	
	Robinette				Eaton		
		Hart		Hayes			

The 1966–67 Morris Harvey College Basketball team is the best team in the history of the college, reaching the NAIA final four. The two black players are Gerald Martin (32) and Chuck Dawson (22) (courtesy of the University of Charleston Athletic Department).

ginia, while not perfect, went better than at all of the southern and border states and better than many of the northern colleges that practiced *de facto* segregation. The ease of integration of the small colleges of West Virginia is to the credit of the people of the state, both white and black.

7

From Hal Greer to Randy Moss:
The Integration
of Marshall University Sports

No one will recognize December 8, 1954, as a date with historical importance in the civil rights movement when compared with the 1954 *Brown* decision or Rosa Parks' refusal to give up her bus seat in Montgomery, Alabama less than a year later. But it is the day that the Marshall athletic teams were integrated. Hal Greer, a knife slender six-foot, three-inch forward who had graduated from the segregated Huntington Douglass High School, took the floor with his four white teammates for the Marshall College freshman basketball team.

That evening, the Marshall "Little Green" (the varsity was then called the "Big Green") took the floor against the B & B Market team. The B & B Market was one of the first big box grocery stores in Huntington, and the enterprising owner sponsored a basketball team for publicity. The B & B team consisted mainly of former college players who wanted to play a few more seasons of basketball. The game was close through the first three quarters, but in the fourth quarter the Marshall freshmen pulled away for an 83–76 victory. Jack Freeman, a highly touted recruit from Huntington High School, led Marshall in scoring with 29 points. Greer hit for 16 points. Later that evening the Marshall varsity met the Chinese National team, which was on a tour of the United States, and defeated them 91–58 in the opening game of the season. In that Cold War era, the Communist government in control of mainland China was not recognized by the United States, and the Chinese National team that Marshall played hailed from the island of Formosa, later called Taiwan. The team Marshall played that night would go on to represent China in the 1956 Olympic Games. The game against the Chinese garnered most of the local newspaper's attention. The *Herald-Dispatch*'s small six-inch story about the freshman game made no mention of Hal Greer integrating Marshall sports teams.[1]

There had, however, been a significant amount of interest when Greer reported for the first day of basketball practice at Marshall two months earlier. The campus gym where the basketball team practiced was built in the 1920s style with a running track around the top of the gym. The gym floor was so small that there was no seating available at floor level, so spectators had to climb the stairs to a small set of bleachers built behind the second floor running track. Anyone watching from the bleachers had to lean forward and peer down through the rail of the running track. The tiny gym was packed for the first day of practice. Ernie Salvatore, the longtime Huntington sportswriter and editor, observed that the only black faces in the crowded gym that day were Greer and the janitor. Greer's pull-up jump shot was impressive. Cam Henderson, the Marshall basketball coach, told Salvatore, "Before that young man is through here, he'll become one of the greatest players in Marshall history and one of the greatest in the country," recalled Salvatore of that day.[2] Hal Greer, with deep roots in the Huntington community, was the perfect choice to integrate the Marshall basketball team.

* * *

Harold "Hal" Greer was born on June 26, 1936. His father, William Garfield Greer, worked for the C&O Railroad. Hal was the second youngest of eight children, six boys and two girls, and the family lived in the heart of the black section of Huntington, West Virginia. Greer's five older brothers and two sisters were all excellent athletes, setting a high standard for young Hal. His oldest brother William was a football and basketball star for Huntington Douglass High School. Brother Phillip played on the 1940 Douglass Wildcat state championship basketball team with Charles, the third of the Greer brothers, and was All-State in the black high schools' West Virginia Athletic Union in both football and basketball.

Jim "J.D." Greer led Douglass High School to two state high school football championships before graduating in 1949. Jim went on to play football at North Carolina's all-black Elizabeth City State College (now Elizabeth City State University), the only Greer brother before Hal to play college sports. Following a couple of years of football in the Army, J.D. tried out for the Cleveland Browns and Philadelphia Eagles, before playing a season in Canada.[3]

Hal was tall at six feet, three inches, but very thin. He was an end on the football team, center on the basketball team, and played first base on the baseball team. All of the Greer brothers played for Z.L. Davis, the legendary coach at Douglass from 1915 through 1954. "They don't come any better than those Greer boys. They were all good clean kids and fine athletes," remembered Davis in a 1959 interview.[4] Hal was not the best athlete in the family, but he was on the Douglass High School basketball teams that won the West Virginia Athletic Union state basketball championships during his freshman and junior seasons in 1951 and 1953. In his senior basketball season, Douglass lost in the opening round of the eight-team WVAU state tournament to Amigo Byrd Prillerman High School, the eventual runner-up, in a close 46–43 game. Greer was named to only the "honorable mention" list on the WVAU All-State team.

In 1959, Douglass coach Z.L. Davis observed that "Harold came along at an opportune time and has really taken advantage of a chance the others didn't get. But I am sure all of them could have gone on and played more if they had gotten the chance."[5]

* * *

Greer was undecided if he wanted to accept an offer from Marshall or instead follow in his brother Jim's footsteps and attend Elizabeth City State Teachers College in North Carolina. His brother had been both successful and happy at the black college in the South. At Elizabeth City State, Hal could continue to study and play in a familiar segregated world where he would have limited interaction with an often-hostile white environment. However, a number of leaders of the black community met with Greer and encouraged him to accept the scholarship offer to demonstrate that integration could work.

For the leaders of the Huntington black community who favored desegregation, Greer represented an excellent candidate. He was mannerly, if a little shy, from a good family, a good student, and an excellent basketball player. They also realized that because the legendary Cam Henderson recruited Greer, his decision would not be openly questioned by the Huntington community. Henderson had a record of unorthodox recruiting that was part of his mystique and generally approved of by the Marshall fan base. Henderson was not a liberal in any sense of the word, but he was a coach who recruited good players, and Greer would be given a fair chance to succeed. Henderson had the political capital to bring about the integration of the Marshall basketball team in 1954.

* * *

Eli "Cam" Henderson had become a legend in Huntington because of his many years as a successful coach at Marshall. Spending his early years on farms in Marion and Harrison counties in West Virginia where he attended one room schools, he graduated from Glenville State Normal School in June 1911 with a two-year teaching diploma. At Glenville he played on the football, basketball, and baseball teams, and met Roxie Bell, his future wife.

Henderson coached and taught at Bristol (West Virginia) High School (1913–1916), where he also invented the zone defense. Bristol won so easily that Henderson continued to use the zone defense despite the fact that few, if any, other teams did so until well into the 1940s. He later coached at Shinnston West Virginia High School (1917–1918).[6] At age 26, Henderson finished his bachelor's degree at Salem College. He coached three more years at Bristol High School (1918–1920) before moving to Muskingum College in New Concord, Ohio. Henderson spent three seasons at Muskingum before he returned to West Virginia for the coaching job at Davis & Elkins College.[7]

Henderson quickly built a football powerhouse at D&E. His 1923 team went undefeated. In 1928, Henderson got the reputation of being an unethical recruiter. Henderson and his wife were on a driving vacation to the West Coast when they stopped at the Haskell Indian School in Lawrence, Kansas. Haskell was a boarding school for Native Americans where high school and trade classes were taught. Henderson talked two Haskell athletes into coming to Davis & Elkins that next fall to play football. When they reported for practice in the fall, they brought two friends with them. The recruitment of the Native Americans was considered to be shady because most people believed that Haskell was a college because they played college teams (including West Virginia University in 1928). Also, many people held the racist belief that Native Americans were not smart enough to attend college and that they were there just to play football.[8]

With four Haskell students added to the returning D&E veteran players, Henderson had a powerful football team. D&E defeated West Virginia University, 7–0, and Navy, 2–0, on successive weekends. D&E finished the season with a 6–2–1 record and claimed the state college championship with a 14–7 win over West Virginia Wesleyan. In addition, Henderson put excellent basketball teams on the floor although college basketball had yet to reach any level of importance.

In June 1935, in response to the economic effects of the Depression, the D&E Trustees Executive Committee instituted changes that de-emphasized the athletic program to the point that Henderson was forced to leave.[9] A number of powerful supporters at Marshall College wanted a new football coach who they hoped could help Marshall compete in the Buckeye Conference. They targeted Henderson, but there was no position open. Henderson had strong support in Huntington from the newspapers, local and state politicians, and the business community, most notably the American Business Club. Even West Virginia governor Herman Kamp from Elkins supported Henderson. In response to the pressure, the West Virginia Board of Education fired Marshall president Morris Shawkey and replaced him with the Davis & Elkins president Dr. James E. Allen. Athletic Director Roy Hawley resigned to take a position at West Virginia University before he could be fired. Coach Tom Dandelet's position was changed to that of chairman of physical education to make room for Henderson. On June 22, 1935, the West Virginia Board of Education announced the hiring of Henderson as the football, basketball, and baseball coach, as well as the athletic director.[10]

Henderson proved to be an excellent football coach, as the team won the Buckeye Conference championship in 1937 and played in the Tangerine Bowl in 1947. After amassing a 68–46–5 record, Henderson was encouraged to resign as football coach following the 1949 season so that he could concentrate on basketball. Until the 1930s, college basketball was a minor sport in most colleges. The development of the Madison Square Garden doubleheader basketball games in New York in 1931, the subsequent founding of the National Association of Intercollegiate Basketball (NAIB, later NAIA) national tournament in Kansas in 1937, the NIT in New York in 1938, and the NCAA tournament in 1939 brought national attention to college basketball. However, football remained the king of college sports.

Although the Huntington powerbrokers had wanted Henderson to coach football, he proved an even better basketball coach, leading Marshall to Buckeye Conference championships in 1937 and 1938. At the December 1938 Buckeye Conference meeting, some of the colleges accused Marshall of using ineligible players. At the end of the meeting, the colleges voted to disband the conference at the end of the 1938–39 academic year. However, before the conference closed its doors, Marshall won a third straight Buckeye Conference basketball championship with a 22–5 season record in 1939.[11]

Henderson continued coaching winning teams throughout the 1940s. After an excellent 1946–1947 regular season in which the Big Green had a 22–5 record, Marshall was invited to participate in the 10th annual NAIB Tournament in Kansas City. Marshall marched through the tournament, winning the national small college championship and ending the season with a 27–5 record.[12] The Huntington powerbrokers who had paved the way to bring Henderson to Marshall in 1935 saw it as Huntington's finest hour and the vindication of their efforts to hire Henderson.

* * *

In the 1950s Huntington was booming, with a population of more than 85,000, and was then the largest city in the state. It was rich with varied industries such as metals, glass, clothing, and railroads. Marshall College, located on the edge of the downtown, was the pride of the community.

Although Greer lived at home, only five blocks from Marshall, each day when he walked under the railroad viaduct and on to campus he stepped into a foreign white world. Located in Appalachian West Virginia across the Ohio River from southeastern Ohio and 10 miles from Kentucky, Huntington was well below the Mason-Dixon Line and had a southern mindset. The city was tightly segregated. The black community was located in a four by six block area bounded by railroad tracks, Twentieth Street, Sixteenth Street, and a steep hillside.

Huntington's black community was vibrant and, with a population of

4,500, bigger than most towns in West Virginia. Retail businesses, clustered along Sixteenth Street and Eighth Avenue, flourished. Jobs were plentiful for African Americans in the railroad industry, hotels, and as janitors and domestics. The town had a black doctor, dentist, and photographer, and an integrated school of nursing was attached to the black hospital. Douglass High School had a long tradition of providing an excellent education. African Americans could venture into the larger white world of downtown Huntington, but their conduct was carefully controlled by a set of unwritten segregationist rules, such as not being able to try on clothing in the downtown department stores, not being served at lunch counters, separate seating areas in the movie theaters, and "colored" restrooms and water fountains. The white hotels excluded African Americans from accommodations and dining, except for visiting athletic teams from the Mid-American Conference that included their African American players, a testament to the power of Marshall athletics. The racial climate in Huntington was worse than the northern part of West Virginia, but better than most areas in the southern United States. The presence of Marshall College was somewhat of a moderating force despite being segregated and providing little support to civil rights even through the mid–1960s. African Americans also had voting privileges in West Virginia, which provided some political power. Hal Greer was a child of segregation and well knew the unwritten racial rules of Huntington. But those rules were changing quickly and in an uneven pattern that made life difficult for a young man caught between two worlds.

* * *

Greer's first year at Marshall, while a success on the basketball floor, was difficult for him on campus. As George Reger notes in his master's thesis, "Integration and Athletics: Integrating the Marshall Basketball Program, 1954–1969," African American students who had attended all-black high schools faced difficult adjustments at integrated white schools where they were an often-unwanted minority.[13]

Greer was not the only black student to enroll at Marshall in the fall of 1954. Thirty-four other black students were in attendance in a student body of 2,926, which made Marshall the most integrated of West Virginia's former all-white colleges. All of the other formerly white colleges were integrated that fall except Glenville State College.[14] Despite the presence of other black students, Greer felt the pressures that came from being the only black basketball player. Greer's grandmother Tula Greer remembered her grandson's feelings that first year: "He'd come home at night too tired and too upset to eat, and he'd tell me he didn't want to go back 'over there,' that he felt like an outsider and that he wished he had gone to Elizabeth City Teachers College like he planned. But I'd say to him, 'Harold, don't be foolish. You've got to go back tomorrow. If you don't, you'll be making a big mistake.' And, so he'd get up in the morning, eat his breakfast, and I'd hurry him along through the door to make sure he got 'over there' on time. That's how he got his nickname in the papers, 'Hurryin' Hal' Greer."[15]

* * *

In 1949, Marshall joined both the NCAA and the Ohio Valley Athletic Conference (OVC). The move to the NCAA gave Marshall the prestige of being an NCAA college and the opportunity to play in NCAA championship events. The OVC, a conference of six colleges located in Kentucky, Tennessee, and Indiana, offered ease in scheduling and conference championships.

Marshall spent two unsuccessful seasons in the OVC. The extensive travel over Appalachian Mountain roads in Kentucky and Tennessee where the conference colleges were located made trips to away games difficult. Marshall was on the far eastern margin of the OVC and, with little history of playing OVC teams, Marshall had a conference rivalry only with Morehead (KY) State. Resigning from the OVC in December 1951, Marshall was admitted to the Mid-American Conference (MAC) in November of 1952 and began to play a full MAC schedule in 1953–54. The MAC offered an additional perk because it was considered a "major college conference" while the OVC was considered a "small college conference."[16]

* * *

Joining the MAC proved to be a huge factor in supporting the integration of the Marshall basketball program. In 1952, none of the OVC colleges, which were located in border states, had black players on their teams. In addition, traveling through Kentucky and Tennessee with an integrated team would have been difficult because most of the hotels and restaurants did not accommodate African Americans. The MAC schools, with colleges located in Ohio and Michigan, had always been integrated. Before Marshall joined the MAC, the question of how black athletes on MAC teams would be treated in Huntington became an issue. Of particular interest was the housing of the visiting black athletes since Huntington had the reputation of being a segregated city. In fact, in 1938 the famous coach Clair Bee, who was from Grafton, West Virginia, brought his Long Island University basketball team to Huntington to play against Marshall. LIU was one of the premier teams in the country and had just come off a 43-game winning streak. This was the biggest college basketball game played in West Virginia to date. But the Long Island team was denied accommodations at Huntington's Governor Cabell Hotel because of the presence of Dolly King, an African American player. Bee threatened to return to New York without playing the game unless King was allowed to stay with and eat with the team. After intervention by the mayor of

Huntington and Henderson, the hotel management relented, allowing King to stay and eat at the hotel. The game was played that evening before a standing room crowd.[17] Later, LIU won the 1939 and 1941 NIT tournaments which was then considered equal to the NCAA Tournament in prestige.

In 1953, after secret negotiations between the Huntington Hotel, Marshall, and the MAC, the hotel agreed to house and feed visiting college athletic teams with black players. But, during the 1950s and early 1960s, African American athletes remained a thorny issue in Huntington. Some hotels and restaurants in the city accommodated black athletes on visiting MAC teams, while these same hotels and restaurants would not accommodate or serve African Americans who were not part of MAC teams.

"That was true," said Phillip Carter, a Marshall basketball player from 1960 through 1963. "I know that the MAC teams stayed in the Huntington hotels when they came to town for games and the black players stayed in the hotel. The black players from Marshall would sometimes go down to the hotel to meet with the black players from the visiting team after the game. But if we went to the hotel any other time we were asked to leave. There were also restaurants in Huntington where we would sometimes have team meals, black and white players together, but if the black players went back later to most restaurants, they would be refused service. Jim's Restaurant was one of the exceptions. Segregation was very uneven."[18]

This policy was never made public; however, the MAC, together with Marshall, must have negotiated the agreement to allow all of the members of MAC teams, regardless of race, to stay and eat together in Huntington as a condition for Marshall to be admitted to the conference. Marshall, for its part, was anxious to do everything it could to join the MAC. The prevailing opinion in Huntington was that what was good for Marshall was good for Huntington. The agreement between the MAC, Marshall, and the Huntington Hotel to accommodate black players was a small triumph of sports over racism. Unfortunately, that same accommodation was not extended to other African Americans until much later.

* * *

In a landmark move in the spring of 1954, Henderson signed Hal Greer to an athletic scholarship to play for Marshall College, but Greer would never have a chance to play for Henderson. In the winter of 1955, Henderson turned 65 years old. An excellent basketball season was spoiled when lowly Western Reserve upset Marshall 70–58 in Cleveland in the final game of the season. That loss denied Marshall a share of the MAC championship and a possible NIT bid. Henderson had appeared to be drunk when he entered the arena. After the disappointing loss, he struck some of the players with his fist in the Marshall locker room. The week after the game, Marshall president Stewart

Smith interviewed the players and talked by phone with the Western Reserve staff. He then called Henderson to his office and asked for and received Henderson's resignation. It was a sad ending to a successful career.[19] Henderson died at his daughter's house in Cedar Hill, Kentucky, near Lexington, on May 3, 1956. His death occurred a little more than a year after he coached his last basketball game.

* * *

After Henderson resigned, Marshall president Stewart Smith interviewed and hired Jules Rivlin, a former star basketball player at Marshall, for the coaching position. Julius Leon Rivlin was born in Washington, Pennsylvania, on February 2, 1917, to Dan and Celia Rivlin, who were Jewish-Lithuanian immigrants. The Rivlin family moved to Wheeling, West Virginia, where Jules was an exceptional athlete at Triadelphia High School. He won the 100- and 220-yard dash events in the West Virginia state high school track meet and was also named to the All-State Basketball team.[20]

From 1938 through 1940, Rivlin proved to be an exceptional basketball player for Cam Henderson's Marshall teams. In his sophomore season Rivlin led the Big Green to a 28–4 record (10–0 Buckeye Conference) and the Buckeye Conference championship, scoring 434 points to place second in the nation in scoring behind Chet Jaworski of Rhode Island State College. The following year, Marshall won a second Buckeye championship with a 22–5 record (8–1 Buckeye Conference). Rivlin was named to the All-Buckeye Conference team for the second straight year. In 1940, Rivlin's senior season, the Buckeye Conference had disbanded. Marshall played an independent schedule, defeating the powerful City College of New York coached by Nat Holman, the University of California, and the University of Tennessee on the way to a season record of 25–4. Rivlin was named to the "Small College All-American" team. He finished his career with 1,093 points, then a Marshall record.[21] Rivlin spent four years in the military during World War II. Later he played industrial league basketball and opened a sporting goods store in Wheeling where he also coached high school basketball before taking the Marshall job.

* * *

As a sophomore, Hal Greer was in the starting line-up for the opening game of the 1955–56 season. Marshall started slowly but came on to beat Spring Hill College from Mobile, Alabama, 83–69. Greer led the Big Green in scoring with 20 points. The Huntington press handled Greer's debut with grace, writing, "Greer became the first Negro to perform for Marshall in intercollegiate athletics and he covered himself with glory as he proved to be a good scorer and his performance on defense was just about all you could ask for."[22] Marshall won the MAC championship with a 10–2 record and earned an NCAA Tournament bid.

In the 1950s the NCAA Basketball Tournament paired teams by location, so Marshall drew Morehead, located in rural Kentucky less than two hours from Huntington. Morehead had beaten Marshall twice during the regular season for two of the Big Green's only four losses. To make things even more difficult for Marshall, Charlie Slack, Marshall's starting center and the leading rebounder in the country, was ruled ineligible for post-season play. Slack had played on the varsity team as a freshman when Marshall was a member of the NAIA, so the NCAA ruled that he had used his three years of eligibility. Morehead, coached by Ellis Johnson, who would later coach at Marshall from 1963 to 1970, defeated the Big Green for the third time that year, 107–92. Marshall finished the season with an 18–5 record. The season was a huge success for rookie coach Jules Rivlin and his sophomore star Hal Greer, who averaged 15.5 points a game and 6.6 rebounds and was second in the nation with a 60 percent shooting percentage.[23]

Rivlin was the toast of Huntington. Marshall basketball fans loved him because he was the heroic athlete who had returned to coach the team to its first MAC conference championship. Huntington's small but vigorous Jewish community revered him. "Jules was a leader in the Jewish community," said one of his best friends, Herb Colker, who was 93 years old when interviewed in 2014. "Jules attended services on a regular basis, directed small theatrical performances, and sang in the choir with me on high holy days."[24] Many of Huntington's business leaders, who were of Lebanese, Italian, or of Eastern European descent, strongly supported Rivlin because he was a minority and, like them, proud of his heritage. And the African American community loved him because he was Hal Greer's coach. Rivlin's first three seasons on the bench and in the community were his best years in Huntington.

* * *

The 1956–57 Marshall team was loaded with talent. Returning from the previous year's team were Paul Underwood, Cebe Price, and Jack Freeman, along with Hal Greer. A new addition to the team was sophomore Leo Byrd, a former Huntington High All-State player who led the Pony Express to the state tournament finals in 1955. Unfortunately, the team had no height. Greer was forced to play center at six feet, three inches. While he performed well, the Big Green had difficulty when matched against taller, more physical teams. Even without height, the Big Green finished the season with a respectable 15–9 record and an excellent second place finish in the seven-team MAC. Greer was named to the All-MAC second team.

Rivlin was perhaps more sensitive to discrimination because he had faced it as a Jew. He tried to shield Greer and his team from potential incidents by scheduling most of Marshall's games against northern teams, but there were inevitable incidents that he could not control. The two most notable housing incidents occurred in Greer's junior season. When Marshall played in the Watauga Invitational Tournament in Johnson City, Tennessee, the Marshall team did not stay in the same hotel as the other teams. "We ended up staying in a place that looked like the past," recalled Greer's teammate Jack Freeman, in a 1996 interview with George Reger. "It was just an old run-down motel. We knew immediately it was because of Greer. But nobody said anything about it. We just took it in stride."[25] Likewise in the annual trip to Morehead, Kentucky, the team was relegated to staying in the worst of Morehead's two hotels. "We'd go to Morehead and play, we'd stay in a horrible hotel down there, just horrible … because of Greer," recalled Sonny Allen, also in a 1996 interview.[26]

There were also times when Greer and his teammates felt the sting of discrimination at restaurants. In a 2012 interview with the *Herd Insider*, a newspaper published by the Marshall Athletic Department, Charlie Slack recalled one incident at a restaurant from the 1955–56 season. "We were driving back from playing Morris Harvey, by car five of us in a car. We stopped at a restaurant coming out of Charleston somewhere. The restaurant wasn't busy. The five of us walked in and sat down, and the waitresses were all standing around the counter. Finally, I went up to the counter and asked what was the problem, why no one was waiting on us. And one of them said, 'We can feed you (four guys), but we can't feed the one fella.' I said 'Well, if you can't feed all of us, we're leaving.' And we all got up and walked out."[27] Racially motivated incidents also occurred during Greer's senior year (1967–68) in Virginia and Kentucky. A Virginia motel owner agreed to provide accommodations for the team but told them to stay in their rooms, and a hotel in Lexington, Kentucky, served the team dinner, but in a private dining room on the second floor.[28]

* * *

In Greer's senior year he was named as a co-captain along with Jack Freeman, who was also from Huntington. Rivlin recruited three African American players for the freshman team, but since the freshman team practiced separately from the varsity and Greer continued to live at home, there was little interaction between Greer and the new players. The season went well for Marshall. The Big Green played an upgraded schedule including the Cincinnati Tournament and finished the season with a 17–7 record and another second-place finish in the MAC. Marshall led the nation in scoring during the regular season, averaging 88 points per game. Greer had a superlative season, averaging 23.8 points per game with a 54 percent field goal average. He also led the team in rebounding with an average of 11.7 rebounds per game. Both Greer and Jack Freeman were named to the All-MAC second team.

In the final home game of the season at the Memorial Field House, co-captains Greer and Freeman were recognized at halftime and received a standing ovation. Near the end of a 92–69 beat down of Toledo, Greer was taken out of the game and received a standing ovation that lasted almost four minutes. Veteran sportswriter Ernie Salvatore admitted in his newspaper column "Down in Front" that he had to fight back tears. He wrote, "This was a booming, thundering, rolling, roaring appreciation to Greer for blazing a trail for Negroes at his hometown college and doing it in such a scintillating fashion...."[29]

That spring, Greer was selected in the second round of the NBA draft by the Syracuse Nationals. He went on to a phenomenal 15-year NBA career with the Nationals and Philadelphia 76ers, being named 10 times to the All-NBA team. He retired as a player in 1973 and was inducted into the Naismith Basketball Hall of Fame in 1982. In 1978, Greer was honored by the city of Huntington. Sixteenth Street, the street that led from his old neighborhood under the viaduct and on past the Marshall campus, was renamed Hal Greer Boulevard.[30]

Marshall 1957–58 co-captains Jack Freeman (40) and Hal Greer (32). Greer was the first African American athlete to earn an athletic scholarship at Marshall College. He played on the 1954–55 freshman basketball team and had a stellar career at Marshall from 1954 to 1958. Greer played in the NBA for 15 years, was named an NBA All-Star in 10 seasons and was named to the NBA 50th Anniversary All-Time Team (courtesy Marshall University Archives and Special Collections Marshall University Libraries).

* * *

The integration of Hal Greer into the Marshall basketball team was a huge success. Greer played his role well. His experience was somewhat easier because he was from Huntington and familiar with the racial boundaries in the town. He did not challenge those barriers other than attending class and playing basketball at Marshall. He was only challenging segregation on one front. In a way Greer was much like the black entertainers who through the first half of the 20th century appeared on the stage in front of white audiences and then disappeared back into the black world. As with the black singers and dancers, Greer's presence on the basketball floor was not a political or an economic challenge to the white power structure. He did not try to buy a house in a white neighborhood, date white girls, or protest for equal treatment. For a commuter student at Marshall, one of 34 black students on the 2,926-student campus, it seemed to be manageable integration. This was particularly true when he returned to the black community after classes and practice. Plus, Hal Greer brought Marshall winning basketball teams and was entertaining on the basketball floor. The black basketball players who followed Greer at Marshall comprised a much different set of pioneers.

While the integration of Marshall basketball appeared to be a win for everyone, it was difficult for Greer. With the support and protection of the black community, he could disappear into that community when the pressure of integration became too great for him to bear. He remained stoic in the face of many racial slights. Some racial incidents were confrontational and significant and some small and seemingly casual. Quiet, modest, and unassuming on the outside, he was a proud man sensitive to racial slights. For Greer to stay within the shifting racial boundaries while integrating Marshall was often difficult. Though he knew well the racial climate of Huntington, he was uncertain of what to do in many of the new "partially integrated" situations that he encountered. He felt the pressure of representing his race under the microscope of white scrutiny. At times Greer expressed his regret at attending Marshall and wished he had gone instead to segregated Elizabeth City State, despite his success on the court and in the classroom at Marshall. Hal Greer's career was significant because when he joined the Marshall freshman basketball team in 1954, he was among the first black players to play on a college basketball team in any of the 16 states which had segregated schools and colleges. Many of the other segregated states took a decade or more to integrate any college sports teams.

* * *

Following Greer's 1954–55 season with the freshman basketball team, four African American freshmen joined the Marshall freshman/junior varsity football team for the 1955 season. The players were Ray Crisp, Howard Barrett, Walter West, and Roy Goines. The next year only Goines joined the Marshall varsity football team in the fall of 1956.

Goines, who grew up in Barboursville, a small suburb of Huntington, was bused to Douglass High School until his family moved to Huntington in his senior year. Barboursville had only two black families, so he grew up with white boys as playmates. At Douglass he was a high school teammate of

Greer. Later at Marshall, Jimmy Maddox, his white boyhood friend from Barboursville, became his teammate on the Marshall football team and the team's quarterback.[31]

In the opening game of the 1956 season at Xavier University in Cincinnati, Goines became the first African American to play in a varsity football game for Marshall. He lettered three years and had a stellar football career. His greatest moment of gridiron glory came in his junior year. The Marshall Big Green scheduled West Virginia State in an historic game, because it was the first football game that Marshall had ever played against a historically black college. In an ironic turn of events, Goines played a crucial role in the 12–7 Marshall win. *The Chief Justice*, Marshall's yearbook, reported, "After an even third quarter Roy Goines, who played an outstanding game for the Big Green, broke away for a 37-yard touchdown run which proved to be the downfall for the Yellow Jackets."[32]

By 1958, Goines's senior season, there were two other African Americans on the varsity team and five Afri-

In 1956 Roy Goines became the first black athlete to play on the Marshall College varsity football team. Goines had played on Huntington Douglass High School teams with Hal Greer. He earned an academic scholarship and played three years on the varsity football team (1956–1958). Goines was the second in command of the ROTC unit his senior year. Photograph dated 1957 (courtesy Marshall University Archives and Special Collections Marshall University Libraries).

can Americans on the freshman team. Goines, who was also an outstanding student attending Marshall on an academic scholarship, closed out his Marshall academic career by being nominated to Who's Who Among Students and being named the second in command of the Marshall ROTC unit. Both were firsts for black students at Marshall.[33]

Goines's integration of Marshall football followed the pattern of most of the athletes who were pioneers in the integration of West Virginia college sports teams. He was a local athlete who was well known in the white community, where he had strong ties. He lived at home because his family moved to Huntington for his senior year at Douglass. "When I got to Marshall, it was not strange to play with the whites I knew as kids, like Jim. It was not a strain to integrate," said Goines.[34]

But because he was in a small minority at Marshall, campus life was difficult. "There was no social life for blacks on the campus. There were only about 40 blacks among 4,000 students at Marshall College at that time. Our social life was in the black community and with our families," said Goines.[35]

Huntington remained segregated, but some exceptions were made for athletes. "We couldn't eat in certain restaurants. I wouldn't have dared to go into Jim's Spaghetti House. We always had a place in town to go eat after games, though, and I never had any problems at any of them, because I was Roy Goines, the football player. Even if I went alone," said Goines.[36]

Goines did run into a situation that he believed had undertones of racial discrimination. "About the only real problem I had with racism I found my senior year. Coach Royer told me he thought with the Dean's List and the ROTC on top of football, asking me to be captain might be too much. Then, the ROTC told me that with football and the Dean's List, being commander of the ROTC might be too much for me. They really sugarcoated it and played off each other. I knew what was going on, but I was getting an education that was not costing me a penny. I was big in our community, and with kids, and just made it part of my business," he said.[37] Goines graduated with a degree in business management. Following a tour of duty in the Army he had a long career as an executive with the Ford Motor Company.

Hal Greer integrated the Marshall baseball team in 1955. In 1958 Vernie Bolden integrated the track and cross-country teams, along with Charles Gordon, a basketball player who also ran cross-country. In the 1959–60 season there were four black varsity football players, two black basketball players, and four black members of the track team. Until 1965, that number remained about the same.[38]

* * *

The African American recruits who followed Greer, however, faced a more difficult situation. The Marshall varsity basketball team did not have any other African American players during Greer's first three years on the team. Later, in the fall of 1957, Rivlin recruited three African Americans for the freshman team: Bruce Moody, Charles Gordon, and Charles Griffin. Willie Tucker and Phillip Carter also joined the basketball team in 1959.

Bruce Moody was an All-City player from the Bronx, New York City, and the other three were from northern West Virginia. Moody had academic issues, which made other colleges hesitant to grant him immediate eligibility, but Marshall accepted his grades and ruled him immediately eligible to play.[39] Charles Gordon was from Wheeling, where he had played for two years for segregated Wheeling Lincoln High School before it closed. He then finished his basketball career at newly integrated Wheeling High School, where he led the team to a regional championship and a berth in the four-team state finals.

Wheeling lost the first game in the state tournament, but Gordon was named to the All-Tournament team.

The three black players played well on the freshman team and seemed ready for varsity play in the 1958–59 season. Griffin, however, did not return to school in the fall. Both Gordon and Moody had limited playing time on the 1958–59 varsity team that fell to a 12–12 record, the first non-winning record in eight years. The white players on the team were friendly with Gordon and Moody, but there was little socializing off the court. African American student-athletes found sanctuary in Hodges Hall, where athletes lived, and Eighth Avenue, the "downtown" section of the black community. Interviewing Moody and Gordon in 1996, George Reger recalled that they both talked about spending most of their free hours in the Huntington black community and specifically at the Bison Club, a fraternal organization of prosperous African American men.[40]

When Gordon was injured in the 1959–60 season, Moody was the only African American on the varsity team. To add to Moody's discomfort, the team record fell to 10–13, making it the first losing season since 1935–36, which was Henderson's first season at Marshall. In the fall of 1959, Willie Tucker and Phillip Carter joined the Marshall freshman basketball team. Tucker, from the Northern Panhandle town of Weirton, was a member of the Weir High School team that qualified for the final four basketball tournament in West Virginia.

Phil Carter, from Clarksburg, attended Kelly Miller High School through the ninth grade, when it was integrated into the formerly all-white Washington Irving High School. School integration changed Carter's life completely and his experience was similar to that of many other African Americans who integrated during that period. "I never again played for a black coach, had a black teacher, was cheered by a black cheerleader or saw a black majorette in high school or college. It was very different from playing for Kelly Miller. I did not socialize with my white teammates. We did not go to the same church or live in the same neighborhood," he said.[41]

Although tall at six feet, five inches, and a successful high school basketball player who made the high school All-Big Ten Conference team in his senior year of high school, Carter received no offers to play college basketball when he graduated in 1959. "I had enough money for one year, but I needed a basketball scholarship to be able to finish," he said. The opportunities for a basketball scholarship open to Carter in West Virginia were limited. West Virginia University had yet to have a black basketball player, and the WVIAC colleges did little recruiting outside of their local areas. His only in-state options were West Virginia State, Bluefield State, and Marshall. "I really wanted to go to WVU like everyone else in Clarksburg, but I knew that that would not work out. I talked with Coach Cardwell at State, but he did not seem very interested. Then I read a sports magazine about Hal Greer at Marshall. In Clarksburg we did not know anything about Marshall because it was so far away, but that article convinced me that Marshall was my best chance for a basketball scholarship."[42]

Carter enrolled at Marshall for the fall 1959 semester and walked on the freshman team, since freshmen were not eligible to play on the varsity. Tall, agile, and with a good shooting touch, Carter was offered a basketball scholarship by Coach Rivlin in November after only a few months on the team.

* * *

Between 1960 and 1964 the civil rights movement increased in intensity. Four students began a sit-in at a lunch counter in Greensboro, North Carolina, the Freedom Rides in the south were started to register black voters, and "The March on Wash-

A three-year letterman in basketball at Marshall from 1959 through 1963, Phil Carter was named to the MAC second team All-Conference in 1963. He was active in the civil rights movement while a student-athlete. Carter returned to Marshall University as a professor of social work in 1980. Carter was a four-term president of the Cabell County/Huntington NAACP. Photograph dated 1963 (courtesy Marshall University Archives and Special Collections Marshall University Libraries).

ington," where Martin Luther King delivered his "I Have a Dream Speech" in August 1963, all occurred within that five-year span of time. Following the passage of the Civil Rights Act in 1964, the West Virginia Civil Rights Commission reported a "general response of compliance." Exceptions were places such as the White Pantry Restaurant in Huntington, the Rock Creek Lake Swimming Pool in Charleston, and even at lunch counters in stores like the Diamond Department Store in Charleston, the largest department store in West Virginia. African Americans staged protests in those establishments.[43]

In the 1960s, civil rights demonstrations rocked Huntington. By then Marshall had three African Americans on the 15-man varsity team, including Phil Carter. "I really became politically aware when Ken Heckler, a congressman from Huntington, got me appointed to work for the Capital Police in Washington, D.C. during the summer of 1962, after my junior year at Marshall. That was an eye opening experience for me in terms of the civil rights movement," Carter said.[44] Often led by Carter or Bruce Moody and including other Marshall black athletes, sit-ins or demonstrations were conducted at Bailey's Cafeteria, a traditional Southern downtown cafeteria; the White Pantry, a greasy spoon restaurant; Thabit's, a downtown family restaurant; the Palace Movie Theatre; and the city-owned Olympic swimming pool. The students and student-athletes received little if any help from Marshall University in challenging the racial environment in Huntington, which was typical of the position of many colleges at that time. But Marshall president Stewart Smith went so far as to allow the playing of the song "Dixie" at football games and supported the Kappa Alpha fraternity's "Old South" week. He even participated in a ceremony where he turned the keys of the campus over to fraternity brothers dressed in confederate uniforms. Those events created an uncomfortable atmosphere on campus for African American students.[45] Black athletes and other students protested those activities on campus in 1963, which brought a halt to the university participation in the "Old South" activities. The white students were divided on the issue of the band playing "Dixie" and Old South Week, although the majority of students who were from southern West Virginia saw no harm in either tradition.

Conservatives in Huntington viewed the Marshall athletes who participated in the demonstrations as being in the class of "outside agitators." They were critical of the athletic department for bringing in what they considered an overabundance of black athletes and particularly those with strong political views. In addition, the football and basketball teams were posting losing records, which only further eroded community support for the university and the athletic teams.

Carter was in the starting line-up on the basketball team his sophomore year, but by his senior season he was seeing less playing time while still leading the team in scoring, rebounding, and shooting percentage. Despite limited playing time, he was named to the MAC All-Conference second team. "The coaching became very erratic by my senior season. Coach Rivlin was under pressure to win and there was a lot of anti–Semitism developing. I did not start some games and when I did play, I would be taken out frequently. The coach would substitute the sophomores who were nicknamed the 'Baby Bombers,' but they did not produce any wins. I think that part of the reason I was not playing more was my involvement in civil rights activity," said Carter.[46]

After graduation in 1963, Carter worked as a paid civil rights worker for the Congress of Racial Equality (CORE). Later, he earned a master's degree in social work and enrolled in the doctoral program at the University of Pittsburgh. In 1980, he returned to Marshall as a professor in the Department of Social Work, where he taught for more than 30 years.

The final blow for Rivlin was the 1962–63 season when Marshall's record fell to 7–16 with a dismal 1–10 record in the MAC. Rivlin resigned at the end of the season. Some of the reason for the decline in the Marshall sports programs could be traced to a decline in the fortunes of the state of West Virginia. During the decade of the 1950s, West Virginia's population shrank from a little more than 2 million to 1.8 million, while states where MAC colleges were located, Ohio and Michigan that continued to grow. Likewise, enrollments in regional state universities, which comprised the MAC, as well as regional universities nationwide were growing. Between 1950 and 1970 most grew to between 15,000 and 20,000 students, while Marshall struggled to reach an enrollment of more than 7,500. In addition, Marshall's athletic facilities were woefully inadequate. The football stadium, basketball arena, track facility, and baseball field were all off campus and shared with three high schools. President Smith was embarrassed to report that Marshall did not have the facilities to host the MAC spring sports championships.[47] All of those factors, added to a minuscule recruiting budget, brought an end to Jules Rivlin's coaching career. After leaving Marshall, he became the activity director of a synagogue in Los Angeles.

In 1967, Marshall hired Ed Starling, who was the first African American assistant coach at Marshall. Starling was from Williamson, West Virginia, and graduated from West Virginia State, where he had played on the basketball team under coach Mark Cardwell. A successful high school coach at the black Williamson Liberty High School, Starling was assigned to coach junior high school basketball when Mingo County integrated. He jumped at the chance to move to the college ranks, and was eventually promoted to Associate Athletic Director, a position he held for many years.

Dwight Freeman became the first African American head basketball coach at Marshall in 1990. When head coach Dana Altman left Marshall after only one year, Freeman, a 31-year-old assistant coach on the Altman staff, was elevated to the head job. Raised in Washington, D.C., Freeman had played college basketball at Southern Methodist University and Western State (Colorado). Coming to Marshall with six years of experience as a college assistant coach, Freeman was the head coach at Marshall from 1990 to 1994, producing a 44–69 record. Freeman was let go after four years.

* * *

Marshall was one of the pioneering colleges in women's sports in the 1970s. In 1969, Marshall hired Dr. Dorothy Hicks, who had a doctorate from the University of Tennessee, as the chairperson of the Women's Physical Education Department. Dr. Hicks was a strong advocate of intercollegiate sports for women and moved quickly to institute an intercollegiate program at Marshall, hiring Donna Lawson to start a woman's intercollegiate basketball team. Lawson, a Marshall graduate, had never played high school or college basketball because neither East Bank High School nor Marshall had teams in the pre–Title IX era. But Lawson had extensive experience playing industrial league basketball and softball.

She struck gold in her first coaching season when Beverly Duckwyler, a five-foot, 10-inch sophomore African American, joined the team. "Duck just showed up," said Lawson. "Of course, I did not recruit her because I did not have any scholarship to give."[48] Duckwyler, a graduate of Charleston High School, had not played high school basketball because Charleston High School did not have a team; also, the West Virginia Secondary School Activities Commission (WVSSAC) did not officially recognize girls' basketball as a high school sport. With Duckwyler leading the team, Marshall went undefeated, winning nine games over Morris Harvey College, West Virginia State College, Ohio University, Morehead State College, and Glenville State College.

That spring, Coach Lawson took the Marshall team to an AAU tournament in Indiana. Brenda Dennis, an African American point guard on a team from Louisville, Kentucky, was one of the outstanding players in the tournament. A graduate of Loretto High School in Louisville, Dennis had played high school basketball because the Catholic high schools had girls' basketball while the Kentucky public schools did not. "I talked Brenda into coming to Marshall because she could play. She had been going to a junior college in Kentucky that did not have a team and she was anxious to get on a college team," said Duckwyler.[49]

Over the next three seasons, with Duckwyler under the basket and Dennis handling the ball, Marshall dominated women's basketball in the state and region. In 1971–72, the team went 15–0, won the State College Tournament, and won two of three games in the Association of Intercollegiate Athletics for Women (AIAW) Midwest Regional Tournament. Marshall won the first three state college basketball championships sponsored by the newly formed West Virginia Association of Intercollegiate Athletics for Women.[50] Duckwyler said that she remembered few racial incidents. "We played most of our games in West Virginia and Kentucky. I can only remember one time when they would not serve us at a restaurant so Coach Lawson just took the whole team out of the restaurant. There may have been more incidents, but I think the coaches protected us from that kind of thing," said Duckwyler.[51] Hicks saw the situation differently. "We had a devil of a time finding places to eat and stay with black players on the teams in the early 1970s."[52]

In 1970–71, Marshall started a volleyball team. That team included Beverly Duckwyler and Brenda Dennis along with Deloris Morrow and Judy Allen. "Those four black players were the most we had on any team at Marshall until 1974–75," remembered Duckwyler. That 1974–75 volleyball team included Brenda Dennis, Stephanie Holman from Logan, Latrica Smith, and Regina Melton. "The early Marshall women's teams were well integrated," said Stephanie Holman.[53] By then, Duckwyler was again a pioneer; becoming an assistant basketball coach, she was the first black woman to coach at Marshall University.

Beverly Duckwyler played on Marshall's first women's basketball team in 1968–69 and in 1971–72 led the team to a 15–0 season and women's state college basketball championship. As an assistant basketball coach in 1974–75, she was the first black woman coach at Marshall. Photograph dated 1972 (courtesy Marshall University Archives and Special Collections Marshall University Libraries).

The women's athletic program at Marshall struggled to get financial support from the university. "We fought to get the program started because there were no scholarships and no support for women's sports. We drove our own cars to games, and often had to spend our own money for food or the cafeteria would pack lunches for us. Early on we wore our gym uniforms for games."[54] In 1972, Title IX of the Educational Amendments Act mandated equal educational opportunities for women, which were interpreted to include athletics. Dr. Hicks was able to get the Student Fees Committee to assess the students

a small fee for women's athletics. Finally, in 1973, the women's intercollegiate athletic program was merged with the Department of Athletics under Joseph McMullen, the director of athletics, and Dr. Hicks was named the associate director of athletics.[55]

* * *

In the 1970s and 1980s, the number of African American athletes at Marshall increased rapidly. Their success on the fields, courts, mats, and in the classroom, in addition to their leadership, led to the grudging acceptance of African American athletes by the Marshall fans and the townspeople of Huntington. The resurgence of the men's basketball team, led by African Americans George Stone and Bob Redd in the late 1960s, brought the recognition of African Americans as team leaders and heroic performers. Likewise, African Americans wrestlers Sam Peppers and David Carr, women's basketball and volleyball stars Beverly Duckwyler and Brenda Dennis, and football players Reggie Oliver, Michael Peyton, Troy Brown, Paul Toviessi, Tim Martin, and many others demonstrated the best of what a student-athlete should be.

By the 2000s, the representation of African Americans on Marshall's athletic teams reflected the distinct cultural pattern of major college sports in America. The starting offensive and defensive teams in football, the men's and women's basketball squads, and the women's track team were significantly African American, while the softball, baseball, women's swimming, men's and women's golf, cross-country, men's and women's soccer, and women's tennis were predominantly white and, in some cases, exclusively white. Most of Marshall's athletes were recruited from outside of West Virginia.

* * *

The successful integration of Marshall athletics following the 1954 *Brown* decision was due to a number of factors, including the respect for the legendary coach Cam Henderson, the personality of Hal Greer, the support of coach Jules Rivlin, the success of the basketball team, and the help of Greer's teammates. The difficulties that the African American athletes following Greer faced were typical of the difficulties that African Americas faced in the era of integration. But as each African American athlete successfully entered the field of play and the classroom, they made it easier for the generation of African American athletes who followed.

8

Two Historically Black Colleges Join the White Intercollegiate Conference

Changes came swiftly to both West Virginia State and Bluefield State in the 1950s. On November 1, 1952, Dr. William J.L. Wallace was named as president of West Virginia State College, replacing John W. Davis, who had been president for more than three decades.[1] "Wallace was the perfect choice to lead West Virginia State through integration," said Elizabeth Scobell, a longtime Wallace friend and also the former head of the college library at West Virginia State. "He was President Davis' handpicked successor who Davis trained to take over. Davis was a strong believer in desegregation," she added.[2]

A number of changes occurred on the West Virginia State campus. One of the most radical was the influx of white commuter students in the fall 1954 registration. State's enrollment increased greatly from integration. By 1956–57, enrollment reached 2,223 full- and part-time students. West Virginia State became the third largest college in West Virginia behind only West Virginia University and Marshall College. In 1960, roughly half of the student population at West Virginia State was white.[3]

There were two additional consequences of integration. The first was that West Virginia State had to give up its designation as a land grant college. In 1957, the West Virginia Board of Education voted to discontinue the matching funding required of land grant colleges. Because they could not provide state money to match the federal money West Virginia State was forced to surrender the land-grant status. All of the land-grant personnel and the remaining funds were transferred to West Virginia University. This move made West Virginia University the only land-grant institution in the state. Later, State fought to regain its land-grant status, beginning the process in 1988. In 1991, the West Virginia legislature passed a bill to re-designate West Virginia State as a land-grant institution and, in 2001, the United States Congress approved West Virginia State as a land-grant college under the Second Morrill Act of 1890.[4]

The third consequence of integration was that West Virginia State High School, which had been a part of the college almost since the beginning, was closed in 1957, in part because of the nationwide trend in colleges to discontinue on-campus "laboratory schools." But the closing of the on-campus high school moved more quickly than at most colleges because black students who had attended the all-black laboratory high school were integrated into the white high schools in Kanawha County by 1955. The former high school classrooms were soon needed for the growing student body of the college.[5]

West Virginia State received national publicity for the influx of white students. The anomaly of white students integrating a black college merited a *New York Times* article published on January 6, 1957, and titled "Integration in Reverse." The article described the various reasons that white students chose to enroll at West Virginia State.[6]

* * *

The situation was much different for Bluefield State, where only three white students registered for classes in 1954. Bluefield State was the only college in West Virginia to experience a decrease in enrollment following integration. The decline was not due to location, given that enrollment at white Concord College, located only 20 miles away in the tiny village of Athens, West Virginia, increased 50 percent from 831 to 1,227 by 1957.[7] The decline in enrollment at Bluefield State was caused by a number of factors. The first was a decrease in the population of African Americans in southern West Virginia. The coal mining counties that surrounded Mercer County, in which Bluefield is located, had significant African American populations which supported nine black high schools. Bluefield State drew most of its students from those high schools. But in the 1950s the mines moved to an aggressive plan to mechanize, significantly reducing need for labor. The number of miners fell to less than half in 1960. Unemployment was rampant and many former miners migrated out of state to seek jobs. In 1960 the population of West Virginia had decreased by 200,000 in 10 years. Between 1950 and 1960, the population of Bluefield declined by almost 10 percent to 19,256, and the population of Mercer County, West Virginia, also fell by about 10 percent, from 75,013 in 1950 to 68,206 in 1960.

African Americans left the state in greater numbers than whites. Between 1950 and 1970 the African American population in West Virginia dropped from 114,000 to 73,000, a decline of almost 36 percent. In the 1952 *Report of the State Superintendent of Schools*, C.E. Johnson, State Supervisor of Negro Schools, noted the decline in enrollment in black schools, particularly in mining areas, and the subsequent decline in demand for black teachers.[8] This decrease in the black population and in the need for black teachers (teacher training was the biggest program at Bluefield State), as well as increasing opportunities for black students to attend formerly all-white colleges, in part caused Bluefield State to be the only West Virginia College to have a declining enrollment between 1950–51 and 1956–57.[9]

In addition, few white students enrolled at Bluefield State through the late 1950s. The culture of segregation in southern West Virginia was a deterrent to white students enrolling at Bluefield State. The counties around Bluefield were among the last West Virginia counties to integrate their public schools. Of the counties bordering Mercer, McDowell and Wyoming counties integrated in 1965, and Raleigh County integrated in 1967. In 1969, Mercer became the last West Virginia county to fully integrate its public schools. Bluefield Park Central High School, which closed in the spring of 1969, was the last black high school in West Virginia. The tardy integration of southern West Virginia's public schools speaks to a strong segregationist feeling and was one reason that only three white students enrolled in Bluefield State in the fall of 1954. In addition, the proximity of Concord State College, a white state college, which offered the same courses at the same tuition as Bluefield State, provided strong competition for students. Integration did not come easy in Mercer County.

* * *

In late 1954, President Wallace of West Virginia State declared his intention to the West Virginia Board of Education, the governing body for all of the public state colleges except West Virginia University, to withdraw from the Colored Intercollegiate Athletic Association (CIAA) and to apply for admission to the West Virginia Intercollegiate Athletic Conference (WVIAC). In his recommendation to the board of education, Wallace wrote, "This is necessary because of integration. We feel that West Virginia State College should make application, be accepted fully for membership in this conference before withdrawing from membership in any other conference."[10] At the May 1955 meeting of the WVIAC college presidents in Wheeling, the applications by Bluefield State and West Virginia State to join the conference were accepted.

This was a courageous move by the WVIAC because national associations such as the NAIA and the NCAA did not encourage black colleges to join through the 1940s in part because of the objections of southern colleges. NCAA member colleges in the South often refused to schedule teams from the North unless the northern college agreed to leave their black players at home. Some southern states even had local laws prohibiting mixed racial athletic contests well into the 1950s. Finally, in March 1952, the NAIA announced that membership was open to black universities/colleges, and more than 20 black colleges soon established full membership. No other historically black universities or colleges in the United States joined a white conference at the time West Virginia State and Bluefield State joined the WVIAC. Subsequently, Lincoln University of Missouri joined the Mid-American Intercollegiate Athletics Association in 1970 and Tennessee State University joined the Ohio Valley Conference in 1986.[11]

West Virginia State changed conferences because President Wallace was a strong believer in desegregation and viewed leaving a segregated athletic conference and joining a white conference as part of the desegregation process. In addition, State would be able to play most of their games in West Virginia and not have to travel as far as they did when they played CIAA games in Virginia, North Carolina, Maryland and Pennsylvania.

"Dad thought it was a blessing to join the WVIAC because he did not have to travel so much, but he did continue to play some of the black schools that he had played before," said Mark Cardwell, Jr. "The integration into the new conference went well because Dad had strong friendships with the conference coaches like Neil Baisi and Rex Pyles. He played practice games with Baisi's Tech teams even before integration," Cardwell Jr. added.[12]

Most people believed that leaving the CIAA for the WVIAC was a positive move—but not all. Bob Wilson, a former star basketball player for West Virginia State in the late 1940s, spoke for some when he said, "Leaving the CIAA was a bad move. Who had ever heard of the WVIAC?"[13] Wilson was correct in the sense that the CIAA represented the top athletic conference for black colleges, and winning the CIAA often meant being named the national black college champion. The name of the winning college was carried in all of the black national weekly newspapers and also in many white newspapers. By joining the WVIAC, West Virginia State and Bluefield State moved from the highest level of black college athletic competition to the small college level of intercollegiate competition among white colleges and to a conference that was little known outside of West Virginia.

* * *

The West Virginia Intercollegiate Athletic Conference was at its height from 1950 through the mid–1970s. A tightly knit conference of West Virginia's public and private colleges, the WVIAC had been in existence since 1924. In 1935, the WVIAC was one of the first college conferences to hold a basketball tournament; an 11-team event played in Fairmont, preceding the NAIA (originally the NAIB-1937), NIT (1938), and the NCAA (1939) tournaments.

The WVIAC remained a basketball-driven conference throughout its existence. In the early 1950s, George King of Morris Harvey College led the nation in scoring and drew capacity crowds in the small towns and rural villages that the conference colleges called home. Legendary coaches such as Rex Pyles at Alderson Broaddus College matched wits with Neil Baisi, whose

West Virginia Tech team played up-tempo basketball and occasionally led the nation in team scoring. In 1963, Joe Retton, a homegrown West Virginia boy, became the basketball coach at Fairmont State and led the Falcons to numerous top 10 small college rankings in his 18 years at Fairmont.

Because of the in-state rivalries fueled by local West Virginia players such as Carl Hartman (Alderson Broaddus-Ridgeley, WV), Joe Miller (Alderson-Broaddus-Linn, WV), Mike Barrett (West Virginia Tech–Richwood, WV), and George King (Morris Harvey–Charleston Stonewall Jackson), conference games were always exciting. In 1960 the conference tournament moved to the new Charleston, West Virginia, Civic Center. Located in the state capital and media center of the state, the WVIAC featured three days of games that drew large crowds to the Civic Center every year.[14]

West Virginia State and Bluefield State, with mostly homegrown players, were at first a curiosity, but quickly fit into the WVIAC. "When State came to play at Glenville our gym was packed. Everyone in Gilmer County went to the game. It was a rural county and most of the people had never seen a black person. They were curious to see an all-black basketball team," said Larry Barker, an All-WVIAC basketball player at Glenville State during the early 1960s.[15]

* * *

West Virginia State's entrance into the WVIAC went smoothly because of the positive position on integration from W.W. Trent, the superintendent of West Virginia Schools; West Virginia State's president Wallace; and Coach Cardwell, who had taken his team on the trips to California in 1949 and 1950 to play white schools. Cardwell's friendship with the white coaches in the WVIAC no doubt curtailed any objections about West Virginia State's membership from the conference coaches.

West Virginia State fully embraced membership in the WVIAC and quickly integrated the athletic program. The 1956 football team had seven white players. By 1959, State was playing a conference football schedule of four games and rounding out the rest of the schedule with games against black colleges.

The State basketball team played a conference schedule of seven basketball games in 1956–57, which increased to a full schedule of 16 games by 1957–58. West Virginia State participated in other sport's conference championships; in 1959, the Yellow Jackets had a banner year, winning the WVIAC championships in baseball, tennis, and track.

The WVIAC was a strong basketball conference, and in their first five years in the conference, West Virginia State teams had mostly break-even records during regular season play. The State basketball team had difficulty winning games in the WVIAC basketball tournament, losing the first-round game in each of the four tournaments from 1956 through 1959. Finally, in 1960, State beat Salem, 96–82, in the first round before falling to West Virginia Wesleyan, 108–90, in the second round.

In 1960–1961, however, the Yellow Jackets caught up with the level of conference play with a 19–10 season record. West Virginia State won the WVIAC tournament championship, earning a berth in the NAIA national tournament in Kansas City. In the first round of the NAIA, State upset the number-eight seed, Whitworth College of Washington, 90–89, but was eliminated, 86–76, in the second round by the historically black Winston-Salem State College.

In 1962–63, State had a 17–8 record and won the WVIAC regular season championship, earning another trip to Kansas City. Unfortunately, the Yellow Jackets drew the number two seed, Augsburg (Minnesota) College, but lost by a respectable 67–57 score.

Coach Mark Cardwell was attending the West Virginia State High School Basketball Championship Tournament in Morgantown in March 1964 when he suffered a fatal heart attack at age 63.[16] Cardwell was a seminal figure in West Virginia history. He was deeply respected in the African American community in West Virginia because he was extremely successful as a coach at both the high school and college levels. He was also recognized as being a man of character and wisdom. He stood with other coaches and educators as strong role models for youth in the African American community. He led the integration movement in sports by demonstrating that African Americans could be successful in integrated competition not only by being skillful, but by being smart. By insisting that his players play as gentlemen with sportsmanship, even when they were not treated the same way, he taught his players the best of what America stands for, which also taught them how to be successful in life. A.L. "Shorty" Hardman, the long-time sports editor of the *Charleston Gazette-Mail* and one of the deans of West Virginia sportswriters, wrote of Caldwell, "Every inch a gentleman, Cardwell was one of the kindest, most thoughtful and talented coaches we ever ran across in our span of writing sports."[17]

* * *

Bluefield withdrew from the CIAA and joined the WVIAC in 1955–56 along with West Virginia State, but did not embrace the WVIAC in the same way. "We really played a schedule of both the CIAA and the WVIAC colleges in 1957–58," said Frank Beach, a basketball player on that team.[18] Bluefield finished fourth in the WVIAC and would have finished third in the CIAA if it had remained an official conference member.

"The Alumni were concerned because we had been in the CIAA forever and this was a change. But it showed progress in integration and it was the

West Virginia State basketball coach Mark Cardwell (left) receiving the 1961 WVIAC tournament championship trophy from West Virginia's governor Wallace Barron. West Virginia State was the first black college to win the WVIAC basketball championship, defeating West Liberty 67–66. Cardwell coached at State from 1945 until his death in 1964. His teams won CIAA conference championships in football, basketball and boxing (courtesy West Virginia State University Archives and Special Collections).

best for Bluefield State," said Ergie Smith, a football star and a 1952 graduate of Bluefield State. Smith later coached state finalist basketball teams at Gary District High School and at Gary High School.[19] Bluefield State retained ties with the CIAA colleges and was slow to fill its schedule with WVIAC colleges. Because of Bluefield's location along the southern border of West Virginia, traveling to Virginia and North Carolina was not as difficult for Bluefield State as it was for West Virginia State because of the shorter distance. Conversely, playing other West Virginia colleges was more of a challenge for Bluefield State because it required long trips over West Virginia's poor road system. From 1955 through 1961 Bluefield State played only a limited number of regular season games against WVIAC teams, while filling out the rest of their schedule with black colleges from the CIAA. From 1955 through 1963, Bluefield State played two football games each season against WVIAC teams, one of which was West Virginia State. From 1955–56 through 1961, the Bluefield State men's basketball schedule was limited to between four to 10 regular season basketball games with WVIAC opponents. During the late 1950s, the Bluefield State coaches felt more comfortable in filling their football schedules with the more familiar black colleges. However, Bluefield State had difficulty continuing its football success of the early 1950s.

Bluefield State integrated its athletic program in the fall of 1957 when Frank Beach, a white basketball player who had played at West Virginia State High School, was offered and accepted a basketball scholarship. Beach had integrated West Virginia State High School in the fall of 1954 and graduated in 1957. "I played the 1957–58 season for Bluefield State and then dropped out to play baseball in Mexico. I returned to Bluefield in 1959–60, but left Bluefield State again because they did not have a baseball team," said Beach.[20]

Bluefield State was initially more successful in the WVIAC basketball tournament than was West Virginia State. In the first game in the new conference tournament, Bluefield State defeated neighboring Concord College, 92–83, before losing the second-round game to Morris Harvey College, 88–79. Bluefield State player Don Galloway, a graduate of Williamson Liberty, became the first black player named to the all-tournament team.

In 1957 and 1958, Bluefield State again won first round games but was eliminated in the second round. In 1959 and 1960, the Blues did somewhat better, winning two games before losing in the semi-final round. "We were getting some good athletes from New York and New Jersey in the late 1950s because we would take athletes who could not get in to other schools. A lot of the northern schools had quotas on the number of black players that they would accept, and most of the schools in the South would not take black athletes until much later," said Ergie Smith.[21]After an initially low enrollment of white students, by 1967 Bluefield State had an enrollment of 1533 students, of whom 586, or a little more than 38 percent, were black. By 1968, both West

Virginia State and Bluefield State had a majority of white students. They were the only two HBCUs in the United States to have a majority of white students.

The appointment of a white president, Wendell G. Hardway, by the West Virginia Board of Education in 1966 and the growing number of white students caused tensions on the Bluefield State campus. While other campuses erupted in protests over the Vietnam War, Bluefield State's black students protested what they believed was a move by the state of West Virginia to make Bluefield State a white college and to erase its cultural heritage as a historically black college. Tensions between the increasingly white administration and the black students soon escalated. In 1967, a number of demonstrations occurred, including sit-ins, swim-ins, and a march to the county seat in Princeton, and a demonstration at the president's house. Broken windows, slashed tires, and other acts of vandalism occurred on campus. The administration believed that those activities were dangerous and out of control and seriously disrupted normal campus activities. A power struggle developed between the administration and the black students, with the administration reacting by suspending nine students and placing others on probation.

As the conflict worsened, West Virginia governor Hulett Smith requested that the West Virginia Human Rights Commission (WVHRC) investigate the situation at Bluefield State. The WVHRC's report was extremely critical about the West Virginia Board of Education's treatment of Bluefield State and the performance of the college's administration. The report said that the college had been administered with "ineptness, poor judgment, and insensitivity, and the discipline had been haphazard and unfair." The report also contended that Bluefield State College was the "stepchild of higher education in West Virginia." The WVHRC recommended amnesty for those students who were suspended or on probation. The college administration refused, claiming that some of the cases were in the judicial system.[22]

The situation at Bluefield State worsened when in November 1968 a bomb was exploded in the Ned Shott Physical Education Building. No injuries occurred, but the campus was immediately closed to visitors and all activities on campus were suspended. Only students who were going to class or to use the library were permitted on the campus. At the end of the fall term, the dormitories were closed because the administration blamed the bombing on "outside agitators" and dormitory students. The college attempted to find off-campus housing for the displaced dormitory students, but that proved difficult because of the history of segregation in the community. Only 47 of the 200 dormitory residents, all of whom were black, returned to school for the spring semester. At the end of the fall 1968 semester, only 450 of the 1450 students at Bluefield State were black, some 30 percent.[23] The dormitories were never reopened on campus. Bluefield State essentially became a white commuter college with white presidents. A list of 41 demands by the students was posted on the bulletin board in the Student Union after the bombing, one of which was the demand for more black coaches.[24]

"The African American students and the alumni believed that President Hardway had been sent to eliminate Bluefield State. Everything he did from suspending students to closing the dorms and closing the cafeteria on campus reduced the number of black students on campus," said Ergie Smith. "I did not send my daughter who graduated from high school in 1969 or my son who graduated from high school in 1976 to Bluefield State because there was no place to stay or eat on campus. There was no campus life. I wanted them to be proud of the activities on campus. It was like punishment to send a child to Bluefield State then. My daughter went to West Virginia State and my son went to West Virginia University," Smith added.[25]

A proposed merger with white Concord College in the 1970s hinted at the possible demise of Bluefield State. To African Americans it looked like a repeat of the integration of the high schools. In every instance in West Virginia, when black students went to the white high school, the black school and its traditions subsequently disappeared. The ill-conceived merger failed, but tensions continued as a series of white presidents followed Hardway. A black population of only 3 percent in the state, and only 7 percent in Mercer County, along with a hostile atmosphere for black students, made it very difficult for Bluefield State to recruit black students. In 1996, Bluefield State hit a low of only 6 percent black students.[26]

Because there was no on-campus housing, it became extremely difficult to recruit athletes to Bluefield State. The coaches tried to arrange housing for athletes with alumni or in converted motels, but neither was very satisfactory. From the mid–1970s, Bluefield State struggled on the football field. The once proud program had won national championships in the 1920s, beating archrival West Virginia State, and drew 8,000 fans to Bluefield's Mitchell Stadium as late as 1950. In 1976 and 1977, the Big Blues had a record of 6 wins and 13 losses. Then things got worse. In the three seasons from 1978 through 1980, Bluefield State won two and tied two games, while losing 25 for a dismal winning percentage of a little more than 6 percent. The head coach requested a five-year commitment of funds, and when that was not forthcoming, he resigned. Bluefield president Jerod O. Duggars retaliated by disbanding the football program, to the dismay of alumni.[27]

Basketball at Bluefield became the game of choice. Recruiting mostly black players from out of state, the Blues generally posted break-even seasons through the late 1970s and into the 1980s in the WVIAC. In 1979, Bluefield's best team posted a 13–4 record to finish as the WVIAC regular season runner-up. Bluefield State also produced runner-up teams in 1987 and 1988. The 1996 Big Blues team won the WVIAC championship and advanced to the

NCAA Division II Regional tournament, where they lost in the first round to Fairmont State.

The Lady Big Blues basketball team was by far the most successful of the Bluefield State athletic teams. They began to play in the WVIAC in 1984, posting a 14–2 record, and went on to win the WVIAC Tournament that year. In 1986, the Bluefield State women's basketball team raced to a 15–1 conference record and, in 1990, had a stellar 18–1 conference record. In both 1986 and 1990, the Lady Big Blues finished as runner-up in the WVIAC Tournament. In 1993, the Lady Big Blue team had a perfect 19–0 regular season record and won the WVIAC Basketball Tournament, defeating Wheeling Jesuit College, 66–48, in the championship game. After a second-place finish in 1996, with a 15–4 conference record, the Lady Big Blues basketball team spent most of the subsequent seasons at or near the bottom of the standings of the WVIAC, along with the consistently unsuccessful Bluefield State volleyball team.

When the WVIAC folded in 2013, Bluefield struggled to find a conference home. Without a football team they were not welcome in the newly formed Mountain East Conference, which housed most of the defectors from the WVIAC. Bluefield finally settled in the East Coast Athletic Conference (ECAC), remaining at the NCAA Division II level.

* * *

West Virginia State also became a predominantly white college in the 1970s, but the college did not struggle with the same level of identity crisis as did Bluefield State. Within 10 years of integration, 78 percent of State's students were white. Most of the white students were from Kanawha and the surrounding counties. While there was concern that the college would lose its black identity, West Virginia State continued to have black college presidents and the administration made a concerted effort to recruit black faculty despite the high cost created by competitive demand.[28]

The football team at West Virginia State struggled in the WVIAC. The only conference championship in the post–Cardwell era was in 1968 under coach Colin Cameron, when the Yellow Jackets went 5–1 in the conference and 8–1 overall. However, none of the 11 coaches since Cardwell has generated a winning record, despite having coaches with outstanding credentials such as Oree Banks, a veteran coach who held assistant coaching positions at major colleges such as Wisconsin, Grambling, South Carolina, and Virginia. Banks did have four winning seasons, but in the seven seasons he coached at West Virginia State he finished with a 32–36 record. Carl Lee, who played at South Charleston (WV) High School and Marshall University and was an All-Pro defensive back for the Minnesota Vikings, had a 10-year coaching record at West Virginia State of 34–75.

The West Virginia State basketball and baseball teams have fared better than the football team and the women's sports teams. After Coach Cardwell led the Yellow Jackets to the WVIAC tournament championship in 1961, West Virginia State did not win the tournament title again until 1987. In the intervening 26 years, though, State was very competitive in the WVIAC, winning the regular season championship in 1963 with a 21–2 record and placing second in the regular season three times and runner-up twice in the conference tournament. The Yellow Jackets won the regular season championship in 1987 with an 18–2 record and easily defeated Bluefield State, 116–89, for the WVIAC tournament championship to qualify for the NAIA national championship tournament in Kansas City. Led by All-American Ron Moore and All-Tournament selection Wayne Casey, the Yellow Jackets rolled through the NAIA tournament with wins over Harding (98–86), Oregon Tech (92–90 OT), Waynesburg (Pennsylvania) (73–67), and over Georgetown (KY) (74–67) in the semi-final to put State in the finals against Washburn (KS). West Virginia State lost 79–77 in an evenly matched game. In the 2000s, State has experienced a basketball resurgence under coach Bryan Poore. The Yellow Jackets won two regular season and three tournament championships between 1999 and 2014, and Poore's teams have had an excellent record of 267–152. The 2009 team finished the conference season with an outstanding record of 19–1, and the 2010 team was 20–2.

Baseball has been the most successful sport at West Virginia State. Winning 17 conference championships during the 36-year tenure of the legendary coach Cal Bailey, whose team has won more than 1,000 games, in 1999 the Yellow Jackets advanced to the NCAA Division II national championship tournament, where they finished third. Bailey retired following the 2014 season.

The West Virginia State women's teams did not fare as well in the WVIAC. Volleyball has been the most successful women's sport, with WVIAC championships in 2006 and 2008. The women's basketball team spent most seasons between the middle and the bottom of the WVIAC standings. The rare exception was in 2004 when, behind Carmella Suggs and junior college transfer Doye Byrd, the Lady Yellow Jackets finished third in the conference with a 14–4 record. When the WVIAC disbanded following the 2013 season, West Virginia State moved with the football-playing colleges from the former WVIAC into the newly formed Mountain East Conference in 2013–14.

* * *

The difference between the difficulties that Bluefield State faced and the ease with which West Virginia State integrated speaks to the vast regional differences in West Virginia and the differences in the colleges' locations and their recruiting strategies. West Virginia's marked regional differences, a small but vibrant black population with the right to vote, and a state administration that for the most part embraced integration, also affected the integration experience. The number of African Americans in the student body at West Virginia State remained steady through the 1980s and into the 2000s at between 13 and 15 percent. State continued to aggressively recruit African American students from inside West Virginia, and also continued to draw out-of-state African American students. By the 1990s and into the 2000s, white commuters filled the campus, while the dormitories primarily housed African American students, and much of the on-campus life reflected the African American traditions of the college. In 2004, the college was granted university status and was renamed West Virginia State University. The State campus remains a center of African American history and culture in West Virginia.

Bluefield State has aggressive marketed off-campus centers in the West Virginia towns of Beckley, Lewisburg, Summersville, and Welch in a concerted effort to increase enrollment and to recruit black students. Both Bluefield State and West Virginia State retained their designation as Historically Black Colleges and Universities (HBCU), despite having a majority of white students, through a loophole in the law that essentially says "once a HBCU always an HBCU." That designation moved National Public Radio's *Morning Edition* to air an October 19, 2013, show on Bluefield State titled "The Whitest Historically Black College in America." The program carefully traced the history of the college.

West Virginia State and Bluefield State are the only two HBCUs in the United States with a majority of white students. In 2010, 72 percent of West Virginia State University's students were white. Bluefield State College had a white enrollment of 75 percent. The next closest HBCU in white enrollment was Kentucky State, with an enrollment of 34 percent white students. The integration of a majority of white students was both a blessing and a curse for West Virginia's two black colleges. However, in 2017, both had small but solid enrollments: West Virginia State had 3,107 students and Bluefield State had 1,486 students. In September 2012, Dr. Marsha Krotseng became the first female president at Bluefield State. "There seems to be an air of optimism and inclusiveness on campus. It seems much better than before," said Ergie Smith.[29] This optimism is captured in the new Bluefield State motto, "Honoring Our Past, Forging Our Future."

9

Black High Schools
in the White Basketball
Tournament, 1957–1969

West Virginia's first official football game between a black high school and a white high school took place only four months after the *Brown* decision. On September 30, 1954, Fairmont West High School, a white school, and Fairmont Dunbar High School, a black school, met on West's football field. The teams had scrimmaged against each other previously, but this was the first game with won-loss results that would be in the record books. Although Huntington St. Joseph, an all-white Catholic school, and Huntington Douglass, a black high school had played each other in basketball since 1948, this was the first interracial football game between white and black public schools.

Both teams' coaches and both principals approved of the game, and the sports editors for both the *Fairmont Times* and the *Fairmont West Virginian* heralded the game as a positive step in race relations. The editor of the *Fairmont West Virginian* wrote, "Within a year or so, the boys will be playing together on the same team."[1]

Fairmont West was a Class A school, the largest class in West Virginia high school sports at that time, while Fairmont Dunbar, with an enrollment of only 500 students in grades 1–12, was a Class B school. However, Dunbar had been undefeated with a 6–0 record in 1953 and had been named the West Virginia black high school football champions. The game gave Fairmont West a full schedule of 10 games, but Fairmont Dunbar had a schedule of only six games, all against black high schools except West. The black high schools played fewer games because of the distance between the black schools.

West had a record of 1–1–1 and Dunbar was 1–0. The historic game, played in front of a large crowd, was scoreless in the first half, but, in the middle of the third quarter, Dunbar recovered a West fumble, scoring a touchdown, but missed the extra point, giving Dunbar a 6–0 lead. The West Polar Bears had dominated the statistics but were unable to score until a short Dunbar punt was returned to the 26-yard line late in the third quarter. In the first play of the fourth quarter, Johnny Fargo, a center converted into a fullback, plunged two yards for the Polar Bear touchdown. The extra point kick was successful to set the final score at 7–6.[2]

In his column in the following days *Fairmont West Virginian* sports editor Emlyn Thomas praised the crowd's behavior, the sportsmanship of the teams, and the clean play of both teams. He concluded with "proof that the integration problem, if there is such a thing, can be handled smoothly with a little cooperation from both sides."[3]

In 1959, the Guin brothers, Moses and Curtis (who had played for Dunbar in that 1954 game), and three other African Americans were playing for the integrated Fairmont State College football team. That season, the Guin brothers were the stars of the team and helped the Falcons to an undefeated 8–0 season and the West Virginia Intercollegiate Athletic Conference football championship.[4]

* * *

In January 1954, West Virginia was one of 16 states with a segregated school system. Of the 446,000 students attending West Virginia schools, only 26,000 or 5.7 percent were African Americans. The African American population was unevenly distributed in the state. The largest concentration of West Virginia's African Americans lived in Kanawha and Greenbrier counties, the Eastern Panhandle, and in the southern counties bordering Virginia.[5]

Integration in the West Virginia public schools took until 1969 to complete. In the Northern Panhandle, north central West Virginia, and Kanawha County, integration was completed in three years. The counties along the Virginia and Kentucky borders took longer to integrate. Bluefield Park Central in Mercer County was the last black high school in West Virginia to close, 15 years after the *Brown* decision. One factor that moved integration along in West Virginia was that, unlike many of the Southern states, West Virginia's African Americans had never lost the right to vote, and in many parts of the state they had political clout. But the unevenness of school integration underscored the often-extreme sectional differences in attitude about race in West Virginia.

* * *

On the day following the Supreme Court decision, May 18, 1954, West Virginia governor William C. Marland held a press conference. At that conference Marland stated, "Gentlemen, the decision of the Supreme Court is the law of the land and we shall abide by it."[6] W.W. Trent, the longtime and powerful state superintendent of schools, attended the press conference and stood firm with the governor on integrating West Virginia schools and colleges. The state superintendent of schools was an elected position in West Virginia. Trent, a shrewd politician, had served as the superintendent of schools since he was elected as a Democrat in 1932. He became a powerful force in West Virginia politics, often receiving more votes than any other state-wide candidate. Trent's stand on integration was not surprising since he had historically been a strong supporter of providing a quality, separate but equal education for West Virginia's African American children.

During Trent's 22 years in office he had taken a number of steps to support African American schools in the state. During his first term of office he led the movement for establishing the county unit system of education, which was put in place in 1933–34. This gave the West Virginia Department of Education only 55 county units to administer instead of the hundreds of small school districts which often slighted black education. Some counties, though, did attempt to cut costs for African American education by farming students out to other counties, black colleges with high school programs, or other states, rather than building high schools.

In his 1960 book *Mountaineer Education: A Story of Education in West Virginia, 1885–1957*, Trent contended that he had hired an African American as the state supervisor of Negro schools, when many states hired white people in that position and that he had specified that county school systems with more than 50 black students could hire an African American assistant county superintendent.[7]

Both Marland and Trent were deluged immediately with anti-integration mail and telephone calls. Undaunted, Trent sent a letter to each county superintendent with a carbon copy to the county boards of education advising them to "begin immediately to re-organize and re-adjust their schools to comply with the Supreme Court decision." However, he added, "in some instances a number too large for convenient accommodation, considerable time may be required before segregation is entirely eliminated."[8] Some counties used that excuse to delay integration for more than 10 years.

During the first year following the *Brown* decision, 31 of West Virginia's counties had fully integrated or began to implement their plan for integration, 15 did not integrate their schools, and nine had no African American students, reported the *Journal of Negro Education* in the summer 1955 issue. Nineteen black schools closed. Two black elementary schools that were scheduled to close remained open at the request of black parents. Only 10 percent of West Virginia's white students and 4 percent of black students attended integrated schools that first year. The *Journal of Negro Education* writer concluded, "desegregation has taken place only in counties with few Negro students."[9]

Unfortunately, during that first year 15 African American school personnel lost their jobs. Most notably were six principals, seven teachers, and one coach. There were 973 black teachers in West Virginia in 1955. No white teachers lost jobs that year because of integration.[10]

In the 1956 election Trent, who by that time had served in the position of superintendent of schools for 24 years and had been elected six times, was defeated by the Republican candidate R. Virgil Rohrbough. Part of the reason for his defeat was the Republican landslide led by President Dwight Eisenhower running for his second term and Republican Cecil Underwood who easily won the governor's race. But a significant factor in Trent's defeat was his strong stand on advancing integration. Trent's defeat in, the election was a blow to integration in West Virginia.

* * *

Integration occurred fairly quickly in the counties in the northern and central part of West Virginia. Morgantown Monongalia and Elkins Riverside were integrated into the white high schools by the fall of 1954–55. Two years later, in the fall of 1956, the West Virginia Department of Education reported that 22 counties had completed integration, 21 had partially integrated, three had taken no action, and nine had no Negro pupils. The report also stated that there were 33 fewer Negro teachers than the previous year.[11] The decline in the number of black teachers indicates that a number of black teachers were not kept on to teach or did not accept the position offered in the integrated schools. Superintendent Trent had contended that on the average the black teachers had better academic preparation with more college degrees than white teachers, because there were fewer jobs for college trained African Americans.[12] By the fall of 1956, Charleston Garnet, London Washington, Wheeling Lincoln, Parkersburg Sumner, Weirton Dunbar, and Fairmont Dunbar students were all absorbed by formerly all-white high schools.

In Clarksburg, black students began attending Clarksburg Washington Irving High School in the fall of 1957. Phillip Carter, who had attended Clarksburg Kelly Miller School from sixth through ninth grade, was a sophomore at Washington Irving that fall. "The Washington Irving principal came to Kelly Miller in the spring of 1957 to personally enroll all of the Kelly Miller students. The school board made every effort to make integration go smoothly. Everything went well except that all of the black teachers and administrators were demoted to lesser positions in the white schools. That demotion really hurt the black middle class in Clarksburg," said Carter.[13]

Carter played basketball at Washington Irving and in his senior year made the All-Big Ten Conference team. "Playing for Washington Irving was really different than playing at Kelly Miller. The thrill wasn't there. You did not know the cheerleaders, you did not go to church with your classmates, and you did not hang out on weekends with your teammates. It was as if we were there to do a job," said Carter.[14]

* * *

In the spring of 1957, the last WVAU Tournament was held at Bluefield Park Central High School. Park Central won the 12-team event. But five of the black high schools (Beckley Stratton, Logan Aracoma, Accoville Buffalo, West Virginia State High School, and Huntington Douglass) chose instead to play in the formerly all-white WVSSAC basketball tournament. The black schools quickly proved that they could compete successfully in the white tournament. Douglass High School was the most successful of the black schools that played in that first integrated tournament. Douglass easily defeated three teams in the sectional tournament, including Huntington Vinson, 83–62, in the championship game, to win the Class B Section 32 tournament. The following week Douglass won two more games, defeating Winfield 68–42 for the Region 8 championship, and advancing one game from the state Class B championship game. However, Douglass's Cinderella ride ended in the Class B area championship game when they lost by 74–62 to Burch High School, denying Douglass the honor of being the first black high school to reach the WVSSAC state championship finals. Burch went on to win the Class B state championship.

* * *

By the mid–1950s basketball was changing to reflect the impact of the *Brown* decision and the advancing civil rights movement. West Virginia was not the first state to integrate black high schools into the white state tournament. Randy Roberts in *But They Can't Beat Us: Oscar Robertson and the Crispus Attucks Tigers* told how Indiana integrated black high schools into the Indiana High School Athletic Association (IHSAA) tournament. Indiana had a strange racial make-up for high schools in a border state. In the small towns and rural areas, where there were few African Americans, the schools were integrated; black students attended the predominantly white school and played in the IHSAA tournament. But all-black high schools were built in the large cities of Indiana and all of the black students in that city were required to attend the one black high school. Lincoln High School in Evansville, Roosevelt High School in Gary and Crispus Attucks in Indianapolis were three examples of the big black high school movement in Indiana cities.[15]

Those high schools were excluded from membership in the IHSAA tournament, using the logic of Arthur L. Trester, the longtime head of the IHSAA. Randy Roberts wrote, "As he told a delegation of Indianapolis black community leaders in 1927, Crispus Attucks was not really a public school since it catered only to black students. And since it was not a public school it was not eligible to join the IHSAA."[16]

However, in 1942, in a burst of patriotism following the bombing of Pearl Harbor, the IHSAA extended membership to the black high schools and included them in the state basketball tournament. By 1953, out of the 750 Indiana high schools, Crispus Attucks advanced as far as the state semi-finals. But in 1955 in an historic all-black state final, Crispus Attucks defeated Gary Roosevelt, 97–74, for the state championship, led by the legendary Oscar Robertson, to become the first black high school to win the IHSAA basketball championship. That same evening Bill Russell and K.C. Jones and the University of San Francisco Dons won the NCAA championship. The following year, Robertson, now a senior, led Crispus Attucks to a repeat championship.[17] Those victories helped to dispel the myth that black athletes could not win basketball championships.

* * *

In 1958, nine black high schools played in the WVSSAC tournament. The black schools were very successful, winning 12 of 21 games. Amigo Byrd Prillerman and Bluefield Park Central both won sectional championships, but lost in the regional finals, and Douglass again lost in the area championship game, this time to Baileysville, 85–76.

The 1959 tournament drew 16 black high schools. The success of the black schools, particularly in the Class A Tournament (by then the WVSSAC was divided into AAA, AA, and A classes), drew resentment from a number of white schools who, following tournament losses, retaliated by appealing player eligibility to the WVSSAC. In 1959, Byrd Prillerman was disqualified for using an ineligible player after defeating Clear Fork, 80–41, in the Sectional Tournament. Byrd Prillerman had used that same player during the regular season without protest. Meanwhile, Williamson Liberty High School advanced through the tournament, beating Lenore, 65–59, for the sectional championship and Huntington Douglass, 58–53, for the regional championship. Liberty went on to defeat Anstead, 54–51, in the area playoff and qualifying for a berth in the final-four state championship tournament. This victory made Williamson Liberty the first black school to qualify for the WVSSAC state tournament finals. However, after losing the area playoff game, Anstead protested the eligibility of one of the Liberty players. Liberty's coach Ed Starling explained the situation. "The black WVAU was less formal about birth dates. They accepted things like family Bibles as documentation. In this situation, someone from Anstead went into Kentucky and found a birth certificate, which supposedly proved one of our players was over the age limit. The WVSSAC upheld Anstead's protest and they replaced us in the state tournament. That really hurt, but there was nothing we could do about it."[18]

* * *

In 1960, West Virginia adopted the policy of free choice. Under the free choice provision, students could choose whether to continue to attend a formerly all-black school or a formerly all-white school.[19] The black communities were not monolithic in favor of integration. The choice by black students was not always to transfer to the white school. As a result, 14 black high schools continued to play in the 1960 WVSSAC tournament. There were threats of violence in some of the counties that did not want to integrate. African American parents felt that integration would place their children in a hostile environment and possibly in physical danger; more commonly, the treatment of black pupils in the integrated schools by the white teachers was very racist. Many African Americans wanted to keep their beloved all-black schools, which were controlled by their community and were the center of black life.

Huntington Douglass High School, located in Cabell County, was typical of the counties where a choice was offered. Initially, most of the African American students continued to attend Douglass High School. This began to change in the late 1950s. Dolores Johnson attended Douglass until 1957, but in the fall of 1957, she transferred with five of her female friends, none of whom were on athletic teams because Cabell County did not have girls' sports, to Huntington High School for her junior year. "The coaches were recruiting the black athletes to come to Huntington High," she said. "And the coaches made sure that everything went ok for them. The white students mostly ignored us. We went home for lunch rather than eat lunch at school. Some people in the black community called us traitors," Johnson added.[20] Johnson graduated from Huntington High School in 1959 and later returned as an English teacher.

Despite losing some athletes, Douglass continued to play successfully in the WVSSAC basketball tournament. As late as 1960, Douglass and 13 other black high schools entered the WVSSAC basketball championship tournament. Douglass marched through the tournament, winning the Sectional and Regional championships, and was only defeated in the area playoff, by state runner-up Anstead, 62–55. In 1961, the Huntington High School Pony Express won the WVSSAC State Class AAA basketball championship with three black players, the Allen twins (Paul and Bill) and Melvin Jennings, in the starting lineup. Both Bill Allen and Jennings made the All-Tournament team. Douglass High School did not have a basketball team in 1961 because there were not enough boys left at the school to have a team. The Cabell County Board of Education closed the school at the end of that year because of low enrollment.

In the fall of 1962, Lewisburg Bolling School was closed and its black students were sent to nearby white schools. Integration was difficult in Greenbrier County. Bolling School was located in Lewisburg, but served all of the

African American students in the entire Greenbrier County from grades 1 through 12. "White parents stood at the school bus stops and kept black kids from getting on the buses," said Opal Jones, a 1950 graduate of Bolling High School, who sent 12 of her children to the integrated schools in Greenbrier County. "We had to go to court to get integration."[21]

The Greenbrier County schools began integration in the fall of 1954, but, following protests by parents and students in White Sulphur Springs, the Greenbrier County Board of Education rescinded integration and sent the students back to the schools they had attended in 1953–54. The NAACP then filed an injunction and federal judge Ben Moore recommended that the process of integration begin before January 18, 1956. The board of education agreed.[22]

The mixed feelings about integration among African Americans in Greenbrier County mirrored those of much of the rest of West Virginia. "We wanted integration because we needed to know what everyone else knew. And the kids were excited because they could take classes like typing and foreign languages which we did not have at Bolling. Lewisburg had a gym too. We did not have one at Bolling and had to use the Lewisburg gym when they were a not using it. But we lost our school which was the center of the black community. It was hard on my children because many of the white teachers were very mean to the black kids. The teachers at the white schools really did not seem to care if the black kids learned or not," said Opal Jones.[23] The last Bolling High School class graduated in 1961. The school remained open, but with only a handful of elementary students, until finally closing in 1963, bringing an end to school segregation in Greenbrier County.

* * *

Gary District High School in McDowell County played in the WVAU Tournament from the very beginning in 1925 through the demise of the tournament after 1957. Gary District won two WVAU tournaments and finished as runner-up four times. In 1956, McDowell County began a very limited process of integration. But integration was slow because of white resistance in the form of protests, particularly at Welch High School.[24]

African Americans in McDowell County were somewhat ambivalent. "There were mixed feelings in the black community about integration. We had a lot of pride in our schools and a desire to keep our schools open. We fought for integration, but we knew that we would lose a lot. Integration without parity and equality is not integration. We lost our sense of community with integration," said Ronald Wilkerson, a student at Gary District during the 1960s.[25]

Gary District, coached by James Wilkerson and Ergie Smith, was one of the most successful black high schools in the WVSSAC tournament. "One thing that really helped the later teams at Gary District was when they added Ergie Smith to the staff in 1953. That was the first time I ever had a paid assistant," said James Wilkerson. "He deserves credit for most of the success our teams achieved."[26]

A graduate of Kimball High School, Smith had played on the Kimball team that lost 45–44 to the Bob Trice–led Weirton Dunbar team in the 1947 WVAU semi-final game. He graduated from Bluefield State College, where he earned All-American honors as a halfback on football teams that finished 7–3 and 8–2 his junior and senior years. Wilkerson was so pleased with his new assistant coach that he made Smith his co-coach in 1960. "They would not give me a raise so Coach Wilkerson had them add our two salaries together and divide it and give each of us half. He reduced his own coaching salary, but he was that kind of person," said Smith.[27]

"We played in the black state tournament clear up to 1957, and then we began to play in the white tournament," said Wilkerson. "We made it to the regional tournament the first couple of years." In 1961, Gary District had one of their best teams but was eliminated in the regional finals by Oceana. The next year, 1962, Gary District qualified for the state tournament and became the first black school to reach the tournament finals. "We finished second because we lost in the championship game to Lenore [66–51]," said Coach Wilkerson.[28]

Following Gary District's second place finish in 1962, it became increasingly clear that the black schools would be formidable competitors in the tournament. Even though black schools had closed and there were fewer black schools in the tournament, the remaining schools were more successful. In 1961, 14 black schools had been in the WVSSAC tournament. By 1963, there were only 10 black schools in the tournament out of a field of 109 Class A, 82 Class AA and 39 Class AAA schools. With the exception of Page-Jackson High School from Berkeley County in West Virginia's Eastern Panhandle, the black schools in the tournament were from the very southern part of the state in Mercer, McDowell, Mingo, Raleigh, and Wyoming counties. One of the southern schools, Bluefield Park Central, advanced through the Class AA tournament, losing to eventual champion Oceana, 73–66, in the regional final.[29]

Mullens Conley High School was much more successful in the Class A tournament. Conley defeated Glen Rogers, 66–61, for the sectional championship, Kermit 78–76 for the regional championship, and Fort Gay 70–57 in the area playoff to advance to the state championship tournament held in Huntington's Memorial Field House.

Conley, located in Mullens, West Virginia, drew from all of Wyoming County, which was a hotbed of high school basketball. The white schools in the towns of Glen Rogers, Mullens, and Oceana had developed strong basketball programs. Conley, named for former West Virginia Governor William Conley, became a high school in 1932. By 1950, the black population of Wyoming County, approximately 3,100, was in decline because the mechanization of the coal fields severely reduced the number of coal mining jobs. However, despite the declining economy of the county, a new high school building was completed for Conley in 1950.

Conley was coached by the veteran Leonard Valentine, who began coaching at Conley in 1944. A graduate of Byrd Prillerman High School, Valentine went on to become an All-American end at Bluefield State College. He coached the Conley Blue Devils to the 1951 WVAU state football championship.[30] "In the summer Coach Valentine was the playground director in our part of town. He never coached us in the off-season but he always made sure that we had basketballs even when the playground was not open. We were close. He watched us grow up and knew our parents," said Ronald Booker, a senior and the captain of the Conley team.[31]

The 1963 Mullens Conley team made it to the West Virginia Class A state championship tournament. "The reason that Conley was still open in 1963 was that Wyoming County began integrating from first grade up. In 1963 integration was up to ninth grade," recalled Ronald Booker.[32] That 1963 Class A tournament field was one of the strongest in history. The field had four teams with a combined record of 89 wins and 6 losses, led by White Sulphur Springs High School, with a record of 25–0. One of the first-round games matched Barrackville, the 1961 state champion, coached by Joe Retton, with Mullens Conley. In 1961 Retton was three years from becoming the basketball coach at Fairmont State College, where he had an 18-season storybook career. His teams achieved a number of small college top 10 rankings and he collected national coach of the year awards. But before that he would have to beat Mullens Conley.

Mullens Conley was a speedy high-scoring team that averaged 90 points a game and had surpassed 100 points on eight occasions during the season. Conley had an exceptionally tall team led by six-foot, two-inch Booker and six-foot, four-inch William Crews, both of whom were averaging over 20 points a game. The championship was rated a toss-up, as none of the teams had played each other in the regular season.[33]

After a close first half, with Conley on top by 26–23, the Conley Blue Devils opened up the game in the second half. "Our strategy was to win by 10 or 15 points because we knew that we could not win close games because of the biased officiating," said Booker.[34]

"Conley really gave the crowd a thrill with its fast-breaking, shoot crazy ball club," wrote George Springer, the sports editor of the *Beckley Post-Herald*. "They shot up and down the floor with the speed of lightning."[35] By the end of the third quarter, Conley had increased its lead to eight points and continued to increase the lead in the final quarter to set the final score at 57–46. The deciding factor in the game was the huge difference in rebounding as Conley pulled down 44 rebounds to Barrackville's 25, giving Conley a 66–49 edge in shots from the floor. William Crews led Conley with 14 points and 15 rebounds. Booker chipped in with 13 points and 13 rebounds.[36]

The championship game between Conley and Piedmont, who had upset undefeated White Sulphur Springs, was played before 4,000 fans in Huntington's Memorial Field House. Neither team could find the basket through two and one-half quarters. Then Conley caught fire and hit a 17–3 run late in the half to take a 12-point lead over a tiring Lions team. The Blue Devils held on for a 43–39 victory and the first WVSSAC championship by an all-black school. Again, the deciding factors were Conley's 51–40 edge in rebounding and the superior conditioning of the Blue Devils. William Crews led Conley with 16 rebounds and 13 points.[37]

That same day Oceana High School, also from Wyoming County, won the Class AA championship, making Wyoming County the center of West Virginia basketball. Weirton High School won the Class AAA championship led by the school's All-State player Ron "Fritz" Williams, who in two years would be one of four African American players to integrate West Virginia University basketball. A celebration of the two Wyoming County teams lasted two days. A caravan of cars greeted both teams at the Wyoming County line on Sunday and escorted them to Oceana High School, where a joint celebration was held. On Monday morning, the Conley team captain, Ron Booker, presented the championship trophy to the principal of Mullens Conley High School in an all-school assembly.[38]

During the 1964 basketball season, the season following Conley's state championship, Conley lost in overtime, 74–70, in the regional semi-final to Kermit, the eventual state champion. In the fall of 1964, Conley High School was closed after Wyoming County completed its 12-year cycle of integration. In 1966, the integrated Mullens High School team placed second in the WVS-SAC Class AA State Tournament.

* * *

In July 1964, Congress passed the Civil Rights Act. That Act made racial discrimination illegal in schools, the workplace, and in public accommodations. By 1965, the number of segregated high schools in West Virginia stood at nine with the closing of Bramwell Bluestone High School, but the eight high schools in the southern tier of the state, as well as Page-Jackson from the Eastern Panhandle town of Charles Town, remained firmly segregated. The integration of the northern and central counties in West Virginia demonstrated the good faith of the state to integrate, but the lack of integration in the very southern counties mirrored the situation that prevailed in the southern

WVSSAC 1963 championship game between Mullins Conley and Piedmont high schools. Mullins Conley defeated Piedmont 43–39 to become the first black high school to win the integrated state tournament. Conley players Ronald Booker and Lloyd Crews are in the dark uniforms (courtesy West Virginia State Archives).

United States, where as late as 1964 only 2.3 percent of African American children attended integrated schools. The uneven pattern of integration reflected the intense sectional differences that had been so much a part of West Virginia from the birth of the state in 1863.

Tournament victories for black schools in the WVSSAC continued even as their ranks thinned. In 1965, Gary District, under co-coaches Ergie Smith and James Wilkerson, made a run to the state finals. "We had our best team in 1961," said Ergie Smith. "But we lost to Oceana, 68–61, in the Regional Finals. They had a great team and I really like and greatly respect Coach Greer, but the officiating was bad."[39] Even the mild-mannered Coach Wilkerson commenting on the officials said, "We got a raw deal up there and I will never believe otherwise."[40]

Biased officiating against black teams was mentioned by many of West Virginia's black coaches and players. It appeared to be widespread, also reported in other states, including Indiana. Randy Roberts in *But They Can't Beat Us: Oscar Robertson and the Crispus Attucks Tigers* mentions numerous instances when coaches and even the black press complained about questionable calls made by referees in Indiana against the all-black teams.[41] In 1954, the Indiana High School Athletic Association rejected all applications by African American referees.[42]

Ergie Smith discussed some of the problems that the black schools faced on the basketball court. "The two major problems with playing in the WVS-SAC were that the white schools would not schedule us. The only time we played them was during tournaments. We played the other eight black schools in southern West Virginia and made trips into Kentucky and Virginia. Also, the officiating was unfair and very obvious in the sectional and regional tournaments. When we got to the state tournament the officiating was better and got even better overall as time passed. By 1965 our players adjusted to the officiating and just kept on playing. We were treated well in personal relationships. We never heard any name calling or anything like that," said Smith.[43]

In 1962, Gary District had another excellent team. They rolled through the early tournament games, beating Elkhorn, also a black high school, 90–61, in the sectional championship game, and Williamson Liberty, another black high school, 91–53, in the regional championship game. Gary District easily defeated Harts High School, 88–62, in the area playoff to advance to the state finals, held at the Mountaineer Field House in Morgantown.

"I think that we lost the 1962 championship game because I had not experienced handling a team as a coach over a time period and being away from home such as the state tournament encompassed. We tried to see and do too much in Morgantown between the games. I know that I was tired when Saturday rolled around. We just did not have much energy in the second half," said Smith.[44]

Gary District returned to the state tournament in 1965. "We were in Class A in 1965. We drew Fairview High School in the semifinal game, but we never worried about those northern teams. They couldn't stand our defense. We played them a tough, pressing defense and took the ball away from them at midcourt. I think we had them, 23–8, at the end of the first quarter, and just coasted the rest of the way with our subs," recalled Coach Wilkerson.[45] The Gary District coaches knew not to tire the team out between games and the next night beat Fort Ashley, 79–70, in the final, to become the second all-black high school to win the WVSSAC state championship. That championship was the first WVSSAC state championship won by any school, in any sport, in McDowell County.[46]

"The black community was ecstatic, because we felt as if the 1961 championship had been taken away from us," said Ronald Wilkerson, a manager for the 1965 Gary District team. "We had a banquet, but I do not remember any white people celebrating. I might not have been in a position to know, but I do not remember any," he said.[47]

Gary District had little time to revel in the state championship, because at the end of the 1966 school year Gary District High School was closed and the students were integrated into the white McDowell County high schools in their home communities. "The decision was made in the summer to close Gary District. We were all concerned because the teachers did not know if we would have jobs and the students were concerned that they would not have the same opportunities in the new schools. We had a right to be concerned. I was offered a job teaching and coaching junior high school. I did not take it. I worked for the next seven years in community action. And the students did not have the same opportunities. For example, there might be only one black cheerleader out of ten. The same thing occurred with other clubs and activities. It was almost as if there was a quota," said Smith.[48]

Ergie Smith in 1973. Smith coached at Gary District High School from 1953 until the school closed in 1966. He and James Wilkerson guided Gary District to a WVSSAC state basketball championship in 1965. In 1973 he coached the integrated Gary High School to a state championship (courtesy Bluefield State College Archives).

Smith returned to Gary in 1973 as the head basket-

ball coach at Gary High School. He was successful immediately, leading the Coal Diggers to the 1973 Class AA state championship with a victory over New Martinsville Magnolia, 68–50. Smith continued to coach at Gary until 1978 when Gary was consolidated into Mount View High School. Smith coached at Mount View until he retired in 1989.

* * *

By the 1966 tournament, the number of black high schools had dwindled to only five (Park Central, Kimball, Stratton, Elkhorn, and Williamson Liberty). The newly integrated Gary High School lost to the newly integrated Mullens High School, 78–53, in the Class AA regional championship game. Mullens went on to finish as the state runner-up, losing in the final, 58–51, to Huntington Vinson High School.

In 1966, Williamson Liberty, which state champion Gary District had beaten in the 1965 tournament, easily ran through the 1966 Class A tournament. Liberty beat Sharples, 72–39, for the sectional championship and Bramwell, 53–41, for the regional championship and a place in the four-team state championship, held in Huntington at the Memorial Field House. A 69–56 rout of Sistersville put Liberty into the Class A state championship game against Piedmont High School. "I really wanted to win that game," said Liberty's coach, Ed Starling, "because I knew that the next year Liberty would be closed and integrated into Williamson High School."[49] Unfortunately, Liberty had a cold shooting night and Piedmont won, 58–55.

In 1967, Bluefield Park Central and Beckley Stratton were the last two black high schools in the basketball tournament. After Stratton closed in the spring of 1967, Park Central continued for two more years as the only black high school in the WVSSAC tournament. In 1969, Bluefield Park Central, under coach Elhainer Willis, defeated Hinton High School, 66–56, for the Class AA sectional championship, but lost to Gary High School, 91–69, in the first round of the Regional Tournament. This was the last game played by an all-black high school in West Virginia. In the spring of 1969, Park Central closed, bringing to an end the 15-year process of integrating the schools in West Virginia.

During the 13 years from 1957 through 1969, the 18 black high schools that participated in the WVSSAC tournament won 55 percent of their games. Huntington Douglass was the most successful, winning 81 percent. "But the ultimate prizes went to Mullens Conley (1963) and Gary District (1965), when they won Class A state titles," wrote Tim Wyatt in *The Final Score.*[50]

In *The Rise of American High School Sports*, Robert Pruter noted that the 1969 Supreme Court decision *Alexander v. Holmes* ordered the desegregation of the South's school systems, some of which had been resisting integration. Southern states immediately established private schools, which critics called "segregation academies." In many southern states those schools began to play each other in interscholastic sports.[51] In West Virginia, when Bluefield Park Central High School was closed in 1969, West Virginia was fully integrated. Few "segregation academies" were established in the state.

* * *

During the integration of the educational system, none of the coaches from the black schools were made head coaches of the integrated high schools. While most were offered employment, they were demoted to assistant coaches or junior high school coaches. The experience of James Wilkerson was typical; even though he had been an extremely successful coach at Gary District, he became the assistant coach at the integrated Gary High School. Similarly, John Mackey was transferred from Excelsior to Big Creek as an assistant coach. Some of the coaches eventually became head coaches or administrators, even though they were initially demoted. James "Ham" Wares, who was demoted to assistant football coach at Weirton High School and a junior high school basketball coach, later became a school principal. Elhanier Willis was made an assistant coach at Princeton High School, but later became the head track and field coach. Lacy Smith eventually worked his way up from assistant coach to head football coach at Logan High School. Jim Jarrett was an assistant coach at Charleston High School but, in 1969, was promoted to head basketball coach.

Some of the coaches left the public school system rather than accepting a demotion. Ergie Smith turned down a position in a junior high school and took a job as a community organizer. Seven years later the board of education asked him to come back to be the head coach at Gary High School. He accepted that positions and after a successful career at Gary, he went on to further success as head basketball coach at Mount View High School. Fairmont Dunbar's Horace Belmear resigned from public school teaching and coaching, and later worked for Fairmont State College and West Virginia University. Two years after Ed Starling was made a junior high school coach in Williamson, he was offered an assistant basketball coaching position at Marshall University. "The Mingo County Superintendent told me that if I stayed, I would eventually be made the head coach at Williamson High School. I told him that I did not think I would live that long, so I was taking the Marshall offer," Starling commented.[52] He went on to become a longstanding associate athletic director at Marshall.

The post-integration experience of James L. Taylor, a teacher and coach at Charles Town Page Jackson High School, was more painful than most. When Page Jackson was closed in 1965, Taylor was more qualified than most of the white teachers in Jefferson County in both education and experience. "I had just received my masters from West Virginia University that summer so

I thought I would get to teach biology or something. But I was a young black male and they did not know what to do with me. So, I was assigned to teach junior high boys' physical education and coach as an assistant football coach and the JV basketball coach at Charles Town High School. I had to travel after school every day from the school where I was teaching to the school where I was coaching," said Taylor. "They did everything that they could do to discourage me and make me want to quit. I did quit in the middle of the year and went with the Job Corps in Harpers Ferry. I worked there for six years. In 1972 when they built the new Jefferson County High School, I got a call and the school board said 'please come back.' I took a cut in pay to do it, but I went back because I wanted to teach and coach."[53]

* * *

Prior to 1954, the objective of civil rights was to gain equality in a separate system, while integration or desegregation remained a dream. The integration of professional sports—major league baseball in 1947, professional football in 1946, and NBA basketball in 1950—represented a significant step in the integration movement because it was a very visible demonstration of successful integration. However, the number of athletes who integrated in the 1947 through 1953 period was limited. While the integration of professional sports created huge cracks in the wall of segregation, there were questions about how broad the impact would be on a national level.

The 1954 *Brown* decision represented a very different kind of integration than that undergone by professional sports teams. With professional sports the fans had the option of attending or ignoring the game. School integration brought integration into every city, town, and village. In southern and border states, like West Virginia, which had segregated schools as well as segregation in most aspects of life, white and black children in the same classrooms enhanced the fear of "race mixing." Plus, the specter of school integration was part of a trend, they believed, that would lead to integration in other areas of life.

For African Americans in the South, the *Brown* decision had an even more profound impact. The power structure in black America began to shift from those who were successful at gaining equality in a separate system to those who could open up the integrated white world. Those were not always the same people nor was the strategy the same.

Sports were a good platform to test integration because sports are a meritocracy and could also demonstrate teamwork as a cooperative effort between players of different races. But inclusion on sports teams thrust black athletes into many uncomfortable situations because of their visibility and the changing rules on segregation and integration.

For the black communities in West Virginia, integration was a painful experience because the schools, which had served as a focal point of community life for black West Virginians, were dismantled. The black teachers, coaches and administrators, who had been leaders and role models in the black community, were given diminished roles in the integrated system, and the black students were sent into an often-hostile white environment. Black students went from being in schools controlled by black teachers in the black community to being a minority in schools controlled by white teachers, administrators, and coaches. Sports proved to be a better area for integration than most other parts of society, though, because the black athletes played with skill, dignity, and sportsmanship. Plus, there were often white people, coaches and teammates, who courageously stood up for the black athlete.

10

From Dick Leftridge to Major Harris: A Call for Sports Advocacy at WVU

From as early as the 1890s, through the 1950s, only a few African American collegiate football players had gained national visibility for their athletic prowess in integrated play. Some of those notable African American athletes included Henry H. Lewis, the first black All-American who played at Amherst and Harvard in the 1890s; Frederick Douglass Pollard of Brown University, who played before World War I; Paul Robeson, an All-American at Rutgers University in the 1910s; and Duke Slater of the University of Iowa in the early 1920s. In 1939, UCLA, with five black players, including Jackie Robinson, Woody Strode, and Kenny Washington in the starting line-up, was the most integrated team in the United States.[1]

Opportunities for African Americans to play college basketball were also limited during that period. Some white colleges including the Ivy Leagues and some schools in the East, Midwest, the Mid-Atlantic, and on the Pacific Coast, recruited a few black players, but the southern colleges resisted integration. Sport historian Charles M. Martin wrote, "During the late 1940s and 1950s, as other sections of the U.S. abandoned the more blatant forms of racial discrimination the white South firmly resisted any racial change, even in sports."[2]

Most African American athletes who attended predominantly white colleges and universities endured racism, prejudice, Jim Crow laws, and humiliation on the college campus at the hands of their white counterparts and fans. Prior to 1954, it was not uncommon for college teams who had African American athletes on their squads to keep those players out of games against college teams from the South. During the decades of the 1960s, 1970s, and early 1980s, teams in the southern conferences were slow to integrate.[3]

Two events helped the integration of major college sports in the South. The first was the 1966 NCAA basketball championship game between Texas

Western, which had an all-black starting lineup, and the University of Kentucky, which was an all-white university. The second event was the opening game of the 1970 football season between the University of Southern California, which was integrated at the time, and the University of Alabama, again an all-white university. Prior to these events, southern colleges and universities had staunchly resisted integrating their athletic teams with only three integrated major college basketball teams in the South.

During the 1966 NCAA championship, Adolph Rupp, who had adamantly refused to recruit black players, coached the University of Kentucky. The game was televised nationally and was a resounding 72–65 victory for underdog Texas Western, showing that the all-black team could win major championships. Charles H. Martin in *Benching Jim Crow* wrote, "The Miner victory ... delivered a powerful message about the dangers of continued athletic segregation to coaches at white southern universities."[4] That message also encouraged coaches at colleges outside of the South who already had black players to increase their recruitment of black players.

During the decade of the 1970s, the impact that African American college football players was having on the game served to increase the recruitment of African American athletes. In the opening game of the 1970 season, the University of Southern California, led by African American Sam Cunningham, defeated the University of Alabama, 42–21, in front of more than 72,000 fans at Legion Field in Birmingham, Alabama. Black players, of whom USC had 20 on the team that day, scored all of the Southern California touchdowns. In 1968, by court order white teams in Alabama had to permit black players to participate on white high school teams. Alabama's coach Bear Bryant had begun recruiting black players but had not offered any scholarships to black players. Charles H. Martin wrote, "It is true that the USC loss clearly shocked many white fans and made many more of them more willing to accept Bryant's new policy of recruiting African Americans. White Alabamians' desire to win football games would subsequently triumph over their historical preference for maintaining the whiteness of the Tide football team."[5] Alabama had a black player in the starting line-up the following season, and by the 1973 season one-third of Alabama's starting line-up was black.[6]

* * *

On November 28, 1891, West Virginia University played in the first recorded intercollegiate athletic event in the state—a football game against Washington and Jefferson College (W & J). The W & J team, from nearby Washington, Pennsylvania, traveled on a river packet boat down the Monongahela River to Morgantown, West Virginia, the home of West Virginia University. Located in north central West Virginia not far south of the Pennsylvania border, Morgantown in 1891 was a sleepy college hamlet, with a population of little over 1,000.

College football, which had been played in the eastern United States as early as 1875, was already popular among the elite American universities. W & J was a veteran team with almost two seasons of football under its belt. For WVU, it was the first game in the history of the school—and the state. WVU was so inexperienced that only one player had ever played in a football game; none of the others had even seen a game before.[7]

Game day dawned dreary with a cold rain turning to snow early in the game. The field had no fence and many fans pulled their wagons, each with WVU banners of gold and navy, up to the very edge of the playing area. Other fans gathered around bonfires they had built behind the goal posts at both ends of the field. The crowd grew to more than 250 fans, eagerly awaiting the first kick-off.[8]

The WVU team knew little about football formations, rules, or game strategy. The W & J boys proceeded to teach their opponents a football lesson using the power wedge and trick plays that completely confused the inexperienced WVU team. By the end of the game, the score stood at 72–0 and could have been worse. The 1892 *Monticola*, WVU's yearbook, said, "W & J made monkeys of the mountain giants, and only stopped when the score had piled up to 72–0."[9]

No African Americans were on the field that day because West Virginia was a state with a segregated school system. In that age of segregation and past the mid–20th century, no African American would represent West Virginia University on either the football field, the basketball court or on any other athletic team.

* * *

WVU was established in Morgantown on February 7, 1867, as a land grant college initially named the Agricultural College of West Virginia. On December 4, 1868, the college changed its name to West Virginia University.[10]

From then on, WVU was often referred to as "the University" in part because it was the only university in the state until Marshall was elevated to university status in 1961. However, WVU was and has remained the flagship university for West Virginia. WVU has traditionally drawn students and athletic loyalty throughout the state. Mountaineer sports teams were the face of West Virginia. Fans traveled to Morgantown on bad country roads for games or listened to the legendary Jack Fleming describe games on the radio from the Field House or "old" Mountaineer Field. As the flagship university of the state, WVU began to build a football program. Through the first half of the 20th century, WVU played a major college independent schedule with a mix of teams. The most notable opponent was the University of Pittsburgh, a national power that became WVU's biggest rival. Regional teams Duquesne and Washington & Jefferson, which both had seasons when they were nationally recognized, and West Virginia Wesleyan were on most schedules. Flagship state universities Penn State, Maryland, and Kentucky filled out the schedule, but WVU also occasionally played Yale, Princeton, and Navy, who were national powers in the early 20th century. In a 1919 game, WVU received national attention by defeating national power Princeton, 25–0. That season Ira Rodgers was the first WVU player named to the Walter Camp All-American team. This was in part due to the strength of his play in the upset victory over Princeton.

In 1922, Athletic Director Harry Stansbury was granted permission to build Mountaineer Field at the bottom of Falling Run Road. The facility, constructed in 1924 and 1925 and holding 33,000 fans, served the WVU football program until 1980. Mountaineer Field made WVU competitive with other state universities, and WVU continued to play a major independent schedule with mixed success on the field.

When WVU joined the Southern Conference in December 1949, it was still a very competitive conference with 17 teams located in Maryland, North Carolina, South Carolina, and Virginia. However, in 1953, when seven more colleges broke away to form the Atlantic Coast Conference (ACC), the Southern Conference became a shell of its former self. WVU desperately wanted to join the new Atlantic Coast Conference, but was too geographically isolated from the ACC colleges, most of which were located in North and South Carolina.[11] After 1953, only nine second-tier college powers remained in the Southern Conference with WVU—the Citadel, Davidson, Furman, George Washington, Richmond, Virginia Tech, VMI, Washington & Lee, and William & Mary. With the large state universities gone from the Southern Conference, WVU was able to dominate the remaining teams. While West Virginia could easily win conference games and titles in both football and basketball to fatten up season records and to gain an automatic qualifying berth in the NCAA tournament, they commanded little respect nationally.[12]

In 1950, WVU hired Art "Pappy" Lewis as the head football coach. WVU had been home to some good football teams up to that point but had received little national recognition. WVU had never once received a national ranking in the polls, which had begun in 1936, and had never been invited to a major bowl game. Lewis's first two teams were disappointing, with a 7–13 record overall and 3–6 Southern Conference record in 1950 and 1951.

The 1952 season was the turning point for WVU's football fortunes. The 1952 season showed much promise for the future of WVU football with a 7–2 season record and a 5–1 Southern Conference record, good for third place in the (then) 17-team conference. Included in the wins was a victory over arch-rival Pitt, who was having a good season, having defeated

Army, Notre Dame, Ohio State, Iowa, and Indiana on the way to a 6–3 record.

In 1953, for the first time in WVU football history, the Mountaineers were nationally ranked, opening the season at sixteenth in the AP poll. The Mountaineers did not disappoint their fans, finishing the season with a victory over arch-rival Pitt, an 8–1 season record, and an invitation to the Sugar Bowl. The Mountaineers lost in the Sugar Bowl to Georgia Tech, 42–19, but were ranked 13th in the final UP poll and 10th in the AP poll released in January 1954.[13]

* * *

Prior to the 1954 *Brown* decision, WVU admitted only West Virginia African Americans to graduate or professional programs not offered at the state's two historically black colleges. Two Supreme Court decisions, *Missouri ex rel. Gaines v. Canada* (1938) and *Sweatt v. Painter* (1950), required states that had separate educational systems to provide equal opportunities particularly in graduate and professional programs. A February 3, 1956, letter from WVU dean Robert Dustman to WVU president Stewart informed President Stewart that a number of African Americans had enrolled at WVU under those provisions in the law. Dustman wrote, "It seems probable (but is by no means certain) that our first Master's degree awarded to a Negro student was made in 1941. Since that time, we have awarded 142 Master's Degrees, four certificates of social work, and one Ph.D. Degree, to Negro students."[14]

On May 21, 1954 (four days following the *Brown* decision), WVU president Irvin Stewart wrote a letter to the state's attorney general requesting clarification on the *Brown* decision and its potential impact on WVU. By June 1954, the state's attorney general wrote back, saying: "It is our considered opinion that West Virginia University must now admit any person who applies for admission regardless of race, provided that such application fulfilled all requirements then prescribed for entry."[15] By summer 1954, President Stewart noted "that we will have one or more Negroes in classes in the elementary school and in the University High School. If this is the case, these will probably be the first Negro children to attend public schools on a non-segregated basis in West Virginia."[16] Stewart was wrong in his prediction, because for one the Monongalia County School Board closed the black schools, including Monongahela High School, and integrated the county school system. Monongalia and Randolph counties were among the first West Virginia counties to integrate in the fall of 1954 immediately after the *Brown* decision. However, WVU did not have a black athlete on any team until 1961 when Phillip Edwards, a track athlete from Morgantown, became a member of coach Stan Romanoski's track team. Dean Ray O. Duncan (chair of the WVU Athletic Council and president of the Southern Conference) was quoted in the *Daily*

Athenaeum as saying, "There is no policy concerning Negro athletes here. We don't even have the word Negro in our whole vocabulary." He concluded by saying, "They are perfectly welcome to come out."[17] Later, being a member of the Southern Conference was a negative factor in the integration of WVU athletic teams. Nevertheless, being a member of that conference was also a key factor in the rise of WVU's athletic fortunes in the 1950s.

* * *

WVU played an increasingly difficult football schedule with excellent records through 1957 and earned national rankings in both 1954 and 1955. However, after two losing seasons in 1958 and 1959, Lewis was fired.

Gene Corum, who had played football at Huntington High School and then WVU as a guard, and served as an assistant under Lewis, was named WVU's 26th head football coach. Corum and his assistant Ed Shockey recruited the first two African American football players at WVU: Dick Leftridge, a running back from Hinton, West Virginia, and Roger Alford, an offensive guard from Winterville, Ohio. The pair were recruited in the spring of 1962 and played that fall on the WVU freshman football team. They joined the varsity team in 1963.[18]

Leftridge and Alford integrated Southern Conference football at the same time they integrated WVU football. WVU was a pioneer among major southern colleges in integrating college football. Only the University of Maryland of the ACC integrated football in the same year as WVU, while the Southeastern Conference (SEC) and the ACC for the most part integrated their football teams between 1969 and 1972.[19]

Coach Corum believed there were two forces contributing to the integration of sports, especially football, on the WVU campus. In a 1991 interview Corum said, "Number one, it was the right thing to do. There were black athletes who deserved the same chance as all other athletes, and so WVU, I think, wanted to be one of the leaders in integrating athletic programs for this reason. Other factors, to be honest about it, were that the black athletes lend a lot of talent to the different athletic teams at the University, and it had reached a period of time where it was difficult to compete with integrated teams if you didn't also have the service of the black athletes."[20]

Years later, reflecting on the significance of Coach Corum's contributions, John Mallory, an African American safety on the 1964–1966 teams, said, "Gene helped change the culture at the University by bringing in black athletes."[21]

Alford and Leftridge brought new drama to the playing field during the 1963 and 1964 games, according to Ed Barrett, the former longtime WVU sports information director. "As to media reaction to the integration, it was universally positive right off and probably because all the high school athletic teams in West Virginia were integrated, so there was no problem there. There was trepidation about that [integration] because we [WVU] were in the Southern Conference, and the Southern Conference went as far south as Furman and the Citadel in South Carolina, and then the old Virginia schools like Richmond and William and Mary were in the conference. However, I can't recall incidents."[22]

Ed Pastilong, who became the WVU athletic director from 1989 through 2010, was the quarterback on the 1963 team. A teammate of Alford and Leftridge, he said: "Looking back to these two men, the things I can remember are their 'qualities,' what good football players they were, how well they got along with everyone, and how well everyone respected them. I can't recall of any instances with regard to those two gentlemen having any problems encountered on the team."[23]

Former assistant head football coach Ed Shockey recalled a racially charged situation on a trip to Virginia Tech in 1962. "We went to Blacksburg to play [the] Virginia Tech freshmen.... We had a workout in the evening and it was a short walk to the theater. We got down there and I was paying for the tickets, and the girl at the ticket-counter, according to instructions she had been given, said 'the rest of you can go through, but they [Alford and Leftridge] got to go upstairs.' I said, 'The hell, you think. The hell they will.' I said, 'Give me my money back.' So, we just turned around and went back to the campus and walked around and looked at the campus and I think that's maybe the only time I can recall confrontation or something like that."[24]

During his WVU career, Roger Alford was a three-year varsity athlete at right guard. A stalwart offensive varsity athlete during his varsity football career, he blocked for noted African American running backs Dick Leftridge and Garrett Ford. Alford eventually became a dentist, earning a D.M.S. degree (1975) from the University of Pittsburgh.

Richard "Dick" Leftridge's stellar football career was pounded out game-by-game. Leading the team in rushing in the 1963 and 1964 seasons, Leftridge averaged 5.8 yards per rush in his first year. During his junior year, he rushed 125 times for 534 yards and averaged 4.3 yards per carry. In 1966, the Pittsburgh Steelers drafted Leftridge in the first round as the third overall pick in the NFL draft.

WVU continued to recruit African American players, and the Mountaineers fared well on the field and in the Southern Conference. After a 4–6 record in 1963, WVU posted a 7–4 record in 1964. The 1964 WVU freshman football team included two outstanding African American football players: Garrett Ford (halfback) and John Mallory (safety). The next year, in 1965, Ford and Mallory were promoted to the varsity team. In addition, the team finished the season with a 6–4 record. From 1965 through 1967, WVU went 10–0–1 in the Southern Conference.

Despite the team's success, Coach Corum was fired after six years as the head coach following the 1965 season. In fact, in his last two seasons, the Mountaineers were 13–8. Corum's record was respectable, considering the obstacles WVU faced in the form of antiquated facilities, bad roads, and a declining state economy. However, Lewis' success in the 1950s had created high expectations.

Jim Carlen was hired as WVU's head football coach in 1966 and coached until 1969. Having served 10 years as an assistant under Bobby Dodd at Georgia Tech, Carlen took the job at WVU, advocating for WVU leaving the Southern Conference and for all the football players to have rooms at the Towers Dormitory. Finally, Carlen supported the pre-season training camp coming back to campus.[25]

Garrett Ford and John Mallory were two African American players who straddled the Corum-to-Carlen coaching change. Mallory, recruited from New Jersey, was one of WVU's best all-around defensive players and punt returners. In 1967, during his third year, he "scored three touchdowns from his safety spot, two on punt returns and one on an intercepted pass. He ended his career on defense with nine touchdowns, seven from punt returns."[26] In 1968, the Philadelphia Eagles drafted Mallory.

Garrett Ford was a highly rated running back out of DeMatha Catholic High School in Washington, D.C. He proved to be an outstanding running back for WVU from 1965 to 1967. His first contact with football at WVU was Coach Corum. "So, this guy named Gene Corum called me from West Virginia.

WVU defensive back John Mallory in 1967. During his varsity career he intercepted 10 passes and scored seven touchdowns on punt returns and was named to the All Southern Conference team his junior year. He played for four years in the NFL and two years in the World Football League (courtesy West Virginia and Regional History Center, WVU Libraries).

I had no idea who he was. My dreams were to go to Syracuse," Ford said. "Coach Corum invited me down to West Virginia, and I came down here to visit. I would not come by myself. I brought four or five buddies with me.... They put us up in the Hotel Morgan.... The one thing that impressed me about West Virginia was the people that I met when I came here," recalled Ford.[27]

In 1968, WVU left the Southern Conference. WVU was an independent school until 1978 when it joined the Eastern Eight in basketball and joined the Big East Conference in football in 1991. Carlen increased efforts to recruit African American football players. The 1967 sophomore class included Carl Crennel and the 1968 sophomore class included African American student athletes Jim Braxton and Bob Gresham. Carl Crennel was a three-year starter at middle guard and middle linebacker from Lynchburg, Virginia. During his sophomore year, he earned All-American recognition, and in 1970, the Pittsburgh Steelers drafted him. Bob Gresham was a tailback from War, West Virginia. During his junior year, he rushed for 1,155 yards and was ranked 11th in the country. In 1969, Gresham was named Associated Press Honorable Mention All-American, and went on to a six-year NFL career. Jim Braxton, a fullback from nearby Connellsville, Pennsylvania, is considered one of WVU's most versatile football players. During his college football career, he played tight end and running back, and kicked field goals and extra points. During his three years on the varsity team, he rushed for 1,462 yards and made 906 yards in pass receptions. In his senior year, he was selected first-team All-American and named West Virginia's Amateur Athlete of the Year in 1970. That year he was drafted by the Buffalo Bills and is best remembered as the lead blocking back for O.J. Simpson.

As at other colleges with a small number of African Americans on campus and located in towns with small black populations, black students at WVU faced a lack of social opportunities. That problem was particularly acute at WVU in the 1960s and into the early 1970s. Following the 1954 *Brown* decision, WVU made provisions to accept graduate and undergraduate students on campus, yet few if any activities were initiated to address social and cultural needs once African American students arrived on campus. Former WVU School of Physical Education dean J. William Douglas observed conditions on campus as a student in the late 1950s and the 1960s. Douglas wrote "acts of apparent racial prejudice include[d] the flying of the Confederate flag in front of the Kappa Alpha fraternity house on N. High Street (even though it was banned during football weekends in 1965), segregation practices of certain barbershops in the downtown area, and discriminatory practices at one restaurant downtown against Negroes and foreigners."[28]

John Mallory, the WVU defensive back from Summit, New Jersey, recalled that Coach Corum took a chance recruiting black players. Mallory said, "There were certain risks to that, with athletics come more socialization, friendships born in the fire, things like that. All the things people didn't like. He made up his mind to recruit black athletes. It took courage to do that."[29] Garrett Ford recalled the absence of any support system on campus as well as the need to feel that African American athletes were accepted and valued in the community, in the classroom, and on the playing field. Ford also recalled interacting with students and local blacks off-campus. On the WVU campus, he would play basketball on Sundays against blacks who lived on White Avenue; this provided a sense of community. Ford also said, "people talked to you in class, but when they got outside with their friends, they would ignore you."[30]

By 1966, WVU began to address the concerns of black students and athletes both on campus and on the playing field. In 1966 Victoria Louistall, a library science graduate from WVU, became the first African American faculty member. WVU's president James Harlow established the Office of Black Student Advising, acknowledged support for Black Studies classes, and encouraged the selection of African American cheerleaders.[31]

In 1970, Garrett Ford was hired as the first black coach at WVU. Ford

Running back Garrett Ford was among the early African American football players at WVU, playing from 1964 to 1967. As a junior he set a school record with 1,068 yards rushing. After two seasons in the NFL with the Denver Broncos, he became an assistant football coach at WVU in 1970 and assistant athletic director in 1985 (courtesy West Virginia and Regional History Center, WVU Libraries).

returned to WVU as an assistant football coach after he had played two seasons in the NFL for the Denver Broncos. In addition to his on-field coaching,
Ford worked with student athletes to address their academic and social concerns. First year WVU head football coach Bobby Bowden hired Ford. The
relationship between Ford, an African American from Washington, D.C., and
Bowden, a white southerner from Alabama, went all of the way back to Ford's
days as a player at WVU.

Bowden was WVU's offensive coordinator under Coach Carlen. He had
previously coached at white segregated schools, so Ford, a tailback, was the
first African American player he coached. At first Ford regarded Bowden
with suspicion because of his southern roots, but they became comfortable
enough with each other that Coach Bowden invited Ford to eat dinner at
his house with his family. Ford reported this was the first time he had eaten
dinner with a white family.[32] The respect and friendship between the two led
to Bowden's hiring of Ford. In 1977, Ford was appointed assistant athletic director and promoted to associate athletic director in 2001.The integration of
the basketball team was much different than football.

* * *

Men's basketball was slow getting a foothold on the WVU campus. The
first intercollegiate season was a seven-game schedule in 1904. The biggest
problem the team faced was not the opponents but the lack of basketball facilities. The first court was in the Armory, which, unfortunately, had a slick
playing surface that made games almost comical to watch. In addition, the
commanding officer often canceled basketball games for "more important"
military events. The team lost money and canceled the seasons between 1908
and 1914. The next facility was "the Ark," a dining hall without a heating
source. In 1927, Harry Stansbury, the WVU athletic director, prevailed on the
state legislature to provide funds for a gymnasium, which was called the Field
House. Opened in 1929, it was a huge improvement over previous basketball
courts on campus.

The Field House was considered a "state of the art" facility. Activities
such as track and field, baseball, boxing, wrestling, handball, physical education classes, and commencement exercises, as well as intramurals and dances,
were held in this venue. The second-floor housed office space for the dean of
physical education and athletics, a classroom, and shower facilities. The basketball area could hold 2,500 fans, and when the temporary bleachers were
added, it could accommodate 2,000 additional fans. In 1938, Director of Athletics Harry Stansbury resigned. In recognition of his leadership, the Field
House was later named Stansbury Hall.[33]

The program took another step forward in 1939 when the Mountaineers
hired Dyke Raese as the basketball coach. Raese had an offer from Spencer

High School but took the WVU job for a salary of $1,400, which was less than the Spencer offer. Basketball was held in such low regard at WVU that high school coaching jobs paid more money. There were no basketball scholarships, and the team was filled with local walk-ons and football and baseball players looking for a diversion.[34]

Based on its 16–4 record, WVU was invited to play in the eight-team 1941 National Invitational Tournament (NIT) in New York's Madison Square Garden. A first round upset win over defending champion Long Island University and victories over Toledo and Western Kentucky led to West Virginia University winning the national championship.

Raese joined the Navy at the start of World War II, but the basketball program continued to grow. Scholarships for players, invitations to play in Madison Square Garden games and the NIT, and national rankings became part of the basketball program in the 1940s and beyond. WVU hired Fred Schaus, a former WVU player (1946–1949), All-American, and NBA player, as coach in 1955. Rod "Hot Rod" Hundley and Jerry West, iconic Mountaineers, played on outstanding teams during the Schaus era. In 1959, WVU's greatest basketball season, the Mountaineers suffered a heartbreaking 71–70 loss to the University of California in the NCAA tournament championship game.

In 1962, the best basketball player in West Virginia was Ron "Fritz" Williams, an African American sophomore from Weirton, a prosperous steel mill town in the Northern Panhandle of the state. It was clear to George King, the basketball coach who replaced Schaus in 1961, that WVU desperately needed to break tradition and recruit Williams. Ron "Fritz" Williams was a basketball prodigy. Doug Huff, the dean of West Virginia sportswriters, who frequently saw Williams play in high school, said, "He played on the varsity as a freshman. He was muscular and was so much more advanced than kids his age."[35]

Williams lived up to his early promise by leading Weir High to the West Virginia high school AAA state champion game in his next three years, where they won the 1963 crown. A multi-sport athlete, he also led Weir High School to state football championships in 1960 and 1961. Williams averaged 30 points a game as a senior in 1964. So many people wanted to see him play that all of the Weir High games, both home and away, were sold out. He led the Red Riders to an undefeated season and the state championship game, where Logan defeated Weir, 81–73, in a foul-marred game that people in Weirton still complain about. Williams had been the best player in West Virginia for three years and West Virginia University coach George King desperately wanted him to play for the Mountaineers. No African American, though, had ever played basketball at West Virginia University or in the Southern Conference. In addition, Williams did not want to be a pioneer. Williams had his choice of colleges, receiving 102 basketball and 20 football scholarship offers. He was leaning toward Michigan and Ohio State, both of which had integrated athletic teams. The black community in Weirton, West Virginia, encouraged Williams to enroll in West Virginia University and play basketball.[36]

So that Williams would not be alone on the WVU team, Coach King recruited two other African Americans, Jim Lewis, a six-foot, two-inch All-Metro player from Alexandria, Virginia, and Ed Harvard, Williams' teammate at Weir High School. When Williams agreed to play for the Mountaineers, the WVU fans were ecstatic. "He was like a Jerry West coming out of high school," said teammate Ed Harvard.[37] Later that summer, King added Norman Holmes, an ex–Marine from Washington, D.C., to the team. West Virginia University basketball and Southern Conference basketball both were integrated in 1965 with the four WVU African Americans.

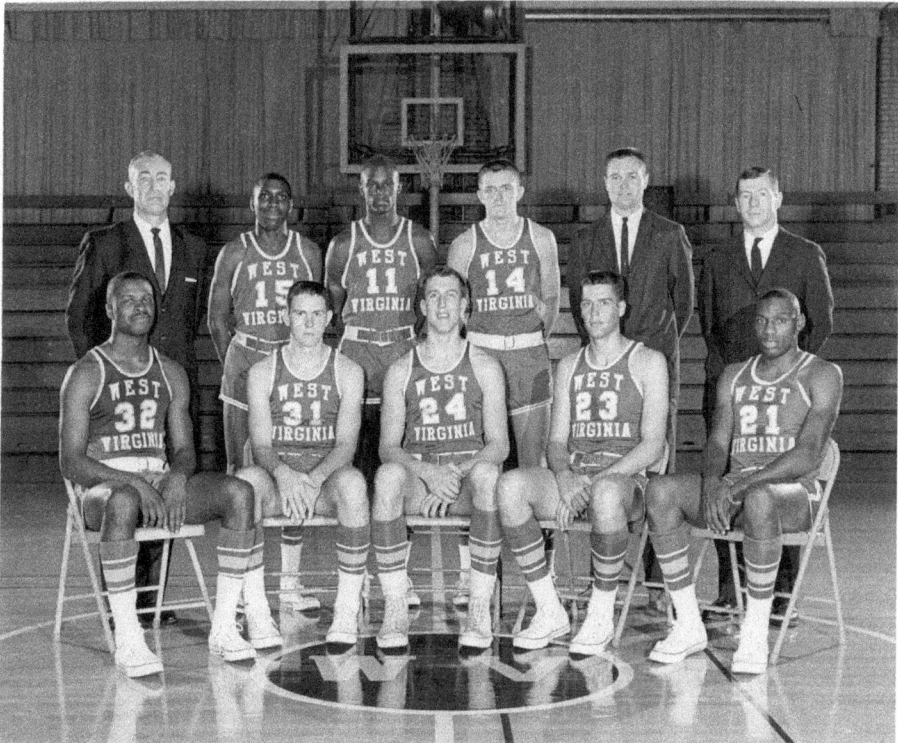

The West Virginia University 1965 freshman basketball team integrated both WVU and Southern Conference basketball. The team had a spectacular 20–1 record. All four of the African American players went on to varsity careers. Front, left to right: Jim Lewis, Letcher Humphries, Dick Penrod, David Reaser, Ron Williams. Back, left to right: Coach Quentin Barnett, Ed Harvard, Norman Holmes, Lewis Hale, Graduate Assistants—Jim Warren and Bucky DeVries (courtesy West Virginia and Regional History Center, WVU Libraries).

The 1965 WVU freshman team was outstanding. With Williams averaging more than 30 points a game, the team went 20–1 against a tough schedule while the varsity went 14–15. Many Mountaineer fans came for the freshman game and left before the varsity took the floor. That spring George King accepted the head coaching job at Purdue University and was replaced with Bucky Walters, an assistant coach from Duke.

The four players who integrated WVU basketball could not help recapture the glory years of Mountaineer basketball, though they did produce good 19–9 records each season from 1966 through 1968. The Mountaineers could no longer dominate the Southern Conference. Coach Lefty Driesell was building a powerhouse program at Davidson College, who beat WVU in the Southern Conference tournament in both 1966 and 1968. In 1967, WVU won the regular season title and beat Davidson, 81–65, in the conference tournament; as a result, they were invited to play in the NCAA tournament.[38]

During their three-year varsity careers Holmes was a part-time starter, Lewis was a solid back up, but Harvard received little playing time. Williams more than lived up to his early promise. He averaged 19.7 points per game as a sophomore and 20 points per game in his junior and senior seasons. He was named to the Southern Conference All-Conference team each year. Ironically, in a conference that was slow to integrate, at the end of his senior year Williams was named Southern Conference Basketball Player of the Year and Southern Conference Athlete of the Year.[39] He was the first African American player to win either one of those awards. Williams played eight NBA seasons and, following his retirement from the NBA, coached at University of California Berkley and Iona College.

The racial situation at WVU was difficult for the four black players. Jim Lewis in an interview with author John Antonik described Morgantown of that time as having nothing for black players. On the road, WVU's black players faced name-calling and threats of physical violence. "Richmond was the worst," said Lewis. "We had to have a police escort and have the cops take us in because those people were vicious back then."[40]

By the mid-1960s, WVU's basketball coaches increased the recruiting of student athletes beyond the borders of West Virginia. In 1967, for the first time the team had more out-of-state than in-state student-athletes. Coach Waters said, "As far as recruiting black players, we tried to get the best players we could." Waters recalled, "It was hard, really hard to bring good players from out-of-state no matter whether they were black or white because our facilities were not good."[41] Recruiting out-of-state players into the antiquated Field House was difficult. Waters insisted that WVU would need to build a new facility if it was to be successful as an independent team after leaving the Southern Conference.

But in 1966, Waters was able to recruit a couple of outstanding African American players, including Carl Head from Dodge City (Kansas) Junior College, whose great jumping ability had earned him selection as a junior college first-team All-American. In 1969, Waters also recruited Wil Robinson from Uniontown, Pennsylvania, who was selected as a third team All-American in his senior year.

The West Virginia Coliseum, a state of the art 14,000 seat basketball facility, was completed in 1970. Although Waters had been a major force in the push for a top-quality basketball venue, he never coached in the new facility because he accepted the head coaching position at Duke University in 1969. The WVU basketball team moved into the Coliseum in 1970. Throughout the 1970s, WVU made a strong effort to recruit outstanding West Virginia high school African American men's basketball players, in addition to out-of-state players. In the late 1970s, several

WVU's Ron Williams (21) was named the Southern Conference Basketball Player of the Year and Southern Conference Athlete of the Year in 1968 (courtesy West Virginia and Regional History Center, WVU Libraries).

West Virginia University African American men's basketball players went on to play in the National Basketball Association. They included Jerome Anderson, Tony Robertson, Will Robertson, and Ron "Fritz" Williams.[42]

The construction of the coliseum in 1970 and the new Mountaineer Field in 1980 improved facilities, and the completion of interstates I-79 and I-68 made it easier to drive to Morgantown because it was connected to the interstate highway system in three directions. The improved facilities and highway access brought WVU into the 20th century and improved the ability of the Mountaineers to successfully recruit on a regional basis.[43]

* * *

Other men's teams at WVU integrated in the 1960s and 1970s. The track and field program was established at WVU in 1898. In 1925, the "old" Mountaineer Field was completed with a cinder track and, in 1929, the new Field House provided an indoor track for the team.[44] Both facilities helped promote and build the program. Long-time coach Stan Romanoski began his coaching tenure in 1958. Under his leadership, Phillip Edwards, from Morgantown, became the first African American athlete to compete in intercollegiate sports at WVU. In a 1961 *Daily Athenaeum* story titled "First Negro Out for Track Shatters University Athletics Color Barrier," coach Stan Romanoski was quoted as saying that Edwards was a talented track and field athlete. Romanoski made no mention of Edwards being African American.[45]

Edwards recalled his WVU career: "When I came out for track, the last thing on my mind was my color. I was welcomed with open arms by Stan Romanoski (head coach), and nothing, nothing was said about my color until I read about it in the newspaper."[46] However, Edwards experienced racism away from the WVU campus. He said, "At VMI I was called a nigger. All those guys apologized to me later. In Richmond I was forced to eat in the basement instead of the dining room at a restaurant called 'The Rebel,' of all things."[47]

The wrestling team and the soccer team were the next teams to integrate when Norman Hill, a 230-pound football player from Morristown, New Jersey, became a member of the wrestling team in 1965. The following year Jim Stevens, the 1965 West Virginia State High School Champion in the 120-pound class from Morgantown High School, joined the team. In 1966, Stevens wrestled in the 137-pound class at WVU and was a member of the WVU team that won the 1967 Southern Conference wrestling championship. George Woods, Jr., also from Morgantown, was a goalie on the 1965 WVU soccer team and played four seasons while on an ROTC scholarship. He played an important role in WVU's winning the 1965 Southern Conference soccer championship.

Baseball, which at WVU began in the 1890s, did not integrate until 1976 when longtime WVU baseball coach Dr. Dale Ramsberg recruited Bruce Clinton from Martinsburg, West Virginia. Clinton enrolled as a transfer student from Potomac State College, arriving on the WVU campus with an ROTC scholarship. After graduation, Clinton became the basketball coach at University High School in Morgantown.

Dual-sport student-athletes, especially among African American men on scholarship, are rare on major college teams. Nevertheless, Fulton Walker, from Martinsburg, West Virginia, who was a running back for WVU and later for the Miami Dolphins, also played two seasons on the WVU baseball team. Walker, who played 1979–81, had a two-year batting average of .244. Darrell Whitmore, who played 1989–1990, was another WVU football player who doubled as a college baseball player. After his college career ended, he was drafted in the second round by the Cleveland Indians and had a professional baseball career.

* * *

The integration of women's athletic teams at WVU did not occur until much later than the men's teams because WVU did not begin a women's intercollegiate athletic program until after the passage of Title IX in 1972. Title IX of the Educational Amendments Act banned sex discrimination in schools receiving federal funds and had a significant impact on the future of women's athletic programs nationally as well as at WVU. Under that federal mandate, Athletic Director Dr. Leland Byrd submitted a proposal in August 1972 to the university administration to organize a women's athletic program on campus. West Virginia University, similar to other colleges and universities across the United States, had until 1978 to implement the law.

Under Title IX, the first three WVU women's teams—gymnastics, tennis, and basketball—were established in 1973–1974. The coaches were Nanette Schnabel (gymnastics), Martha Thorn (tennis), and Kittie Blakemore (basketball). Volleyball, coached by Judy Thomas, was added in 1974–75. All four coaches held joint faculty and coaching appointments within the School of Physical Education and, thus, were expected to teach physical education classes in addition to coaching. Swimming, coached by Donna Henderson, was added in 1975–76, and in 1978–79, Linda King was hired to coach indoor and outdoor track and cross-country.[48] Since 1973, the participation of African American women on WVU athletic teams has varied by sport, but the women's basketball and track and field squads have accounted for most of the African American women student-athletes.

Women's basketball, under coach Kittie Blakemore, was begun in 1973–74. Home games were played in the Coliseum. The Association for Intercollegiate Athletics for Women (AIAW) governed women's intercollegiate sports for women until 1982–83 when the NCAA took over control of women's college sports.[49] In 1973, with much excitement and anticipation, Kittie Blakemore became West Virginia University's first head women's basketball coach. During the initial year of play, Blakemore faced many challenges and opportunities, such as finding appropriate uniforms for the players and conducting team tryout sessions with a varying degree of talent and playing experience among the players. Yet the common thread that united the players was the desire to learn the game of basketball.[50]

During the initial season of women's basketball on WVU's campus, the Lady Mountaineers played their first game in the Coliseum against West Liberty in 1973. The game was a 59–55 victory for WVU.[51] During the 1975 season, Rachel Crawford, from Hinton, West Virginia, became the first African

American on the basketball team. She played only one year before returning home to Hinton. Unfortunately, Crawford's life ended too soon, when, in 1992, she was murdered in southern West Virginia.[52]

In 1983, when WVU joined the Atlantic 10 Conference, more African American players were recruited from out of state. Three of the outstanding players from that era were J.D. Drummonds (Hallandale, Florida), Cathy Parsons (Hagerstown, Maryland), and Olivia Bradley (Bradenton, Florida). All four scored more than 1,000 points during their college basketball careers. Parsons' honors include WVU all-time leading scorer (2,128 points) and selection as an All-American and three-time team MVP. On December 21, 1984, in a game against the University of Charleston, African American Georgeann Wells (Columbus, Ohio) became the first woman to dunk the basketball in a college game.[53]

The track team was integrated in 1976 when it was still a club team. Cheryl Nabors Phillips (1976–1979), from Institute, West Virginia, participated on the club team and then on the intercollegiate team when it was started under coach Linda King in 1978. African American Connie Ellerbe became WVU's first female track and field athlete to earn All-American status in 1992. She also placed 6th in high jump in the 1990 NCAA championships.

Other women's teams at WVU integrated in the 1980s and 1990s. The tennis team was integrated in 1981 when Shirley Robinson, a graduate of Morgantown High School, walked on the team. "There was the excitement of being able to play when we were trying out, to play with a different caliber of tennis players than I had ever played at that time," Robinson said. "I just enjoyed my experiences coming straight out of high school into college. I wanted to increase my level of play here at the university."[54]

Robinson played only the 1981–82 season on the women's tennis team. Later she became a minister and worked in the WVU Office of the Provost.

In 1993 Dr. Kevin Gilson, who was coaching men's and women's swimming and diving, was made aware of African American twins Valerie and Vanessa Patterson. The Patterson sisters swam for the Philadelphia Aquatic Club, and WVU offered Valerie a full scholarship and Vanessa a partial scholarship. Eventually, Gilson was able to make Vanessa's a full scholarship. Once the Pattersons were on campus, Coach Gilson summarized their behavior as hard working, team-oriented, and disciplined. Valerie set records in free style (500, 1,000, and 1650). Vanessa was a middle-distance sprinter, in the backstroke, and in the medley.[55]

* * *

In 2006, Marlon LeBlanc was named the WVU soccer coach. He was WVU's first African American head coach in any sport, and WVU's only African American head coach. Born in East Windsor, New Jersey, LeBlanc played high school soccer, earning All-State recognition. He played soccer at Penn State University and graduated in 2000 with a degree in economics. LeBlanc was an assistant coach at Penn State from 2001 to 2006, helping guide the Nittany Lions to four NCAA tournaments. At WVU LeBlanc has amassed a 10-season coaching record as of 2017 of 114–84–32, leading the Mountaineers to five NCAA tournament berths while also winning the Big East in 2006 and the Mid-American Conference in 2012. His teams have been consistently ranked in the Top 25. LeBlanc was named one of the *Morgantown Dominion Post*'s 100 most influential people in 2007. He was active on campus in supporting the OneWVU initiative to promote racial diversity on campus.[56]

* * *

From 1891 to 2017, the number of African American student-athletes on WVU's campus increased from zero to 169. Evidence suggests the integration of sports teams at WVU has been and remains uneven. Early African American WVU male student-athletes experienced a variety of social and cultural barriers on and off the playing field. The student-athletes were applauded for their physical prowess yet remained marginalized and isolated in the local community.

Nevertheless, the story of Major Harris illustrates how far WVU had come by the late 1980s. Harris was an exceptional high school quarterback in Pittsburgh, but, in 1986, many colleges still shied away from recruiting black quarterbacks. Harris had numerous offers, but they were for him to play defensive back. WVU coach Don Nehlen made it clear to Harris that he wanted him to come to Morgantown as a quarterback. Harris was interested. "When schools started recruiting me, I looked at whether they had a black quarterback before. John Talley had played quarterback at WVU in 1985 and the school was close to home. Those things sold me," said Harris.[57]

In a bold move, the West Virginia coaching staff decided to start Major Harris, a redshirt freshman, as quarterback to open the 1987 season. When the team slumped to a 1–3 record, with losses to Ohio State, Maryland, and Pitt, some Mountaineer fans became extremely critical of Harris' play, in part because the team was losing, but also because Harris was a black quarterback. As the season progressed, though, the team began to jell. A 5–2 record over the last seven games of the season earned the Mountaineers a Sun Bowl bid.

With Major Harris and 25 seniors, the 1988 Mountaineers were loaded with experienced players. A 51–30 victory over Penn State at State College pushed the Mountaineers to an 8–0 record. By the season's end, WVU was 11–0 and ranked number three in the polls. The Fiesta Bowl that season matched Notre Dame and WVU, the only two undefeated major college teams in the country.

Early in the game, Harris suffered an AC sprain where the shoulder blade and collarbone had come apart at the joint where they meet. "This was a huge blow to our strategy. We had planned to turn Major loose and let Notre Dame try to stop him," said Nehlen.[58] "They asked me if I could go," said Harris. "Of course, I said yes because we were playing for the national championship. I had dreamed about doing that my whole life. But I was in intense pain and I could not lift my left arm above my shoulder."[59]

Notre Dame led, 23–6, at halftime. In the second half, the Mountaineers rallied to score 15 points. Despite his injury and playing in pain, Harris passed for 166 yards and was able to lead WVU to 21 points against Notre Dame with one arm. However, the magic that Harris had conjured all season to lead the Mountaineers in come-from-behind victories was gone with the injury. Notre Dame held on for a 34–21 victory and the national championship. The bitterly disappointed Mountaineers were ranked a very respectable number five in the final national poll.

The next season Harris led the Mountaineers to an 8–3–1 record and was named to the Football Coaches All-American team and finished third in the Heisman voting. His three-year record as the Mountaineers quarterback was an excellent 25–10–1. Major Harris became the face of the WVU team and a heroic figure in the state of West Virginia. However, more importantly, he destroyed the myth that had still been held by some people in West Virginia that African Americans did not have the intelligence or leadership ability to successfully play quarterback.[60]

* * *

A number of negative factors affected both WVU's recruiting of African American athletes and the decision of African American athletes to attend or not attend WVU from 1954 through the 1970s. The most significant of those factors were:

    1. WVU played in the Southern Conference;

    2. WVU recruited players primarily in West Virginia and eastern Ohio and western Pennsylvania;

    3. there were very negative stereotypes about the State of West Virginia; and

    4. there was only a very small support group of African American faculty, staff, students, and coaches on campus and in Morgantown.

WVU integrated the football and men's basketball team more quickly after the *Brown* decision than other states that had segregated school systems. However, it took 10 years before four African American basketball players were on the WVU freshman team. WVU integrated the Southern Conference in both football and basketball, but the rest of the conference was very slow to pursue integration even after WVU broke the color barrier in the major sports. There were strong rumors that the Southern Conference and member colleges discouraged its members from recruiting black athletes. In addition, the travel by integrated teams in the states of North Carolina, South Carolina, and Virginia was difficult in terms of both accommodations and dining. In 1968, WVU withdrew from the Southern Conference to play an independent schedule in part because it was difficult to recruit African American athletes to play in the conference. Black athletes were also hesitant to attend WVU because of the rising tensions and violence over civil rights in the South.

By the mid–1960s, the WVU coaches began to recruit more out-of-state athletes. The population in West Virginia had declined by almost 200,000 between 1950 and 1960 and the black population in West Virginia was small, at around 6 percent. Other states were growing, while West Virginia was shrinking in population. In 1950, the population of West Virginia was a little more than two million. Since then the population of the state has stabilized at around 1.8 million. The African American percentage of the state's population has declined to about 3.6 percent. Both factors encouraged the WVU coaches to expand their recruiting base to larger states and states with larger African American populations. From the mid–1960s, more out-of-state athletes and African Americans were members of WVU athletic teams.

In the 1960s and into the 1970s, negative stereotypes about West Virginia being a poor and backward state discouraged black athletes from selecting WVU. The pictures and stories that came out during President Lyndon Johnson's "War on Poverty" enhanced those images. They showed a state that modernity had passed by. On the WVU campus, the antiquated Field House and old Mountaineer Field were both products of an earlier generation and were showing their wear. They underscored that WVU as well as the state was out of date. At the same time, the lack of interstate highways and the poor roads throughout the state made driving to Morgantown arduous and time-consuming.

The completion of the 14,000 seat WVU Coliseum for basketball in 1970, the completion of Interstate 79 through Morgantown in the late 1970s (east–west Interstate 68 was completed in 1991), and the completion of the new 60,000 seat Mountaineer Field in 1980 brought WVU sports into the 20th century. The completion of the two interstate highways through Morgantown made travel easier. A new coaching philosophy based on talent, the desire by alumni and administrators to produce quality and successful athletic teams, access to quality athletic facilities, and the opportunity for African American student-athletes to play for nationally recognized higher education institutions promoting quality athletic teams were factors leading to an increase in the number of African American athletes on campus. The hiring of African American staff, such as Garrett Ford and Horace Belmear, and African American faculty, along with a vigorous effort to recruit African American students, made the WVU campus more welcoming to black students.

WVU has made progress in hiring African American administrators, faculty, and assistant coaches, but the only black head coach in WVU history was Marlon LeBlanc, the head soccer coach. It is clear that WVU must put a plan in place to promote black head coaches from within the existing assistant coaches or recruit African American head coaches from other colleges. This is not an easy task. For example, in NCAA Division 1 there were 16 black head football coaches and 205 white coaches (data excludes HBCUs). The usual career path to an open head football coaching position is by being a head coach at another college or being a coordinator. In 2015, there were 50 black defensive coordinators in NCAA Division I and 198 white defensive coordinators. During the same time, there were 13 black offensive coordinators and 240 white offensive coordinators. The other best possibilities are men's and women's basketball and women's track, where there are a number of African American athletes on the teams and numerous coaches with playing experience.[61]

Epilogue

In the post-integration era, high schools and colleges in West Virginia have continued to produce outstanding African American athletes. Among those athletes are Randy Moss (football, DuPont High School—Marshall University), Vicky Bullett (basketball, Martinsburg—University of Maryland), Fritz Williams (basketball, Weirton—WVU), O.J. Mayo (basketball, Huntington—University of Southern California), Patrick Patterson (basketball, Huntington—University of Kentucky), Carl Lee (football, South Charleston—Marshall University), Bimbo Coles (basketball, Greenbrier East—Virginia Tech), Curt Warner (football, Pineville—Penn State), Kerry Marbury (football and track, Marion County—WVU), and Garnet Edwards (track and football, Welch—WVU). All of these men and woman were excellent high school and college athletes with significant All-American or professional athletic careers, and there are countless others.

What would have happened to them if they had played in the era of segregation? For example, Randy Moss was voted West Virginia Player of the Year in both football and basketball at DuPont High School in his senior year, 1994–95. He was a college All-American football player and was inducted into the Pro Football Hall of Fame in 2018. He grew up in Rand, a tiny village in Kanawha County 23 miles east of Charleston. During segregation, he would have attended the all-black London Washington High School. Despite being an excellent football and basketball player, he would have been ignored by most white coaches because few white colleges, and no Southern white colleges, recruited black players. Moreover, London is located in the heart of rural West Virginia, which would have made it difficult for most coaches to learn about him. However, Moss would have been very visible to the coaches at West Virginia State when his team would have played in the segregated regional basketball tournament in Charleston and in the WVAU state basketball tournament on the West Virginia State campus. Moss would have been offered a scholarship to West Virginia State, where many athletes played both football and basketball.

While at State, there is no doubt that Moss would have dominated the very competitive CIAA conference, particularly in football. If he had played in the early 1950s, he might have had a tryout for either the NFL or NBA. Prior to that, he would have been limited to playing on a local semi-pro football team, although in basketball he might have played with the Harlem Globetrotters or a semi-professional team like the New York Renaissance. No matter how good he was as an athlete, his options would have been severely limited by the color of his skin. He would have been hidden by the veil of segregation, unknown to all but a few sports fans. With integration, his high school records would have been lost when the records of the black high schools were destroyed, and the memories of his skills would have soon faded.

In an effort to preserve the memories and to celebrate the accomplishments of the black schools, Helen L. Jackson-Gillison led the formation of the West Virginia All Black Schools Sports & Academic Hall of Fame in 2008. The Hall of Fame was founded to do research and to preserve the history of the black schools in West Virginia and to recognize the legacies of the athletic and academic role models that the black schools produced. The Hall of Fame held annual two-day induction ceremonies in Charleston that included social events, historical presentations, and a black-tie induction ceremony. The Hall of Fame stimulated research on the individual black high schools and colleges and published the results in the event program along with profiles of outstanding athletes, leaders, and students. The Hall of Fame inductions were gala affairs that drew African Americans from across the state and brought others home to attend, tying the black communities together just as the WVAU tournaments did during the era of segregation. Unfortunately, because of lack of funds, the last induction was held in 2015.

Integration created many more opportunities for African Americans and African American athletes, but it was a bittersweet experience. Opal Jones, a graduate of Lewisburg Bolling High School, said, "We knew we had to know what everyone else knew, but we hated to lose our schools." An additional loss would be the failure to record the accomplishments of those schools and their students. The *Brown* decision declared that "separate educational facilities are inherently unequal." The implication might be that the black schools were inherently inferior, but a truer reading of the decision might lead us to recognize that everyone loses when the entire community does not have access to its schools. Sports provide a visible and objective measure of achievement, showing the talent that is lost when everyone is not given an opportunity to compete. When schools and their teams, which are the heart and soul of a community, do not include all of its members, we lose an important opportunity to strengthen the bonds which support our institutions and enrich our lives.

Appendix:
Pioneers in the Integration
of College Sports
in West Virginia

Compiled by DANA BROOKS,
RON ALTHOUSE *and* BOB BARNETT

1921–22

Walter Jean (fb)   Bethany College*

1950–1951

William Reape (bb)   WV Wesleyan

1954–1955

Billy Owens (fb)   Concord State
Roy Meeks (fb)   Fairmont State
John Smith (fb)   Fairmont State
Sam Garrison (fb)   Fairmont State
Hal Greer (bb)   Marshall College
Robert Smith (fb)   Potomac State
Roy Watson (base)   Alderson Broaddus
Luvall Wilson (tk)   WV Wesleyan

1955–1956

James Taylor (fb)   Shepherd College
Hal Greer (base)   Marshall College
Roy Goines (fb)   Marshall College
Ray Crisp (fb)   Marshall College

197

Howard Barrett (fb)	Marshall College
Walter West (fb)	Marshall College
William Perry (bb & base)	Potomac State
Raymond Coleman (base)	Potomac State
David Coleman (base)	Potomac State
Jo Ellen Flagg(fh)	WV Wesleyan
William Grant (bb)	Shepherd College (transfer from Storer)
William Miller (bb)	Shepherd College (transfer from Storer)

1956–1957

Ernestine Knox (fh)	Fairmont State
Moses Guin (fb, wr, tk)	Fairmont State

1957–1958

Curtis Guin (fb, bb, tk)	Fairmont State
Roy Johnson (bb)	Fairmont State

1958–1959

Burial Holmes (fb & tk)	West Liberty State
Vernie Bolden (tk & cc)	Marshall College
Charles Gordon (tk & cc)	Marshall College
Lloyd Briscoe (tk bb fb)	Bethany College
Robert Sanders (ten)	Salem College

1959–1960

William Turner (bb)	WV Tech
John Wilson (bb)	Salem College

1961–1962

Bob Douglas (fb & wr)	West Liberty
Phil Edwards (tk)	WVU

1962–1963

Roger Alford (fb)	WVU
Dick Leftridge (fb)	WVU

1963–64

Hugh Hollingsworth (cc)	Potomac State
Amos McKenzie (bb)	Alderson Broaddus

1964–65

Garrett Ford (fb)	WVU
John Mallory (fb)	WVU
Bob Minneweather (bb)	Glenville State
Gerald Martin (bb)	Morris Harvey
Kenny Minor (bb)	Morris Harvey
Glen Long (base)	Davis & Elkins

1965–1966

Samuel Burns (bb)	Glenville State
Ron Williams (bb)	WVU
Ed Harvard (bb)	WVU
Jim Lewis (bb)	WVU
Norman Holmes (bb)	WVU
Norman Hill (fb & wr)	WVU
Ronnie Simms (bb)	Davis & Elkins
Ernie Whitted (fb)	Bethany College

1966–1967

Jim Stevens (wr)	WVU
Jackie Joe Robinson (fb bb base)	Glenville State

1969–1970

Beverly Duckwyler (bb & vb)	Marshall U

1970–1971

Brenda Dennis (bb & vb)	Marshall U
Frankie Nowlin (fh)	Marshall U

1971–1972

Judy Allen (bb &vb)	Marshall U
Deloris Morrow (vb)	Marshall U

1975–1976

Rachel Crawford (bb)	WVU

1976–1977

Bruce Clinton (base)	WVU

1977–1978

Harry Moore (tennis)   WVU

1981–1982

Shirley Robinson (tennis)   WVU

*Mixed race (Father was black—mother was white)

Chapter Notes

Chapter 1

1. West Virginia Archives and History website, www.wvculture.org/history/archivesindex.aspx, accessed 12/04/12.

2. John Alexander Williams, *West Virginia: A History* (Morgantown: West Virginia University Press, 2001): 78.

3. Lawrence V. Jordan, "Educational Integration in West Virginia—One Year Afterward," *The Journal of Negro Education* 24, n. 3 (Summer 1955): 371.

4. Charles H. Ambler, *A History of Education in West Virginia from Early Colonial Times to 1949* (Huntington: Standard, 1951): 404–405.

5. West Virginia Archives and History website, www.wvculture.org/history/archivesindex.aspx, accessed 12/04/12.

6. Joe William Trotter, Jr., *Coal, Class, and Color: Blacks in Southern West Virginia 1915-32* (Urbana: University of Illinois Press, 1990): 78.

7. Joe William Trotter, Jr., *Coal, Class, and Color: Blacks in Southern West Virginia 1915-32*, 78.

8. "Harlem Renaissance," in Eric Foner and John A. Garraty, eds., *The Reader's Companion to American History* (Boston: Houghton Mifflin, 1991): 487–488.

9. Joe William Trotter, Jr., *Coal, Class, and Color: Blacks in Southern West Virginia 1915-32*, 52.

10. *Weirton Daily Times*, July 30, 1976.

11. Robert Pruter, *The Rise of American High School Sports and the Search for Control 1880-1930* (Syracuse: Syracuse University Press, 2013): 193–196.

12. Bob Barnett, *Hillside Fields: A History of Sports in West Virginia* (Morgantown: West Virginia University Press, 2013): 352–354.

13. Bureau of Negro Welfare and Statistics State of West Virginia: Biennial Report, 1951–1952.

14. Joe William Trotter, Jr., *Coal, Class, and Color: Blacks in Southern West Virginia 1915-32*, 164–165.

15. Joe William Trotter, Jr., *Coal, Class, and Color: Blacks in Southern West Virginia 1915-32*, 150, 151.

16. Ancella R. Bickley, *History of the West Virginia State Teacher's Association* (Washington, D.C.: National Education Association, 1979).

17. Charles H. Ambler, *A History of Education in West Virginia from Early Colonial Times to 1949*, 409.

18. David A. Corbin, *Life, Work, and Rebellion in the Coal Fields: The Southern West Virginia Miners 1880-1922* (Urbana: University of Illinois Press, 1989): 69.

19. Bureau of Negro Welfare and Statistics, 1951–52, 71.

20. Joe William Trotter, Jr., "African-American Heritage," in Ken Sullivan, ed., *The West Virginia Encyclopedia* (Charleston: The West Virginia Humanities Council, 2006): 4, 5.

21. Sam Stack, "Integration," in Ken Sullivan, ed., *The West Virginia Encyclopedia*, 363, 364.

22. Sam Stack, "Integration," in Ken Sullivan, ed., *The West Virginia Encyclopedia*, 363, 364.

23. Joe William Trotter, Jr., "African-American Heritage," in Ken Sullivan, ed., *The West Virginia Encyclopedia*, 5.

Chapter 2

1. *Storer Record*, school newspaper, December 1900 and December 1901.

2. See, Lewis R. Harlan, *Booker T. Washington: The Making of a Black Leader: 1856–1901*, vol. 1 (New York: Oxford University Press, 1972); Lewis R. Harlan, *Booker T. Washington: The Wizard of Tuskegee, 1901–1915*, vol. 2 (New York: Oxford University Press, 1983); and Joseph Bundy, "Booker T. Washington," in Ken Sullivan, ed., *The West Virginia Encyclopedia* (Charleston: The West Virginia Humanities Council, 2006): 743–744.

3. See, Manning Marable, *W.E.B. DuBois: Black Radical Democrat* (London: Routledge, 1986); and Paul Cruse, "Accommodation versus Struggle," in Mary Young and Gerald Horace, eds., *W.E.B. Dubois: An Encyclopedia* (Westport, CT: Greenwood Publishing Group, 2001).

4. See, Kofi Lomotey, *Encyclopedia of African American Education* (New York: Sage Publishing, 2009).

5. Ocania Chalk, *Black College Sport* (New York: Dodd, Mead, 1976): 197–198; and Pamela Grundy, *Learning to Win: Sports, Education, and Social Change in Twentieth-Century North Carolina* (Chapel Hill: University of North Carolina Press, 2001): 18.

6. Ocania Chalk, *Black College Sport*, 198, 199.

7. Ocania Chalk, *Black College Sport*, 230.

8. Ocania Chalk, *Black College Sport*, 230–239.

9. Raymond Schmidt, *College Football: The Shaping of an American Sport: 1919–1930* (Syracuse: Syracuse University Press, 2007): 138–145.

10. Ocania Chalk, *Black College Sport*, 41–69.

11. Howard B. Grose, "The Story of Storer College," *Missions: A Baptist Monthly Newsletter* (September 1920): 476–484. (All of the Storer College information cited is located in the Storer College collection.) West Virginia University Libraries, West Virginia and Regional History Collection.

12. Stephanie Shapiro, "A Black College Closed in 1955, but Its Fading Alumni Fight to Pass on a Legacy," *Washington Post Magazine* (October 22, 2015).

13. See, Dawne Raines Burke, *An American Phoenix: A History of Storer College from Slavery to Desegregation, 1865–1955* (Morgantown: West Virginia University Press, 2015).

14. James Green, Jr., personal interview, March 19, 2016.

15. James Green, Jr., personal interview, March 19, 2016; and Storer College, "Annual Report of the President to the Board of Trustees," May 25, 1955, 1–2 and 6. West Virginia University Libraries, West Virginia and Regional History Collection.

16. Robert Pruter, *The Rise of American High School Sports and the Search for Control: 1880–1930* (Syracuse: Syracuse University Press, 2013): 283.

17. *Storer Record*, school newspaper, May 1913.

18. *Storer Record*, school newspaper, December 1900.

19. *Storer Record*, school newspaper, December 1901.

20. *Storer Record*, school newspaper, December 1901.

21. *Storer Record*, school newspaper, December 1912.

22. *Storer Sentinel*, school alumni newsletter, vol. 2, 1909–1910, 35–37; *Storer Record*, school newspaper, May 1911, and May 1912.

23. *Storer Record*, school newspaper, May 1919.

24. *Storer Record*, school newspaper, June 1922.

25. James Green, Jr., personal interview, March 19, 2016

26. *Storer Record*, school newspaper, December 1922.

27. *Storer Record*, school newspaper, December 1926.

28. *Storer Record*, school newspaper, December 1926.

29. "Storer College Ten Year Report, 1930–1939," West Virginia University Libraries, West Virginia and Regional History Collection.

30. "Storer College Ten Year Report, 1930–1939," West Virginia University Libraries, West Virginia and Regional History Collection.

31. Dawne Raines Burke, *An American Phoenix: A History of Storer College from Slavery to Desegregation, 1865–1955*, 136.

32. *Storer Record*, school newspaper, May 1953, 3, 4.

33. Storer College, "Annual Report of the President," October 9, 1954, 3, 7. West Virginia University Libraries, West Virginia and Regional History Collection.

34. Storer College, "Annual Report of the

President," October 9, 1954, 3, 7. West Virginia University Libraries, West Virginia and Regional History Collection.

35. Storer College, "Annual Report of the President to the Board of Trustees," May 25, 1955, 1–2 and 6. West Virginia University Libraries, West Virginia and Regional History Collection.

36. Barbara Rasmussen, "Storer College," Ken Sullivan, ed., *The West Virginia Encyclopedia*, 685.

37. William P. Jackameit, "A Short History of Negro Public Education in West Virginia, 1890–1965," *West Virginia History* 37, n. 4 (July 1976): 311.

38. William P. Jackameit, "A Short History of Negro Public Higher Education in West Virginia, 1890–1965," 315.

39. John Clifford Harlan, *History of West Virginia State College* (Dubuque, IA: Wm. C. Brown, 1968): 129; and *Elojo*, West Virginia State College yearbook, 1923, 92–93.

40. Fred R. Toothman, *Wild Wonderful Winners: Great Football Coaches of West Virginia* (Huntington: Vandalia, 1991): 112–117.

41. *Pittsburgh Courier*, December 6, 1924.

42. Raymond Schmidt, "Another Football World (Part III of III)," *College Football Historical Society Newsletter* XVIII, n. III (May 2005): 9–11; and Ocania Chalk, *Black College Sport*, 236–241.

43. John Clifford Harlan, *History of West Virginia State College*, 135–136.

44. Fred R. Toothman, *Wild Wonderful Winners: Great Football Coaches of West Virginia*, 112–117.

45. *Bluefield Colored Institute Catalogue, 1914–1915*, 41–48; also see, William P. Jackameit, "A Short History of Negro Public Higher Education in West Virginia, 1890–1965."

46. *Rambler*, Bluefield State College Yearbook, 1924, np.

47. Raymond Schmidt, "Another Football World (Part III of III)," *College Football Historical Society Newsletter*, 9, 11.

48. C. Stuart McGehee and Frank Wilson, *Bluefield State College: A Centennial History (1895–1995)* (North Tazewell, VA: Clinch Valley Printing Co., 1996), 74.

49. "West Virginia Board of Control Reports; 1910 through 1930," Bluefield State College Archives.

50. *Starlight*, Bluefield State College Yearbook, 1927, np.

51. *Pittsburgh Courier*, November 18, 1927.

52. *Pittsburgh Courier*, November 11, 1928.

53. *Pittsburgh Courier*, November 13, 1928 and December 8, 1928 and Raymond Schmidt, "Another Football World (Part III of III)," 11, 12.

54. Raymond Schmidt, *College Football: The Shaping of an American Sport: 1919–1930*, 147.

55. C. Stuart McGehee and Frank Wilson, *Bluefield State College: A Centennial History (1895–1995)*, 106.

56. "Harry "Big Jeff" Jefferson," American Football Coaches Webpage, http:wwwafca.com/article, accessed May 5, 2014.

57. C. Stuart McGehee, "Bluefield State College," in Ken Sullivan, ed., *The West Virginia Encyclopedia*, 69–70; also see, "West Virginia Board of Control Reports; 1910 through 1930," Bluefield State College Archives.

58. David K. Wiggins and Chris Elzey, "Creating Order in Black College Sport: The Lasting Legacy of the Colored Intercollegiate Athletic Association," in David K. Wiggins and Ryan A. Swanson, eds., *Separate Games: African American Sport behind the Walls of Segregation* (Fayetteville: University of Arkansas Press, 2016): 146, 147.

59. David K. Wiggins, "Central Intercollegiate Athletic Association," in George B. Kirsch, Othello Harris, and Claire E. Nolte, *Encyclopedia of Ethnicity and Sports in the United States* (Westport, CT: Greenwood Publishing Group, 2000): 95–96.

60. Joe William Trotter, Jr., "African American Coal Miners," in Ken Sullivan, ed., *The West Virginia Encyclopedia*, 3.

61. *Bluefield Daily Telegraph*, April 13, 2011.

62. Unidentified clipping, Stubby Currance, "Bluefield State Big Blues Blast West Virginia State 36–32 in Thrilling Grid Classic," *Bluefield Telegraph*, nd., in C. Stuart McGehee and Frank Wilson, *Bluefield State College: A Centennial History (1895–1995)*, 109.

63. Ergie Smith, personal interview, August 24, 2013.

64. *Charleston Daily Mail*, October 24, 1951.

65. *Charleston Daily Mail*, October 28, 1951; and *Bluefield Telegraph*, October 28, 1951.

66. Ergie Smith, personal interview, December 2, 2014.

67. Ergie Smith, personal interview, August 24, 2013.

68. *Bluefield Daily Telegraph*, April 13, 2011.

Chapter 3

1. *Pittsburgh Courier*, March 28, 1925.

2. Andrew Calloway, personal interview, August 13, 1982.

3. "Gary District High School History," in the *West Virginia All Black Schools Sports & Academic Hall of Fame Program*, 2010, 54. In the authors' private collection.

4. James Wilkerson, personal interview, July 19, 1982.

5. James Wilkerson, personal interview, July 19, 1982.

6. Ergie Smith, personal interview, February 5, 2013

7. See, *Charleston Daily Mail*, March 3, 1925; March 21, 1925; March 22, 1925; and *Pittsburgh Courier*, March 28, 1925.

8. Robert Pruter, *The Rise of American High School Sports and the Search for Control: 1880–1930* (Syracuse: Syracuse University Press, 2013): 193.

9. Lewis Hoch Wagenhorst, *The Administration and Cost of High School Interscholastic Athletics* in Robert Pruter, *The Rise of American High School Sports and the Search for Control: 1880–1930*, 198.

10. Tim Wyatt, *The Final Score*, privately published, 1999, 18–22; and Bob Barnett, *Hillside Fields: A History of Sports in West Virginia* (Morgantown: West Virginia University Press, 2013): 265–266.

11. Robert Pruter, *The Rise of American High School Sports and the Search for Control: 1880–1930* (Syracuse: Syracuse University Press, 2013): 289.

12. Robert Pruter, *The Rise of American High School Sports and the Search for Control: 1880–1930*, 273.

13. Robert Pruter, *The Rise of American High School Sports and the Search for Control: 1880–1930*, 28.

14. Robert Pruter, *The Rise of American High School Sports and the Search for Control: 1880–1930*, 289.

15. Robert Pruter, *The Rise of American High School Sports and the Search for Control: 1880–1930*, 282–289.

16. Louis Stout, *Shadows of the Past: A History of the Kentucky High School Athletic League* (Lexington: Host Communications, 2006); Tennessee State University website, http://www.tnstate.edu/lib/document/ PearlHigh, accessed December 28, 2012; http:hoopedia.nba.com//index.php accessed 12/30/12; Florida High School Athletic Association website, http:www.fhsaa.org, accessed 12/30/12; email from Rick Strunk, Associate Commissioner, North Carolina High School Athletic Association, January 1, 2013; Benjamin Baughman, Curator of the Georgia Sports Hall of Fame, personal interview, December 28, 2012; and Robert Pruter, *The Rise of American High School Sports and the Search for Control: 1880–1930*, 287–288.

17. Charles Herbert Thompson, "The History of the National Basketball Tournaments for Black High Schools" (Ph.D. Dissertation, Louisiana State University, 1980): 15–16.

18. Warne Ferguson, personal interview, January 30, 2013.

19. Tim L. Wyatt, *The Final Score* (Privately published, 1999): 368.

20. Elizabeth Scobell, personal interview, August 13, 1982.

21. Elhanier Willis, personal interview, July 19, 1982.

22. Elhanier Willis, personal interview, July 19, 1982

23. Tim L. Wyatt, *The Final Score*, 368.

24. Andrew Calloway, personal interview, August 13, 1982.

25. John Mackey, personal interview, July 19, 1982.

26. John Mackey, personal interview, July 19, 1982.

27. Robert Pruter, "The National Interscholastic Basketball Tournament: The Crown Jewel of African American High School Sports During the Era of Segregation," in David K. Wiggins and Ryan A. Swanson, eds., *Separate Games: African American Sport Behind the Walls of Segregation* (Fayetteville: University of Arkansas Press, 2016): 80–83.

28. James Wilkerson, personal interview, July 19, 1982.

29. James Wilkerson, personal interview, July 19, 1982.

30. Robert Pruter, "The National Interscholastic Basketball Tournament: The Crown Jewel of African American High School Sports during the Era of Segrega-

tion," in David K. Wiggins and Ryan A. Swanson, eds., *Separate Games: African American Sport Behind the Walls of Segregation*, 83–86.

31. Charles Herbert Thompson, "The History of the National Basketball Tournaments for Black High Schools," 125.

32. Robert Pruter, "The National Interscholastic Basketball Tournament: The Crown Jewel of African American High School Sports During the Era of Segregation," in David Wiggins and Ryan A. Swanson, eds., *Separate Games: African American Sport Behind the Walls of Segregation*, 86–88.

33. Robert Pruter, "The National Interscholastic Basketball Tournament: The Crown Jewel of African American High School Sports During the Era of Segregation," in David Wiggins and Ryan A. Swanson, eds., *Separate Games: African American Sport Behind the Walls of Segregation*, 89.

34. Knute Burroughs, personal interview, July 20, 1982.

35. Robert C. Byrd High School website, http://www.hardcoboe/robertcbyrd highschool, accessed 1/10/13; and Margo Stafford, "Clarksburg," in Ken Sullivan, ed., *The West Virginia Encyclopedia* (Charleston: The West Virginia Humanities Council, 2006): 139, 140.

36. Bob Wilson, personal interview, January 29, 2013.

37. C. Robert Barnett and Rod Bradley, "Mark Cardwell," in Rudy Abramson and Jean Haskell, eds., *Encyclopedia of Appalachia* (Knoxville: University of Tennessee Press, 2006): 1375, 1376.

38. Knute Burroughs, personal interview, July 20, 1982.

39. Bob Wilson, personal interview, January 29, 2013.

40. Fred R. Toothman, *Wild Wonderful Winners: Great Football Coaches of West Virginia* (Huntington: Vandalia, 1991): 49–52; and C. Robert Barnett and Rod Bradley, "Mark Cardwell," in Rudy Abramson and Jean Haskell, eds., *Encyclopedia of Appalachia*, 1375–1376.

Chapter 4

1. See David K. Wiggins and Chris Elzey, "Creating Order in Black College Sports," in David K. Wiggins and Ryan A. Swanson, eds., *Separate Games: African American Sport Behind the Walls of Segregation* (Fayetteville: University of Arkansas Press, 2016): 145–164.

2. Russ Barbour, "World War II." e-WV: *The West Virginia Encyclopedia*. 14 December 2016. Web, 22 March 2017; and *Atlanta Journal-Constitution*, March 14, 2016.

3. Carolyn Matthews, personal interview, February 10, 2011.

4. Ancella Bickley, personal Interview, October 18, 2010.

5. Carolyn Matthews, personal interview, February 10, 2011.

6. Bob Wilson, personal interview, October 29, 2010.

7. Earl Lloyd, personal interview, October 15, 2010.

8. Michael Hawkins, "Moonfixer: Basketball Pioneer Earl Lloyd," *Goldenseal* 35, no. 1 (Spring 2009): 45.

9. Earl Lloyd, personal interview, October 15, 2010.

10. Ancella Bickley, "African American Education," in Ken Sullivan, ed., *The West Virginia Encyclopedia* (Charleston: The West Virginia Humanities Council, 2006): 3–4.

11. Ancella Binkley, personal interview, October 18, 2010.

12. *West Virginia State University Football Media Guide*, 2009, 51–52. West Virginia State University Archives.

13. Mark Cardwell, Jr., personal interview, August 2, 2013.

14. Earl Lloyd and Sean Kirst, *Moonfixer: The Basketball Journey of Earl Lloyd* (Syracuse: Syracuse University Press): 13–14, 21–23, 30, 33.

15. Ocania Chalk, *Black College Sport* (New York, Dodd, Mead & Co., 1976): 133.

16. Earl Lloyd, personal interview, October 15, 2010.

17. Earl Lloyd, personal interview, October 15, 2010.

18. Earl Lloyd, personal interview, September 8, 2010.

19. Bob Barnett, *Hillside Fields: A History of Sports in West Virginia* (Morgantown: West Virginia University Press, 2013): 154.

20. Earl Lloyd, personal interview, September 8, 2010.

21. Bob Wilson, personal interview, October 29, 2010

22. Earl Lloyd, personal interview, October 15, 2010.

23. *Charleston Gazette*, July 20, 1999.

24. Earl Lloyd and Sean Kirst, *Moonfixer: The Basketball Journey of Earl Lloyd*, 54.

25. Earl Lloyd, personal interview, September 8, 2010.

26. David K. Wiggins and Chris Elzey, "Creating Order in Black College Sports," in David K. Wiggins and Ryan A. Swanson, eds., *Separate Games: African American Sport Behind the Walls of Segregation*, 157, 158.

27. *Pittsburgh Courier*, March 6, 1948.

28. *Pittsburgh Courier*, March 20, 1948.

29. Earl Lloyd and Sean Kirst, *Moonfixer: The Basketball Journey of Earl Lloyd*, 57.

30. *Pittsburgh Courier*, January 29, 1949, in David K. Wiggins and Chris Elzey, "Creating Order in Black College Sports," in David K. Wiggins and Ryan A. Swanson, eds., *Separate Games: African American Sport Behind the Walls of Segregation*, 162.

31. Ron Thomas, *They Cleared the Lane: The NBA's Black Pioneers* (Lincoln: University of Nebraska Press, 2002): 94.

32. Charles H. Martin, *Benching Jim Crow: The Rise and Fall of the Color Line in Southern College Sports, 1890–1980* (Urbana: University of Illinois Press, 2010): 69, 78–86.

33. David K. Wiggins and Chris Elzey, "Creating Order in Black College Sports," in David K. Wiggins and Ryan A. Swanson, eds., *Separate Games: African American Sport Behind the Walls of Segregation*, 162.

34. *Charleston Gazette*, February 5, 1949.

35. Personal correspondence, John W. Davis to C.R. Rutherford, February 5, 1949, West Virginia State University Archives.

36. *Charleston Gazette*, February 13, 1949.

37. *Charleston Gazette*, February 18, 1949.

38. Earl Lloyd, personal interview, September 8, 2010.

39. Quoted in David K. Wiggins and Chris Elzey, "Creating Order in Black College Sports," in David K. Wiggins and Ryan A. Swanson, eds., *Separate Games: African American Sport Behind the Walls of Segregation*, 163.

40. Bob Wilson, personal interview, July 31, 2013.

41. Earl Lloyd, personal interview, September 8, 2010.

42. *Charleston Gazette*, March 20, 1949.

43. *Charleston Gazette*, December 16, 1949.

44. Warne Ferguson, personal interview, October 21, 2010.

45. Bob Wilson, personal interview, July 31, 2013.

46. Warne Ferguson, personal interview, October 21, 2010.

47. *Charleston Gazette*, February 8, 1950.

48. Ron Thomas, *They Cleared the Lane: The NBA's Black Pioneers*, 96.

49. *Charleston Gazette*, February 19, 1950.

50. *Charleston Gazette*, March 11, 1950.

51. Earl Lloyd, personal interview, September 8, 2010.

52. Ron Thomas, *They Cleared the Lane: The NBA's Black Pioneers*, 33–38.

53. *Charleston Gazette*, March 12, 1950.

54. *Charleston Gazette*, March 7, 1950.

55. Bob Wilson, personal interview, October 29, 2010.

56. Earl Lloyd, personal interview, September 8, 2010.

57. Bruce Newman, "Yesterday," *Sports Illustrated*, October 22, 1979, n.p.; and John Schleppi, *Chicago's Showcase of Basketball: The World Tournament of Professional Basketball and the College All-Star Game* (Haworth, NJ: Saint Johann Press, 2008): 119, 121.

58. Earl Lloyd and Sean Kirst, *Moonfixer: The Basketball Journey of Earl Lloyd*, 65.

Chapter 5

1. Joe William Trotter, Jr., "African American Heritage," in Ken Sullivan, ed., *The West Virginia Encyclopedia* (Charleston: The West Virginia Humanities Council, 2006): 4–5.

2. Ken Blue, personal interview, March 6, 2013.

3. *Morgantown Dominion News*, March 18, 2013.

4. William Dunlap, personal interview, March 6, 2013.

5. Warne Ferguson, personal interview, January 29, 2013.

6. William Dunlap, personal interview, March 6, 2013.

7. Edward Starling, personal interview, August 24, 1982.

8. *Charleston Daily Mail*, March 17, 1946; and *Morgantown Dominion News*, March 18, 1946.

9. James Wilkerson, personal interview, July 19, 1982.

10. Arintha Poe Hairston, personal interview, April 2, 2013.

11. Dennis R. Jones, "History of Dunbar School, Weirton, WV," Weirton Area

Museum and Cultural Center, pamphlet distributed February 2, 2013.

12. Bob Kelley, personal interview, March 7, 2013.

13. William "Shellie" Trice, personal interview, March 9, 2013.

14. *Times West Virginian* (Fairmont), March 28, 1947; and *Weirton Daily Times*, March 24, 1947.

15. Tim Swarr, personal interview, April 13, 2017.

16. Ancella Bickley, "Sumner School," in Ken Sullivan, ed., *The West Virginia Encyclopedia*, 692, 693; and Tim L. Wyatt, *The Final Score*, privately published, 1999, 370.

17. Shirley Atkins, personal interview, June 27, 2016; *Charleston Gazette*, September 19, 1954; and Tim L. Wyatt, *The Final Score* (Privately published, 1999): 367–371.

18. *Register-Herald* (Beckley, WV), May 16, 2004.

19. Tim L. Wyatt, *The Final Score*, 136–188, 367–371.

20. *The West Virginia All Black Schools Sports & Athletic Hall of Fame Program*, August 27, 2011, 133–135, authors' personal collection.

21. Floyd Jones, personal interview, April 13, 2017.

22. Tim L. Wyatt, *The Final Score*, 136–160, 367–371; *The West Virginia All Black Schools Sports & Athletic Hall of Fame Program*, August 27, 2011, 34–35, authors' personal collection; and Belinda Anderson, "Lewisburg," in Ken Sullivan, ed., *The West Virginia Encyclopedia*, 420.

23. Wilkes Kinney, personal interview, January 31, 2013.

24. See, James W. Loewen, *Sundown Towns: A Hidden Dimension of American Racism* (New York: The New Press, 2005): 71–72.

25. Lacy Smith, personal interview, July 20, 1982.

26. Ruth Jarrett, personal interview, August 13, 1982.

27. Ancella Bickley, "Carter G. Woodson," in Ken Sullivan, ed., *The West Virginia Encyclopedia*, 809.

28. *The West Virginia All Black Schools Sports & Academic Hall of Fame Program*, 2011, 36, 37, authors' personal collection; and Ancella Bickley, "Douglass High School," in Ken Sullivan, ed., *The West Virginia Encyclopedia*, 200.

29. *Herald-Dispatch* (Huntington), December 10, 1948.

30. *Huntington Advertiser*, January 17, 1949.

31. *Herald-Dispatch* (Huntington), January 16, 1949.

32. *Herald-Dispatch* (Huntington), January 17, 1949.

33. *Herald-Dispatch* (Huntington), February 22, 1949.

34. *Herald-Dispatch* (Huntington), January 17, 1949.

35. *Charleston Gazette*, March 21, 1953.

36. *Charleston Gazette*, March 22, 1953.

37. *Charleston Daily Mail*, March 18, 1954.

38. *The West Virginia All Black Schools Sports & Academic Hall of Fame Induction Program*, 2010, 39–40, authors' personal collection; and Hazel P. Wooster, "Garnet High School," in Ken Sullivan, ed., *The West Virginia Encyclopedia*, 269.

39. Knute Burroughs, personal interview, July 20, 1982.

40. Edward Starling, personal interview, August 24, 1982.

41. Horace Belmear, personal interview, September 12, 1982.

42. Claude Harvey, personal interview, March 15, 2013.

43. Lawrence V. Jordan, "Educational Integration in West Virginia—One Year Afterward," *The Journal of Negro Education* 24, n. 3 (Summer 1955): 371.

44. Elhanier Willis, personal interview, July 19, 1982.

45. James L. Taylor, personal interview, March 22, 2016.

46. *Bluefield Daily Telegraph*, March 14–17, 1957.

47. See, *Charleston Daily Mail*, March 13, 1957; March 14, 1957; March 15, 1957; March 16, 1957; and March 17, 1957; *Herald-Dispatch* (Huntington), March 16, 1957; and March 17, 1957.

48. Tim L. Wyatt, *The Final Score*, 140.

49. Ruth Jarrett, personal interview, August 13, 1982.

50. Edward Starling, personal interview, August 24, 1982.

51. Ruth Jarrett, personal interview, August 13, 1982.

52. James Wilkerson, personal interview, July 19, 1982.

Chapter 6

1. Lawrence V. Jordan, "Educational Integration in West Virginia—One Year Afterward," *The Journal of Negro Education* 24, n.

3 (Summer 1955): 372; and Sarah Hendrickson, "The Integration of Marshall University," The Carter Woodson Project website, http://www.marshall.edu/carterwoodson/sarah_hendrickson.asp, accessed March 13, 2016.

2. Lawrence V. Jordan, "Educational Integration in West Virginia—One Year Afterward," 372, 373; W.W. Trent, *Mountaineer Education: A Story of Education in West Virginia* (Charleston: Jarrett Publishing, 1960), n.p.; and Harveyan, Morris Harvey College student yearbook, 1955, 53, 100.

3. W.W. Trent, *Mountaineer Education: A Story of Education in West Virginia*, n.p.

4. Lawrence V. Jordan, "Educational Integration in West Virginia—One Year Afterward," 373.

5. Sam F. Stack, Jr., "Implementing Brown vs. Board of Education in West Virginia," *The Southern School News Reports*, http://textbooks.lib. wvu.edu/wvhistory/files/html/15_wv_history_reader_stack/

6. Bob Douglas, personal interview, July 2, 2016.

7. Cliff Christi, "Who Was Packers First African American Player?" https://www.packers.com, January 28, 2016, accessed May 17, 2019.

8. Kenneth M. Plummer, *A History of West Virginia Wesleyan College: 75 Years in the Service of Christian Higher Education 1890–1965* (Buckhannon: West Virginia Wesleyan College Press, 1965): 95.

9. Kenneth M. Plummer, *A History of West Virginia Wesleyan College: 75 Years in the Service of Christian Higher Education 1890–1965*, 96.

10. Email, Brett Miller, Archivist West Virginia Wesleyan College to Dana Brooks, February 19, 2016.

11. Email, Brett Miller, Archivist West Virginia Wesleyan College to Dana Brooks, February 19, 2016.

12. *Murmurmontis*, West Virginia Wesleyan College student yearbook: 1955, 1956, 1957, 1958.

13. *Bluefield Daily Telegraph*, October 5, 2013.

14. *Bluefield Daily Telegraph*, October 5, 2013.

15. *Bluefield Daily Telegraph*, October 5, 2013.

16. Dinah W. Courrier, *Potomac State College: The College History Series* (Charleston, SC: Arcadia Publishing, 2000): 1–6.

17. *Catamount*, Potomac State College student yearbook, 1955.

18. *Catamount*, Potomac State College student yearbook, 1956.

19. Mike Arcure, personal interview, June 10, 2016.

20. *The Mound*, Fairmont State College student yearbook, Note 1959:

21. Moses Guin, personal interview, June 12, 2016.

22. *The Mound*, Fairmont State College student yearbook, 1958.

23. Moses Guin, personal interview, June 12, 2016.

24. *The Mound*, Fairmont State College student yearbook, 1959.

25. *The Mound*, Fairmont State College student yearbook, 1960.

26. *Fairmont Times-West Virginian*, August 24, 2014.

27. Moses Guin, personal interview, June 12, 2016.

28. Moses Guin, personal interview, June 12, 2016.

29. Mike Arcure, personal interview, June 10, 2016.

30. *The Mound*, Fairmont State College student yearbook, 1961.

31. James L. Taylor, personal interview, June 7, 2016.

32. "Remember When," 1992, West Liberty Alumni Association website. http://www.westliberty.edu.alumni/

33. "Remember When," 1992, West Liberty Alumni Association website.

34. "Remember When," 1992, West Liberty Alumni Association website.

35. "Remember When," 1992, West Liberty Alumni Association website.

36. Bob Douglas, personal interview, July 2, 2016.

37. Bob Barnett, *Hillside Fields: A History of Sports in West Virginia* (Morgantown: West Virginia University Press, 2013): 211–212.

38. Bob Douglas, personal interview, July 2, 2016.

39. Doug C. Huff, *Sports in West Virginia: A Pictorial History* (Virginia Beach: The Donning Company, 1979): 187.

40. See Craig Sesker, *Bobby Douglas: Life and Legacy of an American Wrestling Legend* (Exit Zero, 2011).

41. Brent Carney, *Bethany College: The Campus History Series* (Charleston, SC: Arcadia Publishing, 2004): 1–3; and Lester

G. McAllister, *Bethany: the First 150 Years* (Bethany, WV: The Bethany College Press, 1991): 3–8.

42. Brent Carney, *Bethany College: The Campus History Series*, 28.

43. Brent Carney, *Bethany College: The Campus History Series*, 57–60, 89.

44. *Bethanian*, Bethany College student yearbook, 1963.

45. *Tribune* (Pittsburgh, PA), May 24, 2002.

46. *Observer-Reporter* (Washington, PA), November 10, 1969.

47. Ronald R. Alexander, *West Virginia Tech: A History* (Charleston: Pictorial Histories Publishing, 1992): 31–46; 65–105.

48. Ronald R. Alexander, *West Virginia Tech: A History*, 119.

49. William Turner, personal interview, April 9, 2011.

50. William Turner, personal interview, April 9, 2011.

51. William Turner, personal interview, April 9, 2011.

52. William Turner, personal interview, April 9, 2011.

53. Larry Barker, personal interview, March 22, 2011.

54. Glenville University Athletic Hall of Fame website, www.glenville.edu/athletics/hof.php?gyear=2001, accessed January 27, 2016.

55. Glenville University Athletic Hall of Fame website, www.glenville.edu/athletics/hof.php?gyear=2001, accessed January 27, 2016.

56. John Antonik, "Five for the Ages," January 17, 2011, 5, accessed January 30, 2016, http://www.wvusports.com/page,CFM?sport=mbball&Show=1790S.

57. Gerald Martin, personal interview, September 1, 2016.

58. Gerald Martin, personal interview, September 1, 2016.

Chapter 7

1. *Herald-Dispatch* (Huntington), December 9, 1954.

2. Ernie Salvatore, "Hurrying Hal Greer," *Huntington Quarterly* (Summer 1994): 31.

3. *Herald-Dispatch* (Huntington), January 25, 1959.

4. *Herald Advertiser* (Huntington, WV), January 25, 1959.

5. *Herald Advertiser* (Huntington, WV), January 25, 1959.

6. C. Robert Barnett, "Winning in the Rural Zone: How Cam Henderson Invented the Zone Defense," *Now and Then: The Appalachian Magazine* (Fall 1992): 37–39.

7. Sam Clagg, *The Cam Henderson Story: His Life and Times* (Parsons, WV: McClain, 1981): 97–128.

8. Sam Clagg, *The Cam Henderson Story: His Life and Times*, 203–212.

9. Sam Clagg, *The Cam Henderson Story: His Life and Times*, 230–231.

10. Sam Clagg, *The Cam Henderson Story: His Life and Times*, 238–241.

11. See Robert Crabtree, "Cam Henderson's Marshall Years: 1935 to 1955" (master's thesis, Marshall University, 1975), 6–8.

12. *Herald-Dispatch* (Huntington, WV), March 16, 1947.

13. George M. Reger, "Integration and Athletics: Integrating the Marshall University Basketball Program, 1954–1969" (master's thesis, Marshall University, 1996), 52.

14. Lawrence V. Jordan, "Educational Integration in West Virginia—One Year Afterward," *The Journal of Negro Education* 24, n. 3 (Summer 1955): 373.

15. Quoted in Ernie Salvatore, "Hurryin' Hal Greer," 30.

16. For a more complete discussion of the OVC/MAC affiliation question see, George M. Reger, "Integration and Athletics: Integrating the Marshall University Basketball Program, 1954–1969," 29–34.

17. Dennis Gildea, *Hoop Crazy: The Lives of Clair Bee and Chip Hilton* (Fayetteville: University of Arkansas Press, 2013): 129–131.

18. Phillip Carter, personal interview, January 6, 2014.

19. *Charleston Gazette*, March 9, 1955; and *Huntington Advertiser*, March 5, 1955.

20. Jerry Gargus, "In the Shadow of a Legend: The Jules Rivlin Story," unpublished class paper, spring 1994, 1, 2, and Keith Morehouse, "Jules Rivlin: A Look Back at Marshall's Forgotten All-American," *Huntington Quarterly* (Spring 2013): 18.

21. Jerry Gargus, "In the Shadow of a Legend," 3–5; and Keith Morehouse, "Jules Rivlin," 18.

22. *Herald Advertiser* (Huntington), December 4, 1955.

23. Marshall College Press and Radio Guide, 1956–57, Huntington, WV, 20, in

George M. Reger, "Integration and Athletics: Integrating the Marshall University Basketball Program, 1954–1969," 55.

24. Herb Colker, personal interview, April 9, 2014.

25. Quoted in George M. Reger, "Integration and Athletics: Integrating the Marshall University Basketball Program, 1954–1969," 61.

26. George M. Reger, "Integration and Athletics: Integrating the Marshall University Basketball Program, 1954–1969," 61.

27. *Herd Insider*, October 31, 2012.

28. George M. Reger, "Integration and Athletics: Integrating the Marshall University Basketball Program, 1954–1969," 65.

29. *Herald-Dispatch* (Huntington, WV), February 26, 1958.

30. Stan Bumgardner, "Hal Greer," in Ken Sullivan, ed., *The West Virginia Encyclopedia* (Charleston: West Virginia Humanities Council, 2006): 303.

31. Woody Woodrum, "Roy Goines Broke MU Football Color Barrier," http://www.scout.com/college/marshall/story/573681, accessed April 7, 2017.

32. *Chief Justice*, Marshall College yearbook, 1958, 212.

33. Sarah Hendrickson, "The Integration of Marshall University," The Carter Woodson Project/Marshall University, http://www.marshall.edu/carterwoodson/sarah_hendrickson.asp, accessed March 3, 2016.

34. Woody Woodrum, "Roy Goines."

35. Woody Woodrum, "Roy Goines."

36. Woody Woodrum, "Roy Goines."

37. Woody Woodrum, "Roy Goines."

38. This information is from a review of team pictures in the *Chief Justice*, the Marshall University yearbook, from 1956 through 1965. Marshall University Archives.

39. George M. Reger, "Integration and Athletics: Integrating the Marshall University Basketball Program, 1954–1969," 75.

40. George M. Reger, "Integration and Athletics: Integrating the Marshall University Basketball Program, 1954–1969,"75.

41. Phillip Carter, personal interview, September 21, 2014.

42. Phillip Carter, personal interview, January 6, 2014.

43. *Charleston Gazette-Mail*, June 30, 2014.

44. *Charleston Gazette-Mail*, June 30, 2014.

45. Alex Edelmann, "The Integration of Marshall University Athletics," The Carter Woodson Project/Marshall University, http://www.Marshall.edu/carterwoodson/alex_edelmann.asp, accessed 11/12/13.

46. Phillip Carter, personal interview, January 6, 2014.

47. For a more complete discussion of the decline in West Virginia's sports programs after the 1950s, see, Bob Barnett, *Hillside Fields: A History of Sports in West Virginia* (Morgantown: West Virginia University Press, 2013).

48. Donna Lawson, personal interview, March 4, 2016.

49. Beverly Duckwyler, personal interview, March 5, 2016.

50. Barbara Josten, "A History of Women's Intercollegiate Athletics at Marshall University" (master's thesis, Marshall University, 1974), 36–38.

51. Beverly Duckwyler, personal interview, March 5, 2016.

52. Dorothy Hicks, personal interview, September 20, 2014.

53. Stephanie Holman, personal interview, March 11, 2016

54. Beverly Duckwyler, personal interview, March 5, 2016.

55. Barbara Josten, "A History of Women's Intercollegiate Athletics at Marshall University," 65–69.

Chapter 8

1. John Clifford Harlan, *History of West Virginia State College: 1890–1965* (Dubuque: Wm. C. Brown, 1968): 99.

2. Elizabeth Scobell, personal interview, August 14, 2013.

3. Ron Thomas, *They Cleared the Lane: The NBA'S Black Pioneers* (Lincoln: University of Nebraska Press, 2002): 86, 87.

4. West Virginia State University website, http://www.wvstateu.edu/Research/Gus-R-Douglass-Land-Grant-Institute.aspx, accessed April 26, 2017.

5. John Clifford Harlan, *History of West Virginia State College*, 104–105.

6. Harry W. Ernst and Andrew Calloway, "Reverse Integration," *New York Times*, January 6, 1957.

7. William P. Jackameit, "A Short History of Negro Public Higher Education in West Virginia, 1890–1965," *West Virginia History* 37, n. 4 (July 1976): 322.

8. West Virginia, "Biennial Report of the State Superintendent of Free Schools, 1952," 22, Marshall University Library Special Collections.

9. William P. Jackameit, "A Short History of Negro Public Higher Education in West Virginia, 1890–1965," 322.

10. West Virginia State College Recommendations to the Board of Education by President, January 1, 1954-January 1, 1956, Proposed Budget and Recommendations for 1955–56, Item 6641, West Virginia State University Archives, reviewed August19, 2013.

11. Charles H. Martin, *Benching Jim Crow: The Rise and Fall of the Color Line in Southern College Sports, 1890-1980* (Urbana: University of Illinois Press, 2010): 71–72.

12. Mark Cardwell, Jr., personal interview, August 4, 2013.

13. Bob Wilson, personal interview, July 31, 2013.

14. Bob Barnett, *Hillside Fields: A History of Sports in West Virginia* (Morgantown: West Virginia University Press, 2013): 227–254.

15. Larry Barker, personal interview, August 3, 2013.

16. *Charleston Daily-Mail*, March 21, 1964.

17. *Charleston Gazette-Mail*, March 22, 1964.

18. *Charleston Gazette-Mail*, March 22, 1964.

19. Ergie Smith, personal interview, December 2, 2014.

20. Frank Beach, personal interview, December 2, 2014.

21. Ergie Smith, personal interview, August 24, 2013.

22. West Virginia Human Rights Commission, "Annual Report. 1967–1968," 27–29.

23. C. Stuart McGehee and Frank Wilson, *Bluefield State College: A Centennial History, 1895-1995* (North Tazewell, VA: Clinch Valley Press, 1996): 178–184; and *The Bluefieldian*, Bluefield State College student newspaper, special edition, December 1968.

24. C. Stuart McGehee and Frank Wilson, Bluefield State College: A Centennial History, 178–184; and The Bluefieldian, special edition, December 1968.

25. Ergie Smith, personal interview, December 2, 2014.

26. C. Stuart McGehee and Frank Wilson, *Bluefield State College: A Centennial History*, 182.

27. C. Stuart McGehee and Frank Wilson, *Bluefield State College: A Centennial History*, 184.

28. Arline Thorn, "West Virginia State University," in Ken Sullivan, ed., *The West Virginia Encyclopedia* (Charleston: The West Virginia Humanities Council, 2006): 772.

29. Ergie Smith, personal interview, December 2, 2014.

Chapter 9

1. *Fairmont West Virginian*, September 16, 1954.

2. *Fairmont West Virginian*, October 1, 1954, and Fairmont (W.Va.) Times, October 1, 1954.

3. *Fairmont West Virginian*, October 1, 1954.

4. A longer version of this game story is in Bob Barnett and Lysbeth Barnett, "Black and White: Fairmont West vs. Fairmont Dunbar," *Goldenseal, West Virginia Traditional Life* (Winter 2018): 40–45.

5. Sam Stack, "Integration," in Ken Sullivan, ed., *The West Virginia Encyclopedia* (Charleston: The West Virginia Humanities Council, 2016): 363, 364.

6. W.W. Trent, *Mountaineer Education: A Story of Education in West Virginia, 1885–1957* (Charleston: Jarrett Printing, 1960): n.p. There were no page numbers in Trent's book.

7. W.W. Trent, *Mountaineer Education: A Story of Education in West Virginia, 1885–1957*: n.p.

8. W.W. Trent, *Mountaineer Education: A Story of Education in West Virginia, 1885–1957*: n.p.

9. Lawrence V. Jordan, "Educational Integration in West Virginia—One Year Afterward," *The Journal of Negro Education* 24, n. 3 (Summer 1955): 374–376.

10. Lawrence V. Jordan, "Educational Integration in West Virginia—One Year Afterward," 379.

11. W.W. Trent, *Mountaineer Education: A Story of Education in West Virginia, 1885–1957*: n.p.

12. W.W. Trent, *Mountaineer Education: A Story of Education in West Virginia, 1885–1957*: n.p.

13. Philip Carter, personal interview, January 6, 2014.

14. Philip Carter, personal interview, January 6, 2014.

15. Randy Roberts, *But They Can't Beat Us: Oscar Robertson and the Crispus Attucks Tigers* (Champaign, IL: Sports Publishing, 1999): 39–41.

16. Randy Roberts, *But They Can't Beat Us: Oscar Robertson and the Crispus Attucks Tigers*: 42.

17. See, Randy Roberts, *But They Can't Beat Us: Oscar Robertson and the Crispus Attucks Tigers*, chapters 1, 4, 5, and 6.

18. Edward Starling, personal interview, August 24, 1982.

19. See, *Report of the State Superintendent of Schools and Department of Education, West Virginia Educational Directory*, 1953–54 through the 1961–62 editions.

20. Dolores Johnson, personal interview, April 30, 2013.

21. Opal Jones, personal interview, May 6, 2013.

22. *West Virginia Daily News* (Lewisburg, WV), February 27, 2015.

23. Opal Jones, personal interview, May 6, 2013.

24. Alice E. Carter, "Segregation and Integration in the Appalachian Coalfields: McDowell County Responds to the Brown Decision," *West Virginia History*, v. 54, 1995, 239–253, http://www.wvculture.org/history/journal_wvh/wvh54-5.html. Accessed May 10, 2017.

25. Ronald Wilkerson, personal interview, May 8, 2017.

26. James Wilkerson, personal interview, July 19, 1982.

27. Ergie Smith, personal interview, April 25, 2013.

28. James Wilkerson, personal interview, July 19, 1982.

29. Tim L. Wyatt, *The Final Score* (privately published, 1999): 166–170.

30. Ronald Booker, personal interview, April 27, 2013.

31. Ronald Booker, personal interview, April 27, 2013.

32. Ronald Booker, personal interview, April 27, 2013.

33. *Huntington Advertiser*, March 20, 1963, and *Herald-Dispatch* (Huntington, WV), March 21, 1963.

34. Ronald Booker, personal interview, April 27, 2013.

35. *Post-Herald and Register* (Beckley, WV), March 22, 1963.

36. *Herald-Dispatch* (Huntington, WV), March 23, 1963.

37. *Herald-Dispatch* (Huntington, WV), March 24, 1963.

38. *Post-Herald* (Beckley, WV), March 25, 1963.

39. Ergie Smith, personal interview, April 25, 2013.

40. James Wilkerson, personal interview, July 19, 1982.

41. See, Randy Roberts, *But They Can't Beat Us: Oscar Robertson and the Crispus Attucks Tigers*, pages1–12, 50–51 and numerous other places in the book.

42. Randy Roberts, *But They Can't Beat Us: Oscar Robertson and the Crispus Attucks Tigers*: 81.

43. Ergie Smith, personal interview, April 25, 2013.

44. Ergie Smith, personal interview, April 25, 2013.

45. James Wilkerson, personal interview, July 19, 1982.

46. See, *Register-Herald* (Beckley, WV), January 18, 2015; and *Bluefield Daily Telegraph*, January 14, 2015.

47. Ronald Wilkerson, personal interview, May 8, 2017.

48. Ergie Smith, personal interview, April 25, 2013.

49. Edward Starling, personal interview, August 24, 1982.

50. Tim L. Wyatt, *The Final Score*, 372.

51. Robert Pruter, *The Rise of American High School Sports and the Search for Control 1880–1930* (Syracuse: Syracuse University Press, 2013): 318–319.

52. Edward Starling, personal interview, August 24, 1982.

53. James Taylor, personal interview, March 22, 2016.

Chapter 10

1. "The Goal Post," Football Game Program, UCLA vs. Southern California, December 9, 1939, n.p.

2. Charles M. Martin, "Jim Crow in the Gymnasium: The Integration of College Basketball in the American South," *The International Journal of the History of Sport* 10, no. 1 (April 1993): 68.

3. J. Paul, R. McClure and H. Fant, "The Arrival and Ascendance of Black Athletes in the Southern Conference—1966–1980," *Phelan* 45, number 4 (1984): 284–297.

4. Charles H. Martin, *Benching Jim Crow: The Rise and Fall of the Color Line in Southern College Sports, 1890–1980* (Urbana: University of Illinois Press, 2010): 115.

5. Charles H. Martin, *Benching Jim Crow: The Rise and Fall of the Color Line in Southern College Sports, 1890–1980*: 277.

6. Charles H. Martin, *Benching Jim Crow: The Rise and Fall of The Color Line in Southern College Sports*, 1890: 277.

7. Kent Kessler, *Hail West Virginians!* (Parkersburg, WV: Park Press, 1959): 3–4.

8. Kent Kessler, *Hail West Virginians!*: 3–4.

9. *Monticola*, WVU student yearbook, 1892, 123.

10. For a complete history of WVU, see, William T. Doherty, Jr., and Festus P. Summers, *West Virginia University: Symbol of Unity in a Sectionalized State* (Morgantown: West Virginia University Press, 1982).

11. John Antonik, *Roll Out the Carpet: 100 Seasons of West Virginia University Basketball* (Morgantown: West Virginia University Press, 2010): 57.

12. Bob Barnett, *Hillside Fields: A History of Sports in West Virginia* (Morgantown: West Virginia University Press, 2013): 172–173.

13. Bob Barnett, *Hillside Fields: A History of Sports in West Virginia*, 175–182.

14. Personal letter Dean Dustman to President Stewart, February 3, 1956, West Virginia University archives. Morgantown, West Virginia.

15. Personal letter Dean Dustman to President Stewart, February 3, 1956, West Virginia University archives. Morgantown, West Virginia.

16. William T. Doherty, Jr., and Festus P. Summers, *West Virginia University: Symbol of Unity in a Sectionalized State*, 212.

17. Ralph Izard, "The door has been opened." *Daily Athenaeum*, West Virginia University student newspaper, March 28, 1961.

18. See Tony Constantine, *Mountaineer Football: 1891–1969* (Morgantown: West Virginia University Department of Intercollegiate Athletics, 1969).

19. Keith Patrick Howard, "Desegregation of College Football in the Southeastern United States" (master's thesis, University of North Carolina, 2001): 6 and 13–39.

20. Gene Corum, personal interview, June 13, 1991.

21. Stefanie Loh, Coachwhointegrated-wvufootballteamdiessportsregister-herald.com.

22. Ed Barrett, personal interview, June 17, 1991.

23. Ed Pastilong, personal interview, June 6, 1991.

24. Ed Shockey, personal interview, June 25, 1991.

25. Kevin Keys and Shelly Poe, *Bring on the Mountaineers* (Morgantown: West Virginia University Department of Intercollegiate Athletics, 1991): 126–128.

26. Tony Constantine, *A Record of West Virginia University Football: The First 100 Years* (Morgantown: West Virginia University Department of Intercollegiate Athletics, 1991): 61.

27. Garrett Ford, personal interview, June 12, 1991.

28. J. William Douglas, *The School of Physical Education at West Virginia University: An Historical Perspective 1891–1999* (Morgantown: WVU School of Physical Education, 1999): 56.

29. Stefanie Loh, Coachwhointegratedwvufootballteamdiessportsregister-herald.com.

30. Garrett Ford, personal interview, June 12, 1991.

31. Garrett Ford, personal interview, June 12, 1991.

32. See Mike Freeman, *How Bobby Bowden Forged a Football Dynasty* (New York: Harper Collins, 2009).

33. See J. William Douglas, *The School of Physical Education at West Virginia University: An Historical Perspective 1891–1999*.

34. Bob Barnett, *Hillside Fields: A History of Sports in West Virginia*, 121–129; and John Antonik, *Roll Out the Carpet: 101 Seasons of West Virginia University Basketball*, 38–39.

35. John Antonik, "Breaking Barriers," MSN Sports Net. Com, April 9, 2004, accessed February 17, 2016.

36. John Sorrenti, personal interview, March 25, 2016.

37. John Antonik, "Breaking Barriers."

38. John Antonik, "Breaking Barriers."

39. WVU STATS, "Basketball Roster," http://www.wvustats.com/sport/mbasketball/roster, accessed March 26, 2016.

40. John Antonik, "Breaking Barriers."

41. Bucky Waters, personal interview, December 10, 2005.

42. See, Doug Huff, *Sports in West Virginia: A Pictorial History* (Virginia Beach: The Donning Company, 1979).

43. Bob Barnett, *Hillside Fields: A History of Sports in West Virginia*: 317–341.

44. See J. William Douglas, *The School of Physical Education at West Virginia University: An Historical Perspective 1891–1999*.

45. *Daily Athenaeum*, WVU student newspaper, March 28, 1961.

46. *Dominion Post* (Morgantown, WV), October 15, 2006.

47. *Dominion Post* (Morgantown, WV), October 15 2006.

48. *WVU Women: The First Century* (Morgantown: WVU Women's Centenary Project, 1991).

49. *WVU Women: The First Century*.

50. Kittie Blakemore, https://www.youtube.com/watch?v=IPx-YdSFdhI. Accessed February 17, 2017.

51. *WVU Women: The First Century*.

52. *Hinton (WV) News*, December 1, 1992.

53. Bob Welsh, *20 Years: Women's Athletics* (Morgantown: West Virginia University, Department of Intercollegiate Athletics, 1984).

54. Shirley Robinson, personal interview, November 7, 2005.

55. Kevin Gilson, personal interview, October 27, 2004.

56. John Bolt, "oneWVU" theme of Diversity Week 2008 at WVU, University/Relations/News, October 9, 2008.

57. Major Harris, personal interview, July 6, 2012.

58. Don Nehlen with Shelly Poe, *Tales from the West Virginia Sideline* (Champaign, IL: Sports Publishing, 2006): 149.

59. Major Harris, personal interview, July 7, 2012.

60. Bob Barnett, "A Major Leads His Army: West Virginia University Football, 1960 through the Don Nehlen Years," in Bob Barnett, *Hillside Fields: A History of Sports in West Virginia*: 317–342.

61. NCAA Demographic Data 2013–201

Bibliography

Books

Abramson, Rudy, and Jean Haskell, eds. *Encyclopedia of Appalachia.* Knoxville: University of Tennessee Press, 2006.

Alexander, Ronald R. *West Virginia Tech: A History.* Charleston: Pictorial Histories, 1992.

Ambler, Charles H. *A History of Education in West Virginia from Early Colonial Times to 1949.* Huntington: Standard, 1951.

Antonik, John. *Roll Out the Carpet: 100 Seasons of West Virginia University Basketball.* Morgantown: West Virginia University Press, 2010.

Barnett, Bob. *Hillside Fields: A History of Sports in West Virginia.* Morgantown: West Virginia University Press, 2013.

Bickley, Ancella R. *History of the West Virginia State Teacher's Association.* Washington, D.C.: National Education Association, 1979.

Burke, Dawne Raines. *An American Phoenix: A History of Storer College from Slavery to Desegregation, 1865–1955.* Morgantown: West Virginia University Press, 2015.

Carney, Brent. *Bethany College: The Campus History Series.* Charleston, SC: Arcadia, 2004.

Chalk, Ocania. *Black College Sport.* New York: Dodd, Mead, 1976.

Clagg, Sam. *The Cam Henderson Story: His Life and Times.* Parsons, WV: McClain, 1981.

Constantine, Tony. *Mountaineer Football: 1891–1969.* Morgantown: West Virginia University Department of Intercollegiate Athletics, 1969.

Corbin, David A. *Life, Work, and Rebellion in the Coal Fields: The Southern West Virginia Miners 1880–1922.* Urbana: University of Illinois Press, 1981.

Courrier, Dinah W. *Potomac State College: The College History Series.* Charleston, SC: Arcadia, 2000.

Crabtree, Robert. "Cam Henderson's Marshall Years: 1935 to 1955." Master's Thesis, Marshall University, 1975.

Doherty, William T., Jr., and Festus P. Summers. *West Virginia University: Symbol of Unity in a Sectionalized State.* Morgantown: West Virginia University Press, 1982.

Douglas, J. William. *The School of Physical Education at West Virginia University: An Historical Perspective 1891–1999.* Morgantown: WVU School of Physical Education, 1999.

Foner, Eric, and John A. Garraty, eds. *The Reader's Companion to American History.* Boston: Houghton Mifflin, 1991.

Freeman, Mike. *How Bobby Bowden Forged a Football Dynasty.* New York: HarperCollins, 2009.

Gildea, Dennis. *Hoop Crazy: The Lives of Clair Bee and Chip Hilton.* Fayetteville: University of Arkansas Press, 2013.

Grundy, Pamela. *Learning to Win: Sports, Education, and Social Change in*

Twentieth-Century North Carolina. Chapel Hill: University of North Carolina Press, 2001.

Harlan, John Clifford. *History of West Virginia State College.* Dubuque: Wm. C. Brown, 1968.

Harlan, Lewis R. *Booker T. Washington: The Making of a Black Leader: 1856–1901.* Vol. 1. New York: Oxford University Press, 1972.

Harlan, Lewis R. *Booker T. Washington: The Wizard of Tuskegee, 1901–1915.* Vol. 2. New York: Oxford University Press, 1983.

Howard, Keith Patrick. "Desegregation of College Football in the Southeastern United States." Master's thesis, University of North Carolina, 2001.

Huff, Doug C. *Sports in West Virginia: A Pictorial History.* Virginia Beach: Donning, 1979.

Josten, Barbara. "A History of Women's Intercollegiate Athletics at Marshall University." Master's thesis, Marshall University, 1974.

Kessler, Kent. *Hail West Virginians!* Parkersburg, WV: Park Press, 1959.

Keys, Kevin, and Shelly Poe. *Bring on the Mountaineers.* Morgantown: West Virginia University Department of Intercollegiate Athletics, 1991.

Kirsch, George B., Othello Harris, and Claire E. Nolte. *Encyclopedia of Ethnicity and Sports in the United States.* Westport, CT: Greenwood, 2000.

Lloyd, Earl, and Sean Kirst. *Moonfixer: The Basketball Journey of Earl Lloyd.* Syracuse: Syracuse University Press, 2009.

Loewen, James W. *Sundown Towns: A Hidden Dimension of American Racism.* New York: New Press, 2005.

Lomotey, Kofi. *Encyclopedia of African American Education.* New York: Sage, 2009.

Marable, Manning. *W.E.B. DuBois: Black Radical Democrat.* London: Routledge, 1986.

Martin, Charles H. *Benching Jim Crow: The Rise and Fall of the Color Line in Southern College Sports, 1890–1980.* Urbana: University of Illinois Press, 2010.

McAllister, Lester G. *Bethany: The First 150 Years.* Bethany, WV: Bethany College Press, 1991.

McGehee, C. Stuart, and Frank Wilson. *Bluefield State College: A Centennial History (1895–1995).* North Tazewell, VA: Clinch Valley Printing, 1996.

Nehlen, Don, with Shelly Poe. *Tales From the West Virginia Sideline.* Champaign, IL: Sports Publishing, 2006.

Plummer, Kenneth M. *A History of West Virginia Wesleyan College: 75 Years in the Service of Christian Higher Education 1890–1965.* Buckhannon: West Virginia Wesleyan College Press, 1965.

Pruter, Robert. *The Rise of American High School Sports and the Search for Control 1880–1930.* Syracuse: Syracuse University Press, 2013.

Reger, George M. "Integration and Athletics: Integrating the Marshall University Basketball Program, 1954–1969." Master's thesis, Marshall University, 1996.

Roberts, Randy. *But They Can't Beat Us: Oscar Robertson and the Crispus Attucks Tigers.* Champaign, IL: Sports Publishing, 1999.

Schleppi, John. *Chicago's Showcase of Basketball: The World Tournament of Professional Basketball and the College All-Star Game.* Haworth, NJ: Saint Johann Press, 2008.

Schmidt, Raymond. *College Football: The Shaping of an American Sport, 1919–1930.* Syracuse: Syracuse University Press, 2007.

Sesker, Craig. *Bobby Douglas: Life and Legacy of an American Wrestling Legend.* n,p,: Exit Zero, 2011.

Stout, Louis. *Shadows of the Past: A History of the Kentucky High School Athletic League.* Lexington: Host Communications, 2006.

Sullivan, Ken, ed. *The West Virginia Encyclopedia.* Charleston: West Virginia Humanities Council, 2006.

Thomas, Ron. *They Cleared the Lane: The NBA's Black Pioneers.* Lincoln: University of Nebraska Press, 2002.

Thompson, Charles Herbert. "The History of the National Basketball Tournaments for Black High Schools." Ph.D. dissertation, Louisiana State University, 1980.

Toothman, Fred R. *Wild Wonderful Winners: Great Football Coaches of West Virginia.* Huntington: Vandalia, 1991.

Trent, W.W. *Mountaineer Education: A Story of Education in West Virginia, 1885–1957.* Charleston: Jarrett, 1960.

Trotter, Joe William, Jr. *Coal, Class, and Color: Blacks in Southern West Virginia 1915–32.* Urbana: University of Illinois Press, 1990.

Welsh, Bob. *20 Years: Women's Athletics.* Morgantown: West Virginia University, Department of Intercollegiate Athletics, 1984.

Wiggins, David K., and Ryan A. Swanson, eds. *Separate Games: African American Sport Behind the Walls of Segregation.* Fayetteville: University of Arkansas Press, 2016.

Williams, John Alexander. *West Virginia: A History.* Morgantown: West Virginia University Press, 2001.

WVU Women: The First Century. Morgantown: WVU Women's Centenary Project, 1991.

Wyatt, Tim L. *The Final Score.* n.p.: privately published, 1999.

Young, Mary, and Gerald Horace, eds. *W.E.B. Dubois: An Encyclopedia.* Westport, CT: Greenwood, 2001.

Journal and Magazine Articles

Barnett, Bob, and Lysbeth Barnett, "Black and White: Fairmont West vs. Fairmont Dunbar," *Goldenseal: West Virginia's Traditional Life* (Winter 2018): 40–45.

Barnett, C. Robert. "'The Finals': West Virginia's Black Basketball Tournament, 1925–1957." *Goldenseal: West Virginia's Traditional Life* (Summer 1983): 30–39.

_____. "Winning in the Rural Zone: How Cam Henderson Invented the Zone Defense." *Now and Then: The Appalachian Magazine* (Fall 1992): 37–39.

Carter, Alice E. "Segregation and Integration in the Appalachian Coalfields: McDowell County Responds to the Brown Decision." *West Virginia History* 54 (1995): 239–253, http://www.wvculture.org/history/journal_wvh/wvh54-5.html.

Hawkins, Michael. "Moonfixer: Basketball Pioneer Earl Lloyd." *Goldenseal: West Virginia's Traditional Life* 35, no. 1 (Spring 2009): 44–47.

Jackameit, William P. "A Short History of Negro Public Education in West Virginia, 1890–1965." *West Virginia History* 37, n. 4 (July 1976): 309–324.

Jordan, Lawrence V. "Educational Integration in West Virginia—One Year Afterward." *The Journal of Negro Education* 24, n. 3 (Summer 1955): 371–381. Martin, Charles M. "Jim Crow in the Gymnasium: The Integration of College Basketball in the American South." *The International Journal of the History of Sport* 10, no. 1 (April 1993): 68–86.

Morehouse, Keith. "Jules Rivlin: A Look Back at Marshall's Forgotten All-American." *Huntington Quarterly* (Spring 2013): 18–19.

Newman, Bruce. "Yesterday." *Sports Illustrated* (October 22, 1979): n.p.

Paul, J., R. McClure, and H. Fant. "The Arrival and Ascendance of Black Athletes in the Southern Conference—1966–1980."*Phelan* 45, no. 4 (1984): 284–297.

Salvatore, Ernie. "Hurrying' Hal Greer, "*Huntington Quarterly* (Summer 1994):30–34.

Interviews

Ronald R. Alexander, Mike Arcure, Shirley Atkins, Larry Barker, Ed Barrett, Benjamin Baughman, Frank Beach, Horace Belmear, Ancella Bickley, Ken Blue, Ronald Booker, Knute Burroughs, Andrew Calloway, Mark Cardwell, Jr., Phil Carter, Herb Colker, Gene Corum, Bob Douglas, Beverly Duckwyler, William Dunlap, Warne Ferguson, Garrett Ford, Kevin Gilson, James Green, Jr., Moses Guin, Arintha Poe

Hairston, Major Harris, Claude Harvey, Dorothy Hicks, Stephanie Holman, Ruth Jarrett, Dolores Johnson, Dennis R. Jones, Floyd Jones, Opal Jones, Bob Kelley, Wilkes Kinney, Donna Lawson, Earl Lloyd, John Mackey, Gerald Martin, Carolyn Matthews, Ed Pastilong, Shirley Robinson, Elizabeth Scobell, Ed Shockey, Ergie Smith, Lacy Smith, John Sorrenti, Edward Starling, Tim Swarr, James L. Taylor, William "Shellie" Trice, William Turner, Bucky Waters, James Wilkerson, Ronald Wilkerson, Elhanier Willis and Bob Wilson.

Periodicals and Newspapers

Atlanta Journal-Constitution: 2016.
Bethanian, Bethany College student yearbook: 1963.
Bluefield Daily Telegraph: 1957, 2011, 2013, 2015.
Bluefield Telegraph: 1951.
The Bluefieldian, Bluefield State College student newspaper, special edition: 1968.
Catamount, Potomac State College student yearbook: 1955, 1956.
Charleston Daily Mail: 1928, 1946, 1954, 1957, 1964, 2013.
Charleston Gazette: 1931, 1949, 1950, 1953, 1954, 1955, 1999, 2001, 2003.
Charleston Gazette-Mail: 1964, 2014.
Chief Justice, Marshall College yearbook: 1958.
College Football Historical Society Newsletter: 2005.
Daily Athenaeum, West Virginia University student newspaper, 1961.
Dominion Post (Morgantown, WV): 2006.
Elojo, West Virginia State College Yearbook: 1923.
Fairmont Times: 1954.
Fairmont Times-West Virginian: 2014.
Fairmont West Virginian: 1954.
Harveyan, Morris Harvey College student yearbook: 1955.
Herald-Dispatch (Huntington, WV): 1931, 1947, 1948, 1949, 1954, 1957, 1958, 1959, 1963.
Herd Insider: 2012.
Hinton News: 1992.
Huntington Advertiser: 1949,1955,1959, 1963.
Missions: A Baptist Monthly Newsletter: 1920
Monticola, WVU student yearbook: 1892.
Morgantown Dominion News: 1946, 2013.
The Mound, Fairmont State College student yearbook: 1958, 1959, 1960, 1961.
Murmurmontis, West Virginia Wesleyan College student yearbook: 1955, 1956, 1957, 1958.
New York Times, 1957.
Observer-Reporter (Washington, PA), 1969.
Pittsburgh Courier: 1924, 1925, 1927, 1928, 1948, 1949.
Post-Herald (Beckley, WV): 1963.
Rambler, Bluefield State College yearbook: 1924.
Register-Herald (Beckley, WV): 2004, 2015.
Starlight, Bluefield State College yearbook: 1927.
Storer Record, school newspaper: 1900, 1901, 1921, 1913, 1919, 1922, 1923, 1953.
Storer Sentinel, school alumni newsletter: 1909–1910.
Times West Virginian (Fairmont): March 28, 1947.
Tribune (Pittsburgh, PA): 2002.
Washington Post Magazine: October 22, 2015.
Weirton Daily Times: 1947, 1976.
West Virginia Daily News (Lewisburg, WV): 2015.
West Virginia History: 1976.

Other Resources

Archives

Bethany College Archives, Bethany, WV.

Bluefield State College Archives, Bluefield, WV.

Fairmont State University Archives, Fairmont, WV.

Glenville State University Archives, Glenville, WV.

Marshall University Archives, Huntington, WV.

Shepherd University Archives, Shepherdstown, WV.

Storer College, "Annual Report of the President," October 9, 1954, and 1955. West Virginia University Libraries, West Virginia and Regional History Collection.

Storer College, "Annual Report of the President to the Board of Trustees," May 25, 1955, 1–2 and 6. West Virginia University Libraries, West Virginia and Regional History Collection.

"Storer College Ten Year report, 1930–1939," West Virginia University Libraries, West Virginia and Regional History Collection.

West Liberty University Archives, West Liberty, WV.

West Virginia Archives and History Collection, Charleston, WV.

West Virginia State College Proposed Budget and Recommendations for 1955–56, Item 6641, West Virginia State University Archives.

West Virginia State College Recommendations to the Board of Education by President, January 1, 1954–January 1, 1956.

West Virginia University Libraries, West Virginia and Regional History Collection.

West Virginia Wesleyan College Archives.

Government Publications

Bureau of Negro Welfare and Statistics State of West Virginia: Biennial Report, 1951–1952.

Report of the State Superintendent of Schools and Department of Education, West Virginia Educational Directory, 1953–54 through the 1961–62 editions.

West Virginia, Biennial Report of the State Superintendent of Free Schools, 1952, 22, Marshall University Library Special Collections.

"West Virginia Board of Control Reports; 1910 through 1930," Bluefield University Archives. "West Virginia Board of Control Reports; 1910 through 1930," Bluefield University Archives.

West Virginia Human Rights Commission, "Annual Report. 1967–1968."

Programs and Pamphlets

Dennis R. Jones, "History of Dunbar School, Weirton, WV," Weirton Area Museum and Cultural Center, pamphlet distributed February 2, 2013.

"The Goal Post," Football Game Program, UCLA vs. Southern California, December 1939.

The West Virginia All Black Schools Sports & Athletic Hall of Fame Program 2011. 133–135. Held in the authors' personal collection.

The West Virginia All Black Schools Sports & Academic Hall of Fame Program, 2010. Held in the authors' personal collection.

The West Virginia All Black Schools Sports & Academic Hall of Fame Program, 2008. Held in the authors' personal collection.

Miscellaneous

Bluefield Colored Institute Catalogue, 1914–1915.

Gargus, Jerry. "In the Shadow of a Legend: The Jules Rivlin Story," unpublished paper, Spring 1994.

Marshall College Press and Radio Guide, 1956–57, Huntington, WV.
NCAA Demographic Data (various years).
West Virginia University/Relations/News.

Websites

American Football Coaches webpage, http:wwwafca.com/article; 2014.
The Carter G. Woodson Project website, http://www.marshall.edu/carterwoodson/sarah_hendrickson.asp, 2016.
The Carter G. Woodson Project/Marshall University, http://www.Marshall.edu/carterwoodson/alex_edelmann.asp, 2013.
Fairmont State University Athletic Hall of Fame website, http://fightingfalcons.com/hof.aspx, 2016.
Florida High School Athletic Association website, http:www.fhsaa.org, 2012.
Glenville University Athletic Hall of Fame website, www.glenville.edu/athletics/hof.php?gyear=2001, 2016.
http://www.scout.com/college/marshall/story/573681, 2017.
http://www.wvusports.com/page, CFM?sport=mbball&Show=1790S, 2016.
http:hoopedia.nba.com//index.php, 2012.
https://sportsintegration.wvu.edu.
https://www.youtube.com/watch?v=IPx-YdSFdhI, 2016.
MSNSportsNet.com, 2016.
Robert C. Byrd High School website, http://www.hardcoboe/robertcbyrdhigh school, 2013.
The Southern School News Reports, http://textbooks.lib, wvu.edu/wvhistory/files/html/15_wv_history_reader_stack.
Tennessee State University website, http://www.tnstate.edu/lib/document/Pearl High, 2012.
West Liberty Alumni Association website, http://www.westliberty.edu.alumni/.
West Virginia State University website, http://www.wvstateu.edu/Research/Gus-R-Douglass-Land-Grant-Institute.aspx, 2017.
WVU STATS, "Basketball Roster," http://www.wvustats.com/sport/mbasketball/roster, 2016.

Index

Numbers in **bold italics** indicate pages with illustrations